Rev. Henry Davis

Life in the Son

And this is the record, that God hath given to us eternal life, and this life is in his Son. He that hath the Son hath the life, and he that hath not the Son of God hath not the life.

I John 5:11, 12

Life in the Son

A Study of the Doctrine of Perseverance

by

ROBERT SHANK

Introduction by William W. Adams, Th. D.

WESTCOTT PUBLISHERS
SPRINGFIELD, MISSOURI

© Robert Lee Shank, 1960

———

Westcott Publishers
P. O. Box 803
Springfield, Missouri

———

Library of Congress Catalog Card Number: 59-15488

PRINTED IN THE UNITED STATES OF AMERICA BY
VON HOFFMANN PRESS, INC., ST. LOUIS, MISSOURI

To Him who loves us and freed us from our sins with His own blood.

Revelation 1:5

PREFACE

IN THE DAYS of the Apostles, explicit answers to essential questions of doctrine were available from men to whom our Lord had personally committed "the faith once delivered unto the saints." Exact definition of doctrine is today a more difficult problem. Definitions lie within the Scriptures; but what saith the Scripture? In some important areas of doctrine, sincere men disagree. We cannot appeal to "them that heard Him" for definitions beyond what the Scriptures now afford. Earnest inquiry into the meaning of the Scriptures is therefore imperative.

Few doctrines have been as much the occasion of controversy among evangelical Christians as the doctrine of the perseverance of the saints. This book treats of that doctrine, and is therefore controversial. But controversy is not evil; it is the servant of truth. Only prejudice is evil and the enemy of understanding.

Many volumes have been written on the question of the security of believers. But perhaps there is yet room for others. This volume is sent forth in the conviction that it is the fulfillment, however imperfectly, of a task assigned an unworthy servant by the Spirit of grace and truth. It is in a sense the testimony of one whose study of the Scriptures led him to abandon a definition of doctrine he once cherished, and who sincerely hopes that his endeavor will encourage others to re-examine a doctrine of critical practical importance.

Sometime we no longer shall know in part. The final word awaits the coming of Him who is Alpha and Omega. Meanwhile, believing that to disagree with sincere men is not to dishonor them, and that truth is served by honest inquiry, let us press toward a fuller understanding of the Holy Scriptures and a more accurate definition of saving faith in Jesus Christ.

* * *

I am grateful to my beloved parents, the Reverend and Mrs. Ernest F. Shank, for their prayers and encouragement in my task; to my dear wife and children for their love and patience through many busy days; to the members of the Baptist Church of Louisburg—a small church, and dear—for their understanding and forbearance in the days when their pastor devoted many hours to his writing, and for their noble Berean spirit; to Mrs. Warren Scarbrough for her splendid work in typing the final manuscript; to Dr. William W. Adams for graciously taking time to read the manuscript and to write an introduction, and to my dear friend, the Reverend Roe Matthews, for bringing the manuscript to his attention; to Mrs. Cecil Pitts for valuable assistance in reading the proofs; to other friends who aided in important ways; to the Central Bible Institute and Seminary, Springfield, Missouri, for generous library privileges; to publishers and other owners of copyrights who granted permission to quote; to Bible scholars of other days, from whose labors we continue to benefit; and above all, to Him whose grace has been sufficient and whose strength has been made perfect in weakness, without whom we can do nothing in His holy service. Jesus Christ be praised.

ROBERT SHANK

Louisburg, Missouri
October 12, 1959

CONTENTS

INTRODUCTION

BY WILLIAM W. ADAMS

WE ARE DEEPLY INDEBTED to those people who, rooted firmly in tradition, are orthodox and regular. They are a necessary bulwark against fanatical rebels and reformers whose convictions are weak and unstable, whose interests are in what is new more than in what is true, and whose influence is negative and destructive. If left to themselves, such people would wreck our Christian faith and destroy civilization in one generation. Fortunately they are never left to themselves. Alert and intelligent watchmen, securely rooted in the historic faith, are ever ready to analyze and to challenge every departure from traditional theology, belief, and custom. We are deeply indebted to such people, for they are our defense against the erosions of idle speculations and empty vagaries.

But we are equally indebted to responsible thinkers who dare to challenge tradition. They are the pioneers who explore new areas of truth, clarify concepts, enlarge vision, and enrich our store of knowledge by breaking the paralyzing grip of blind, uncritical enslavement to tradition. But for such men, no progress would be made toward a fuller comprehension of the truth.

Occasionally we come across a book that is loaded with dynamite, one that jars us awake and quickens all our cognitive powers. *Life in the Son* is that kind of book. Seldom is a book published that reflects such bold independence of thought, such freedom from the fetters of tradition, and such complete objectivity in the study of the Scriptures. It is a book to be reckoned with by all serious students of the Bible, and especially by all who teach or preach.

The book appears at an appropriate hour. We live in a time of theological tension. The increasing tempo of human events and the apparent impotence of organized Christianity in the face of a chaotic world are causing thoughtful men to re-examine their theology with candor. It is painfully evident that the forces of evil are gaining all over the world. We are not meeting the issues and mastering the forces that are fashioning our modern world. The crisis of the ages seems close at hand, and we are not ready for it. Is it possible that our tragic impotence derives in part from the fact that we have been using but a small portion of the truth and power available to us in Christ and the Holy Scriptures? Is it possible that a lack of comprehension of revealed truth is a major cause of our ineffectiveness? The appearance of a book that demands that we search the Scriptures afresh and re-examine a doctrine of utmost importance will be welcomed by all thoughtful and responsible men.

Again, *Life in the Son* appears in a time of confusion in ecclesiastical polity. There are nearly three hundred separate denominations in America today, including more than twenty-five Baptist groups, some of which continue to fragmentize. While the shameful multiplicity of sects must in part be attributed to the cultivation of personal interests by ambitious men, it is also true that it must in part be attributed to doctrinal confusion. Surely it can be taken for granted that the Bible does not teach varied and contradictory ideas on any doctrine. We must therefore conclude that contradictory and divisive beliefs and practices among denominations and among groups within denominations are the consequence of ignoring or misinterpreting certain Scriptures. Intelligent and sustained efforts to interpret the Scriptures objectively, contextually, historically, and comprehensively would eliminate most theological conflicts and ecclesiastical divisions. Any book that will provoke men to earnestly re-examine an important area of doctrine in which there long have been divisive opinions and persuasions will serve a constructive purpose and encourage hope for a doctrinal unity that is truly Biblical. The appearance of such a book will be welcomed by all men who care more for the unity of the Spirit and of the faith and the knowledge of the Son of God than for the defense of creed and dogma.

Again, this book appears at a time when many pastors and denominational leaders are becoming increasingly disturbed over the fact that more than half of our church members do not support the local church and the Christian world mission with sufficient regularity to be counted. Why? Is it possible that this tragic situation derives largely from the dearth of expository preaching which blights pulpits everywhere throughout the land? The appearance of a book that underscores the supreme importance of serious exegetical study and the effective expository preaching that can only follow such study will be welcomed by men of discernment and concern.

Surely the time is ripe for new voices to be heard, bringing new insights into holy truth. Now and again in history, in the fulness of time, God has prepared and sent forth prophetic sons to interpret more fully the Son who also came "in the fulness of time." It is altogether possible that an urgently needed prophetic voice is now to be heard through this book.

Mr. Shank has honored me in two ways. First, through a mutual friend, he extended to me the privilege of reading his manuscript before it went to press. Secondly, he asked me to write an introduction. For several reasons, I consented:

First, it gives me opportunity to express publicly my everlasting gratitude to the author for writing one of the most arresting and disturbing books I have ever read.

Again, Mr. Shank's book gives me new faith and confidence in evangelical Christianity. New Testament Christianity possesses its own correctives and remedial resources. They are found in the Bible. In time, the Bible corrects most of the false, incomplete, and unbalanced interpretations of its content.

Again, his book gives me new confidence in my own Baptist heritage. The local church is autonomous in fact, not merely in theory. Mr. Shank is pastor of a local Baptist church which certainly cannot be ignorant of his beliefs. Yet he remains free to challenge and to reject a basic doctrine which long has been traditional among Baptists. This proves anew that we have no hierarchy among us—no ecclesiastical lords who can command our conscience or deprive us of our liberty. Baptists believe and practice the basic Biblical principle of the priesthood of believers. Each believer has the right of private interpretation; and certainly each divinely called minister of the Gospel has the right and the duty to interpret the Scriptures and to preach as he is led by the Holy Spirit, free from the coercion and restraints of men, free from all judgment save that of the Scripture itself. We are free men in a free society, and therefore truly responsible before God. There are, unfortunately, "Baptists" who would silence all challenging and disturbing interpretations of Scripture by placing totalitarian, dictatorial, excommunicating hands on those who are responsible for them. The fact that they cannot do so proves both the reality and the significance of the autonomy of the local church and the priesthood of all believers.

Again, by writing an introduction, I can render a service to those who read books. Time is so valuable and there are available so many books that are both profitable and satisfying that one is not justified in reading books to no profit. Therefore, it is quite in place to state frankly the nature and message of this book and to suggest who should read it, and who should not.

Life in the Son offers a fresh, exacting, and comprehensive study of the Scriptures that concern the doctrine of the perseverance of the saints, commonly defined as "once in grace, always in grace." The author concludes that, when all pertinent Scriptures are carefully examined and fully considered, the doctrine must be rejected. For Baptists and many other evangelicals, this at once classifies his book as revolutionary.

There are certain people who should not read *Life in the Son:*

People who have already decided what they intend to believe and who read only for confirmation of their present opinion should not read Mr. Shank's book. The book was not written for people with spring-trap minds that have already sprung.

People who prefer to determine their doctrine from a few proof texts and ignore or wrest other passages bearing on a given theme should not read *Life in the Son*. This book will not suit them, for it shows no partiality toward any Scripture passages that concern the important question of the doctrine of perseverance.

People who read the Bible with the conviction that they must be dogmatic and final on all matters of doctrine, leaving no place for humility and deferred judgment, should not read *Life in the Son*. It demands that readers re-examine and carefully weigh the evidence before adopting conclusions.

People who read only to augment their comfort and tranquility should not read *Life in the Son*. The book is profoundly disturbing and will not serve the purpose of those who intend to remain "at ease in Zion."

Pastors who never read except to gather material for next Sunday's sermon should not read *Life in the Son*. It would require months, even years, to prepare the average Baptist audience to face the fresh Biblical exegesis this book contains.

There are certain people who should not read *Life in the Son*. On the other hand, there are certain people who, by all means, should read it:

People whose first loyalty is to the Scriptures rather than to traditional interpretations and creeds should read this book. They are people who are willing to think and to weigh evidence, and they cannot fail to profit from the reading of this book.

People who are ready to accept and follow the truth, whatever it is and wherever it leads, should read *Life in the Son*. They are people who can profit from *any* serious study of the Scriptures.

People who have the ability to read a book and accept part of its content without necessarily accepting the book in its entirety should read *Life in the Son*. Regardless of whether they ultimately accept Mr. Shank's thesis, they will benefit from his study.

People who are really disturbed over certain alarming trends and conditions in our churches and contemporary Christianity should read *Life in the Son*. Those who are searching for causes and cures will find much of significance in Mr. Shank's book.

Certainly *Life in the Son* should be read by all professional "contenders for the faith" (ecclesiastical pugilists) who make their living by searching for motes real or imaginary and blacking the eyes of individuals, institutions, and denominations which dare to differ with them, whom they courageously attack in "holy" (and profitable) crusades financed by people who should know better. Regardless of whether they are able to refute Mr. Shank's interpretations and thesis, enterprising "defenders" for whom the faith is a commodity will be able to misrepresent the issue to their patrons and, for some time to come, make merchandise of Mr. Shank, his book, and all who commend it.

I wish it were in my power to place a copy of *Life in the Son* in the hands of every pastor, teacher, leader, and layman who sincerely loves the Bible, the Saviour, the church, and the fulness of spiritual life. My only condition would be that they read it prayerfully, keeping their Bibles open as they read, and following the author's comments as the starting point for a fresh, exhaustive, contextual, patient study of the passages which Mr. Shank discusses in his book. Such a study would produce some wholesome results:

It would teach us the wisdom of guarding against hasty and uncritical acceptance of tradition, regardless of its apparent sanctity, venerable age, or esteemed devotees.

It would cause us to fall on our knees in prayer, rather than to seek opportunities for public argument and debate, and to search the Bible as never before in an earnest quest for truth, the whole truth, and nothing but the truth.

It would lead us to face the causes of the "dead wood" on our church rolls and to inquire whether we have preached the full Gospel of Christ and declared the whole counsel of God to those who have accepted Jesus as Lord and Saviour.

It would compel us, in genuine humility, to re-examine some of our hermeneutical principles, to improve our methods of exegesis, and to sweep around our own theological doors before criticizing others and presuming to correct their interpretations of Scripture.

It would lead us to thank God for men like Mr. Shank who are dedicated to God and truth, who possess intellectual and spiritual insight, and who have the pastoral concern and prophetic daring to speak for God even when it involves calling in question and rejecting one of the most venerable tenets of traditional theology in their denomination, at the risk of possibly having it later proved that they have retreated from one extreme position only to assume another.

It is difficult to write such a book as *Life in the Son*. Nothing can be taken for granted except God, truth, and duty. Everything must be minutely examined and comprehensively interpreted. This demands sustained and exacting work of only the highest order. And there is always the danger that the scholar may become so infused with the invigorating spirit of independent thinking that he sometimes becomes too unsympathetic with tradition and unduly enamored of newness, to the impairment of his work. Only time will reveal how well Mr. Shank has guarded against this peril in his study.

Mr. Shank did not request that I endorse the thesis presented in his book. Had he done so, I should have been compelled at this time to refuse. Certainly no one should either accept or reject Mr. Shank's thesis without reading his book several times and attempting to refute his interpretations from the Scriptures in the same sort of exhaustive and objective study that he has pursued. Whether this can be done remains to be demonstrated.

Mr. Shank asked only that I write an introduction to his book, and I count it a privilege to honor his request. I consider *Life in the Son* one of the most significant books in this generation. I consider it possible that the judgment of time may prove it to be one of the most important books ever written. I earnestly insist on this one thing: Let all who have a sincere concern to understand the truth revealed in the Holy Scriptures get a copy of *Life in the Son*. With open Bibles and minds and hearts, let them read the book carefully and prayerfully at least three times. Taking the utmost care to remain as objective as they are capable of being, let them sincerely endeavor to refute from the Scriptures the interpretations and thesis which Mr. Shank presents. Then, and not before, let them form their conclusions and prepare to declare them to others.

If Mr. Shank is right in his interpretations and thesis, it is of the utmost importance for time and eternity that we come to share his understanding of the Scriptures. If he is wrong, it remains for us to refute his thesis by demonstrating that we are better exegetes and interpreters of Scripture than he has proved himself to be. In any event, a critical re-examination of one of the historic tenets of our theology now becomes mandatory through the publishing of this book. We now have no warrant for entertaining positive convictions on the doctrine of perseverance until an exhaustive objective study has enlarged and clarified our comprehension of all revealed truth that has any bearing on this essential question of doctrine.

I feel that it is now in order for me to address myself to the author with respect to the kinds of response his book will probably receive. Mr. Shank, unless human nature has recently and radically changed, there are some who will do their utmost to give your book the "silent" treatment. Some will be too learned to acknowledge that they have not known all there is to know on the subject. They will consider that their first obligation is to their personal academic reputation and professional interests. With great scholarly dignity, they will carefully ignore your book.

Some will loudly denounce your book merely because you dare to call in question some of their customary interpretations and to challenge their accustomed doctrinal position. They will label you a heretic or a novice. Let me urge you to ignore all criticisms of yourself, and all criticisms of your book that amount to mere general disapproval and denunciation. This will be the resort only of men who are incapable of presenting any serious reply to your interpretations and thesis. Negative criticisms that fail to demonstrate objectively that your interpretations are incorrect will not deserve serious consideration or serve the cause of truth.

Some will consider that "unity" is more important than truth and that, right or wrong, conformity to tradition and popular opinion is the only wise course. Men so easily become enslaved by a vested interest in the *status quo,* and many will refuse to venture the risk of honestly searching for truth at the possible expense of comfort.

Some, thank God, will read your book with growing provocation and an insatiable hunger and determination to see the study through to a conclusion that is unquestionably Biblical. They are the ones (I pray they may be many) who will profit from the reading of your book and from an honest effort to refute it. Whatever the ultimate verdict, their knowledge of the Scriptures will be increased and their lives and Christian witness will be enriched because of your book.

Mr. Shank, there may be other responses to your book which neither you nor I can foresee. But this much is assured: all genuine scholars and searchers after truth will be compelled to take your book into consideration.

WILLIAM W. ADAMS
James Buchanan Harrison Professor of New
   Testament Interpretation
The Southern Baptist Theological Seminary

Louisville, Kentucky
June 19, 1959

By Grace, Through Faith

Not by works of righteousness which we have done, but according to his mercy he saved us, by the washing of regeneration and renewing of the Holy Spirit, which he shed on us abundantly through Jesus Christ our Saviour; that being justified by his grace, we should be made heirs according to the hope of eternal life.

TITUS 3:5-7

For by grace are ye saved through faith, and that not of yourselves: it is the gift of God; not of works, lest any man should boast.

EPHESIANS 2:8, 9

But we believe that through the grace of the Lord Jesus Christ we shall be saved, even as they.

ACTS 15:11

CHAPTER I

BY GRACE, THROUGH FAITH

THEY HAD COME TOGETHER to consider a matter of grave importance. The church at Jerusalem, as elsewhere, was divided. Certain of the sect of the Pharisees who believed (Acts 15:5) were insisting that believing in Jesus was good—as far as it went; but merely to trust in Christ and His saving grace was not enough. It was necessary that Gentile converts be circumcised and assume the obligations of the law of Moses.

Their arguments were persuasive. Was not their Saviour a Jew? Had He not been circumcised? Had He not honored the law? True, He had scorned the vain traditions which men had imposed upon the law; but had He not honored the law itself? He came, He said, not to destroy the law, but to fulfill it. Indeed, only a few days before His death, He had reminded His disciples that "the scribes and the Pharisees sit in Moses' seat: all therefore whatsoever they bid you observe, that observe and do" (Matt. 23:1-3). Were His followers now to abandon Moses and the law?

The legalists had become a powerful faction in the church at Jerusalem. And their influence was spreading. They were sending their apologists everywhere, on the very heels of the Apostles themselves, to ensure that Gentile converts should receive the full truth, and so be lacking in nothing and assuredly saved.

But there were many who were convinced that the Judaizers, despite their zeal, were misguided men. There was Paul, to whom the Lord had given no such instruction in the personal

3

revelation of the Gospel which He had given him and who, with Barnabas, had contended against the apostles of circumcision at Antioch (Acts 15:2). And there was Peter, whom the Lord had sent to the Gentiles in the house of Cornelius at Caesarea, and who there had witnessed the salvation of all who heard the Word, to which salvation God "who knoweth the hearts" had borne witness through the gift of the Holy Spirit (Acts 15:7-9) before ever they had considered the question of baptism, and quite apart from any observance of any physical ordinance.

The dissension was sharp and the issue was decisive, for the implications were fundamental. And so

. . . the apostles and elders came together to consider this matter. And when there had been much disputing, Peter arose and said unto them, Men and brethren, ye know how that a good while ago God made choice among us that the Gentiles by my mouth should hear the word of the gospel and believe. And God who knoweth the hearts bare them witness, giving them the Holy Ghost even as he did unto us, and put no difference between us and them, purifying their hearts by faith. Now therefore, why tempt ye God, to put a yoke upon the neck of the disciples which neither our fathers nor we were able to bear? But we believe that through the grace of the Lord Jesus Christ we shall be saved, even as they (Acts 15:6-11).

Thus Peter gave his inspired definition of the way of salvation. God, said he, had purified the hearts of Cornelius and his companions by faith. And, even as those Gentiles, Peter and his fellow Jewish believers were to be saved through the grace of the Lord Jesus Christ by simple faith, quite apart from the law and fleshly ordinances.

Peter's account of his experience at Caesarea fully agreed with Paul's thesis at Antioch in Pisidia—the cardinal axiom of the Gospel committed to him by the risen Christ: "Through this man [Jesus] is preached unto you the forgiveness of sins: and by him all who believe are justified from all things, from which ye could not be justified by the law of Moses" (Acts 13:38, 39).

This cardinal axiom of justification by faith alone, apart from ordinances or works, Paul later expounded at length in his epistles to the churches in Galatia and at Rome. Indeed, throughout the New Testament the axiom is stated so simply, so forcefully, and so frequently that one wonders at the success of some in our day in bringing multitudes into the bondage of legalism (cf. Gal. 2:4; 5:1). The explanation, however, is quite apparent. The success of twentieth-century legalists stems from the fact that their unscriptural doctrines appeal to a concept which is strongly rooted in the natural man: one dare not presume to trust God to save him in pure mercy and grace!

The idea of self-justification is deeply ingrained in humanity, and as old as human history. Witness Cain. Throughout human history, every false religion has been steeped in the principle of self-justification, including the many perversions of Christianity (with the exception of antinomianism). With what difficulty do men believe that "by grace are ye saved, through faith; and that not of yourselves: it is the gift of God" (Eph. 2:8).

The difficulty prevailed in the days of our Lord's ministry in the flesh. "Then said they unto him, What shall we do that we might work the works of God? Jesus answered and said unto them, This is the work of God, that ye believe on him whom he hath sent" (John 6:28, 29). What shall we do?—how shall we work and win God's favor? The answer is ever, *This* is the work of God: believe on the Saviour whom He has sent!

Many seem quite unwilling to concede that salvation must be by grace. They do not wish to be saved in such an embarassing manner. "When Lady Huntington invited the Duchess of Buckingham to come and hear Whitefield, the Duchess answered: 'It is monstrous to be told that you have a heart as sinful as the common wretches that crawl on the earth; it is highly offensive and insulting.' "[1]

---

[1] A. H. Strong, *Systematic Theology*, p. 832.

As in Paul's day, "the offense of the cross" is more than many
can endure. The cross of Jesus is a reminder of man's inability to
lift himself from the quagmire of his own spiritual depravity.
As the symbol of the grace of God, it is equally the symbol of
the guilt of man. The cross of Jesus demands that we confess
that ". . . all have sinned and come short of the glory of God . . .
There is none righteous, no, not one . . . We are all as an un-
clean thing, and all our righteousnesses are as filthy rags." Well
did Isaac Watts write:

> When I survey the wondrous cross
>   On which the Prince of glory died,
> My richest gain I count but loss,
>   And pour contempt on all my pride.

Accepting Jesus Christ as one's personal Saviour from sin
is a humbling experience. It requires the surrender of all confidence in one's assumed goodness and in the supposed redemptive merit of all his best endeavors. But only thus can one be
saved.

Jesus is a Savior, not of the righteous, but of sinners. . . . He does not
wait until they are pure and holy, then to be spiritually betrothed unto
them; but He betroths Himself unto them that they may become pure
and holy. . . . He says not, "Get thyself clean, wise, and rich; and as a
rich bride I will betroth thee unto Me"; but, "I take thee just as thou art.
I say unto thee, in thy blood, Live. Tho thou art poor, betrothing thee, I
will make thee partaker of Myself and My treasure. But a treasure of thine
own thou shalt never possess."[2]

Someone has well said that we are saved, not through our
attainment, but through His atonement. This seems a hard
truth for many to accept. In his sermon "Christ's Last Invitation From the Throne," Alexander Maclaren said:

. . . the one thing that Christ asks me to do is to trust my poor sinful
self wholly and confidently and constantly and obediently to Him. That
is all. Ah! All! And that is just where the pinch comes. . . . Naaman's

---

[2]Abraham Kuyper, *The Work of the Holy Spirit*, p. 334 f.

strange reluctance to do a little thing in order to produce a great effect, whilst he was willing to take a mint of trouble in order to produce it, is repeated over and over again amongst us. You will see men buy damnation dear who will not have salvation because it is a gift and they have nothing to do. I do believe that great multitudes of people would rather, like the Hindoos, stick hooks in the muscles of their backs and swing at the end of a rope if that would get heaven for them, than simply be content to come *in forma pauperis* and owe everything to Christ's grace and nothing to their own works.[3]

How many there are who, like most of the Jews of Paul's day, vainly seek to establish their own righteousness and thus fail to receive the righteousness of God in Christ, through simple faith. Hodge has well said: "The renunciation of a legal, self-righteous spirit is the first requisition of the gospel. This must be done, or the gospel cannot be accepted. 'He who works,' i.e., who trusts in his works, refuses to be saved by grace...."[4]

But does not James declare that "faith without works is dead" and such "faith" cannot save? He does indeed. But a careful examination of James' discourse (2:14-26) discloses that in no way does it contradict the principle of justification by faith alone, which is everywhere taught in the Scriptures. Actually it serves, not to establish works as a means of salvation, but to quailfy the kind of faith that saves. Melanchthon's dictum is an apt summary of James' contention: "It is faith, alone, which saves; but the faith that saves is not alone."

Saving faith is a living faith in a living Saviour, faith so vital it cannot avoid expression. Paul described it as "a faith which *works* by love" (Gal. 5:6). Lightfoot comments on Paul's words: "These words *di' agapēs energoumenē* bridge over the gulf which seems to separate the language of St. Paul and St. James. Both assert a principle of practical energy, as opposed to a barren, inactive theory."[5]

---

[3]Alexander Maclaren, *Expositions of Holy Scripture: Revelation*, p. 400 f.
[4]Charles Hodge, *A Commentary on the Epistle to the Romans*, p. 99.
[5]J. B. Lightfoot, *The Epistle of St. Paul to the Galatians*, p. 205.

Jesus said, "He that believeth on me, the works that I do shall he do also" (John 14:12). The "faith" of men who have no sincere intention of following in the steps of the Saviour is something less than saving faith. The "faith" of men who have no real concern for the cause of the Gospel and the work of His church is not the kind of faith in Christ which saves. "Faith" is dead that finds no expression in good works.

But even so, all "good works" are vain that are not the fruit of simple faith in Jesus Christ as Saviour, by the grace of God. A barren faith is of no avail; but it is still faith, not works, which saves.

> Not the labors of my hands
> Can fulfill Thy law's demands;
> Could my zeal no respite know,
> Could my tears for ever flow,
> These for sin could not atone;
> Thou must save, and Thou alone.
> Nothing in my hand I bring;
> Simply to Thy Cross I cling.

AUGUSTUS M. TOPLADY

The story is told of a mother who appeared before a general to plead for the life of her soldier-son who had been found asleep at his post. "Sir, I beg of you," she implored, "have mercy on my son." "But your son deserves to die," replied the general. "Sir," answered the mother, "I asked for mercy, not justice."

When we kneel before the cross of Jesus, we appear as supplicants, not for justice, but for mercy. There is no need to petition God for justice. His justice has been declared: "The soul that sinneth, it shall die." The Scriptures everywhere affirm that inexorable justice will be swift and full for every finally impenitent soul. "The wages of sin is death." That is justice. But thank God, there is mercy: "The gift of God is eternal life in Jesus Christ our Lord."

In this was manifested the love of God toward us, because God sent his only begotten Son into the world, that we might live through him. Herein is love; not that we loved God, but that he loved us, and sent his Son to be the propitiation for our sins.

I JOHN 4:9, 10

The High Cost of a Free Gift

For by grace are ye saved through faith; and that not of yourselves: it is the gift of God.

EPHESIANS 2:8

The gift of God is eternal life through Jesus Christ our Lord.

ROMANS 6:23

Thanks be unto God for his unspeakable gift.

II CORINTHIANS 9:15

CHAPTER II

THE HIGH COST OF A FREE GIFT

THE BEST THINGS in life are free, according to the popular maxim. But what is more, life itself is free—life abundant and eternal. In his letter to the Romans, Paul speaks of justification, righteousness, and life as "the free gift" and "the gift by grace" (5:15-18) and declares that, "while the wages of sin is death . . . the gift of God is eternal life through Jesus Christ our Lord." Salvation is offered only as God's free gift to men. It must be so received. This, many seem unable to understand.

An aged Moslem, an influential citizen of Egypt, recently testified of his faith and hope in conversation with an American journalist. "Sir," he said, "all my life I have obeyed the Koran and worshipped Allah faithfully. If, after death, I find that there is no paradise and there are no houris with which a man may be comforted, as the Koran promises, I shall feel that I have been miserably cheated."

There are countless "Christians" whose hope of attaining heaven rests upon their good life, their generous giving of their money, and their faithful attention to "religion." All who propose to bargain with God for a place in his eternal heaven will be disappointed. The gifts of God are not for sale. To Simon of Samaria, who supposed that the gift of the fulness of the Spirit could be purchased with money, Peter replied, "Thy money perish with thee, because thou hast thought that the gift of God may be purchased with money" (Acts 8:20).

Salvation is God's gift to undeserving men. We have but to ask to receive. "If thou knewest the gift of God and who it is that saith to thee, Give me to drink," said Jesus to the woman of Sychar, "thou wouldest have asked of him, and he would have given thee living water" (John 4:10). The last invitation in the Bible is our risen Saviour's gracious appeal, "Let him that is athirst come. And whosoever will, let him take the water of life freely" (Rev. 22:17). ". . . take . . . freely!" The water of life may be had for the taking. What good news for impoverished sinners!

Does salvation, then, cost nothing? Indeed, nothing in all the universe has cost so much. It cost the Word, who from the unbegun beginning was *God* and face-to-face as an equal in the Holy Trinity, the humiliation of exile from the throne room of the universe, the renunciation of the glory and majesty which had been His, and the acceptance of an identification with humanity so complete that He must forever remain the Son of man—a circumstance from which there can be no retreat in all eternity to come.

It cost the Father the sacrifice of His only begotten Son, in whom He was well pleased, on Golgotha's tree where was "laid on him the iniquity of us all," that He who was without sin might be "made sin for us, that we might be made the righteousness of God in him . . . the just for the unjust, that he might bring us to God."

It cost Jesus the patient pursuit of the path of obedience—finally unto death, even the death of the cross where "he bore our sins in his own body on the tree" and "his soul was made an offering for sin," plunging Him into the spiritual desolation of hell itself and drawing from Him the anguished cry that marked the wretched bitterness of the cup of His Father's appointing, "My God, my God, why hast thou forsaken me?"

It cost the Holy Spirit an agelong ministry of patiently wooing the stubborn hearts of sinful men in the call of the sweet Gospel of Christ, and of suffering long with men who treat Him ill—even some He owns as His. Not all the angels of heaven can declare the cost of the glorious salvation which God in grace offers as His free gift to undeserving sinners.

But though salvation is God's gracious gift to spiritual paupers, the acceptance of the gift, like its provision, is costly. It
costs the renunciation of self and of much that men hold dear.
Paul, who gladly paid the cost, expressed it in such statements
as, "I am crucified with Christ. . . . To me to live is Christ. . . .
What things were gain to me, those I counted loss for Christ.
Indeed, I do count all things but loss for the priceless privilege
of knowing Christ Jesus my Lord, for whom I have suffered the
loss of all things and do count them but refuse, that I may
gain Christ and be found in him. . . ." One cannot accept Christ
and His salvation on lesser terms than the complete surrender
of self to him.

We pastors have confused the issue by such pulpit appeals
as, "You have accepted Christ as your Saviour; but have you
really made Him the Lord of your life? Why not dedicate your
life fully to Him?" Such appeals imply that the acceptance of
Christ as Saviour and as Lord are two entirely separate acts.
Much to the contrary, they are inseparable aspects of a single
act. Like repentance and faith, they are mutually involved;
there cannot be one without the other. No man can accept
Jesus as Saviour of his soul without accepting Him as Lord of
his life. Multitudes of "Christians" today seem quite unaware
of this solemn fact.

The church today is paralyzed at the moment of its supreme opportunity
because we have committed the blasphemy of insisting that what is so
costly for God shall come easy to us. We haven't dared face our congregations with a hard gospel.[1]

The Gospel of Christ, though a comfortable Word, is in
a sense "a hard gospel." Jesus warned His hearers that the cost
of discipleship is dear. In Luke 14:25-35 is recorded an instance
in His ministry which seems virtually to be ignored in this day
of easy discipleship:

---

[1]Dr. Paul Calvin Payne, General Secretary, the Board of Christian Educa-
tion, the Presbyterian Church in the U.S.A. Used by permission.

"There went great multitudes with him: and he turned and said unto them, If any man come to me and hate not his father and mother and wife and children and brethren and sisters, yea, and his own life also, he cannot be my disciple. And whosoever doth not bear his cross and come after me cannot be my disciple" (vv. 25-27). Count the cost, warned Jesus, and be sure you intend to finish (vv. 28-30). Salt is good only as it retains its savor (vv. 34, 35). The price of discipleship is high. "What king," asked Jesus, "going to make war against another king, sitteth not down first and consulteth whether he be able with ten thousand to meet him that cometh against him with twenty thousand? Or else, while the other is yet a great way off, he sendeth an ambassage and desireth conditions of peace" (vv. 31, 32). The "condition of peace" granted by a king to a lesser king who dared not meet him in battle was total submission. The lesser king became his vassal, paying tribute, with himself and all his possessions subject to the command of his lord. "So likewise," said Jesus, "whosoever he be of you that forsaketh not all that he hath, he cannot be my disciple" (v. 33).

The lordship of Jesus over self, life, and possessions must be acknowledged if we are to know Him as Saviour. All must be surrendered to Him who gave His all for us. He who said, "Come unto me, all ye that labor and are heavy laden," said also, "Take my yoke upon you." We cannot find rest for our souls in Him unless we take His yoke upon us. "Whosoever shall fall upon this stone," said Jesus, "shall be broken" (Matt. 21:44). Casting ourselves upon the Rock of our salvation involves a painful breaking of self. But the alternative is fearful: "On whomsoever it shall fall, it will grind him to powder." We must fall and be broken, or be fallen upon and forever crushed.

Jesus commissioned His disciples to preach "repentance and remission of sins in his name" (Luke 24:47). There is no remission apart from repentance. And repentance involves the whole of life. It is concerned, not merely with sorrow for the past, but even more with our intention for the future. It is the abandoning of our own selfish way to go God's way in obedience and fellowship with Him.

"Just accept Christ and be saved" is the appeal of many. But receiving Jesus Christ as Saviour is not a matter of "just" accepting Him—"no strings attached." We cannot accept Christ as Saviour apart from a definite change of mind, heart, and will involving the whole of life and all our affections and intentions. There must be full surrender to the lordship of Christ, a sincere acceptance of His yoke.

Thank God, a dying thief with nothing to offer but a confession of need and a plea for mercy can receive forgiveness and the saving grace of God in Christ. But they err who presume to be saved "just like the dying thief"—nothing to be said about "deny self . . . take up your cross daily . . . follow me . . . keep my commandments. . . ." Only a dying man can be saved "just like the dying thief." This does not mean that God has different plans of salvation for different people, according to their circumstances. It means only that, at whatever point in life one comes to Christ for salvation, the whole of life from that point onward is necessarily involved in his decision and must be surrendered to the lordship of the Saviour. Had the thief on the cross met Jesus in the midst of life rather than as a dying man at the gates of death, he would have been confronted with the grave demands of Jesus which He frequently declared as the irreducible terms of discipleship for all who would know and follow Him. There can be no reception of Christ as Saviour apart from a full commitment of oneself to Him. Salvation costs men nothing . . . and everything.

The Christian, to be sure, begins his new life in Christ as a babe. He needs time and nurture for development. He has much to learn in his new life. He lacks understanding and may stumble frequently, displaying spiritual immaturity in many ways. But the windows of his heart will be open toward the Sun of Righteousness, and the basic orientation of his life will be toward God. He will acknowledge, however imperfectly, the lordship of Christ over his heart and life.

A long lifetime will not suffice to teach us all that is involved in true discipleship. But though at best our devotion and obedience will be quite imperfect, they nevertheless must be real and sincere if Jesus is to be our personal Saviour. Solemn indeed are the words of Jesus, "Greater love hath no man than this, that a man lay down his life for his friends. Ye are my friends—if ye do whatsoever I command you" (John 15:13, 14). "He that saith, I know him, and keepth not his commandments," declares John, "is a liar, and the truth is not in him" (I John 2:4). Submission to the lordship of Jesus is not optional for men who would know Him as Saviour.

It costs to follow Jesus. The emblem of our faith is the cross. There was one for Jesus. There was one for Peter. There is one, too, for everyone who would follow Jesus. "If any man will come after me," said Jesus, "let him deny himself and take up his cross and follow me. For whosoever will save his life shall lose it, and whosoever will lose his life for my sake shall find it. For what is a man profited if he shall gain the whole world and lose his own soul? or what shall a man give in exchange for his soul?" (Matt. 16:24-26).

The gift of salvation is costly. It cost God more than heaven can declare. It cost Jesus the cross. It costs everyone who receives it the total submission of self in the acceptance of the rightful claims of Jesus on the lives and souls of all who would be His for time and eternity.

> Jesus, I my cross have taken,
>   All to leave and follow Thee;
> Destitute, despised, forsaken—
>   Thou, from hence, my all shalt be.
>
> Perish every fond ambition,
>   All I've sought and hoped and known;
> Yet how rich is my condition:
>   God and heaven are now my own!
>
>   HENRY F. LYTE (adapted)

Life in the Son

That which was from the beginning, which we have heard, which we have seen with our eyes, which we have looked upon and our hands have handled, of the Word of life. For the life was manifested, and we have seen it and bear witness, and show unto you that eternal life which was with the Father and was manifested unto us.

*   *   *

And this is the record, that God hath given to us eternal life, and this life is in his Son. He that hath the Son hath the life, and he that hath not the Son of God hath not the life. These things have I written unto you that believe on the name of the Son of God, that you may know that you have eternal life.

I JOHN 1:1, 2; 5:11-13

Chapter III

LIFE IN THE SON

It is said that in World War II, a Marine Corps sergeant led his men into action on a precarious beachhead on a Pacific island with the bold challenge, "Come on, men! Do you want to live forever?" The universal answer of mankind is, Yes, we would live forever! The ancient query, "What shall I do to inherit eternal life?" has been in the hearts, if not on the lips, of all men in every generation. Tennyson voiced the longing of every human heart:

> 'Tis life, whereof our nerves are scant,
> O, life, not death, for which we pant;
> More life, and fuller, that I want.[1]

"More life, and fuller" is the desire of every heart. And it is such a life—abundant and eternal—that God in grace deigns to bestow upon men. "This is the record," writes John, "that God hath given to us eternal life, and this life is in his Son."

What is this "eternal life" which God has given to men in His Son? It is something other than mere endless existence. There is no necessity for God to act to bestow endless existence upon men; for from creation, immortality in the sense of endless existence is an inalienable endowment of mankind. The Bible affirms the endless existence of every human being, whether saved or lost. "Eternal life," then, is a particular *quality* of life which emanates from God, rather than a mere ex-

---

[1] Alfred Tennyson, from "The Two Voices."

tension of existence. For man, it is the reception and enjoyment of the essential life of God Himself through Christ, the channel, by the Holy Spirit, the agent. It is a gracious participation in the very life of God. "It is more than endless [existence], for it is sharing in the life of God in Christ."[2]

There is, of course, a sense in which all men, whether saved or lost, derive life from God who "quickeneth all things" (I Tim. 6:13) and is the source and ground of our very existence. "In him we live, and move, and have our being," as Paul declared to the pagan Athenians (Acts 17:28). But the life in which fallen men participate is attenuated and devoid of the essential spiritual quality of the infinite life of the Person of God. The life experienced by men "dead in trespasses and sins" and "alienated from the life of God" is not at all that "eternal life" which God offers men in Jesus Christ, His Son.

For the fulfillment of His eternal purposes, God created man in His own image—a moral intelligence with the faculty of spiritual initiative and volition, a spirit-being with the capacity for knowing his Creator and sharing His life in all its fulness. To provide occasion for the exercise of man's moral and spiritual faculty and to afford him opportunity for worship and faith toward his Creator, God confronted man with a simple, but essential, moral test. To Adam in Eden, He said, "Of every tree of the garden thou mayest freely eat. But of the tree of the knowledge of good and evil, thou shalt not eat of it: for in the day that thou eatest thereof thou shalt surely die" (Gen. 2:16, 17).

The simple test presented a direct challenge to Adam's faith. He knew nothing of death from experience or observation, and the fact of death could be grasped only by faith. Acceptance of the reality of death as an actual peril, solely on the word of his Creator, was tantamount to exercising faith in God Himself as the source of his very life. Thus, through faith, Adam avoided death and participated in the eternal life of

---

[2]A. T. Robertson, *Word Pictures in the New Testament*, Vol. V, p. 50.

God. As long as he continued in obedient faith, he continued in eternal life.

From the beginning of human history, it has been true that "the just shall live by faith" (Heb. 10:38). This cardinal principle enunciated by Habakkuk and thrice repeated in the New Testament, has governed the personal relation of individual men to God in all generations. Although it has had various modes of expression in different ages and under varying circumstances, the principle itself has been constant and fundamental from the creation of man. It governed the spiritual relation of Adam to God in Eden. God had warned Adam that the penalty for transgression was death. "In the day that thou eatest thereof thou shalt surely die" (Gen. 2:17). And thus it occurred:

When Adam sinned, death came at once; but so far as the body was concerned, its complete severing from the soul required more than nine hundred years. But the soul died at once, died suddenly; the bond with the Holy Spirit was severed, and only its raveling threads [remained] active in the feelings of shame.[3]

Though plunged by sin into spiritual death and deprived of the eternal life of his Creator in which he had participated by faith, Adam was not abandoned to everlasting despair. "Though God punished Adam and Eve, He did not curse them, as He did the Serpent, they being candidates for restoration."[4] God immediately promised the coming of a Redeemer, "the seed of the woman" (Gen. 3:15), who would crush the head of the Serpent.

It is evident from the Scriptures (Gen. 3:21; 4:4, Heb. 11:4) that God also instituted the ordinance of animal sacrifice in Eden. It was "by faith," not good fortune, that Abel offered to God an acceptable sacrifice. As "faith cometh by hearing," it is evident that God instituted animal sacrifice as an ordinance to be observed by men, and that He did so prior to Abel's act

---

[3]Abraham Kuyper, *The Work of the Holy Spirit*, p. 281.
[4]E. Harold Browne, *Commentary on the Holy Bible* (ed. F. C. Cook), Vol. I, p. 40.

of faith. The ordinance served as a representation of the "one sacrifice for sins for ever" ultimately to be provided through "the offering of the body of Jesus Christ once for all" (Heb. 10:10-14). It offered sinners a means whereby they might approach a righteous God in repentance and faith and commune with Him and know His forgiveness and gracious salvation.

We need not infer that every person who offered an animal sacrifice was fully aware of the prophetic significance of the ordinance. Indeed, the Apostles themselves failed to associate the ordinance with the approaching death of Jesus, the purpose and significance of which they failed to perceive until after His resurrection. But men's failure to comprehend the prophetic significance of the ordinance of animal sacrifice did not impair its validity in the sight of God.

The offering of every sacrifice was an object-lesson proclaiming the principle of vicarious sacrifice and substitutionary atonement. That much, at least, men could understand and appreciate. Man's offering of the appointed sacrifice constituted a confession of his sin and need for cleansing and redemption. It was an expression of his faith in God and a petition for grace and forgiveness. Although the offering of animal sacrifices did not "make the comers thereunto perfect" (Heb. 10:1), God nevertheless was pleased with the faith of the worshippers, as expressed in the act of sacrifice, and so imputed to them that righteousness which was to be imparted to all believers of all ages through the once-for-all offering of Christ—as yet to be accomplished, but eternal in the purpose of God.

The reconciliation of man to God and his restoration to participation in the eternal life of his Creator required no less than a perfect and complete expiation of all his sin. This, animal sacrifices could not accomplish. "For it is not possible that the blood of bulls and of goats should take away sins" (Heb. 10:4). But a Redeemer "appeared to put away sin by the sacrifice of himself" (Heb. 9:26) and to offer for the redemption of sinners His own precious blood, "as of a lamb without blemish and without spot" (I Pet. 1:19).

The penalty for sin is death, both spiritual and physical. That penalty Jesus paid in full, at dreadful cost to Himself. We cannot imagine the physical pain of crucifixion. But fearful as it was, it did not mark the true measure of "the cup" of His agony. The darkness which covered the land from the sixth hour to the ninth, while Jesus suffered on the cross, was symbolic of the spiritual desolation and death which came upon our holy Saviour when God "laid on him the iniquity of us all" and He who was without sin "was made sin for us, that we might be made the righteousness of God in him." His *soul* was made "an offering for sin" and He "poured out his soul unto death" (Isa. 53:10, 12). Out of the abyss of spiritual desolation and death came His wretched, anguished cry, "My God, my God, why hast thou forsaken me?" Gone was the gracious rapport of the earlier hours on the cross when He could say, "*Father*, forgive them. . . ." No longer was it "Father," but rather, "My *God*." And God had forsaken Him. He was alone in His agony of body and desolation of soul and spirit. The Son of man, made sin for all the guilty sons of Adam and banished from the Fathers' holy presence, cried in all the very anguish of hell itself, "My God, my God, why hast thou forsaken me?" He "poured out his soul unto death."

> But none of the ransomed ever knew
> How deep were the waters crossed;
> Nor how dark was the night the Lord passed through
> Ere He found His sheep that was lost.[5]

"It is finished!" Our Saviour's triumphant cry marked the completion of the offering of His soul for sin. He had drained the bitter cup of its last vile dregs. The angry venom of sin was spent. Gone forever was the dreadful gulf imposed by sin. Once again He knew the Father's gracious presence: "Father, into thy hands. . . ." Bowing His head, He dismissed His spirit, and the body in which He had borne our sins on the

---

[5]Elizabeth C. Clephane, from "The Ninety and Nine."

tree became the prey of death. The full penalty for sin had been paid.

In the life and death of Jesus, the holiness of God and His righteous Law have been vindicated and divine justice has been forever satisfied. In the cross of Christ, wrath and grace have met. "Mercy and truth are met together; righteousness and peace have kissed" at the cross of Him who is our peace. God now can be "just, and the justifier, of him who believes in Jesus." Atonement has been wrought in Christ—an objective atonement efficacious for all who believe.

Even if no man should ever say, "Thou, O Christ, art all I want; more than all in Thee I find," God says it. Christ and His work have this absolute value for the Father, whatever this or that individual may think of them. And as it is only on the basis of Christ and His work that reconciliation becomes an accomplished fact, it is strict truth to say that reconciliation—in the sense of man's return to God and acceptance with Him—is based on an objective atonement. It is because divine necessities have had homage done to them by Christ that the way is open for sinners to return to God through Him.[9]

An objective reconciliation has been accomplished for all mankind. Jesus "gave himself a ransom for all" (I Tim. 2:6) and "by the righteousness of [Jesus] the free gift came upon all men unto justification of life" (Rom. 5:18). For "in Christ, God was reconciling the world to himself" (II Cor. 5:19, cf. Meyer and Lange *ad loc.*). But what has been provided must be appropriated; what is objective must become subjective. Therefore, "be *ye* reconciled to God" (v. 20). Personal reconciliation to God in Christ is actual for individual men only as they trust in Him. It is ever true that "the just shall live by faith."

Men who do not participate by faith in the redemption in Christ are "dead in trespasses and sins" and "alienated from the life of God" (Eph 2:1; 4:18). But such men still bear the image of God (though marred by sin) and still retain the capacity

---

[9]James Denney, *The Christian Doctrine of Reconciliation*, p. 235.

for participation in the life of their Creator. They are the objects of the infinite love of God, who longs to share with them His own eternal life, through Christ.

"This is the record," writes John, "that God hath given to us eternal life, and this life is in his Son. He that hath the Son hath the life; and he that hath not the Son of God hath not the life." Jesus said of all who hear and follow Him, "I give unto them eternal life." But the gift of eternal life can neither be received nor possessed apart from the Giver, who said of Himself, "I am the way . . . and the life: no man cometh unto the Father but by me." To have Him is to have life; for "Christ is our life" (Col. 3:4). Kuyper writes:

It is true that in the soul of the regenerated there is a vital principle, but the source of its energy is outside of ourselves in Christ. There is indwelling, but not interpermeation. The dweller and his house are distinct. Hence in the regenerated man life is extraneous, its seat is not in himself. . . . To obtain gas from the city's gas-works is one thing; to manufacture it at one's own cost, in one's own establishment, is quite another. The regenerated child of God receives life directly from Christ, who is outside of him at the right hand of God, through the channels of faith.[7]

Although He is bodily at the right hand of the Father in heaven, Christ yet dwells in our hearts by faith, spiritually (Eph. 3:17). His gracious promise and invitation is, "Abide in me, and I in you" (John 15:4). His indwelling presence in all who abide in Him is, itself, the bestowal of life. "God hath given to us eternal life, and this life is in his Son. He that hath the Son hath the life."

It is equally true that "he that hath *not* the Son of God hath not the life." There is no eternal life for men apart from Him. Our Saviour's gracious invitation is, "If any man thirst, let him come unto me and drink. . . . Whosoever will, let him take the water of life freely" (John 7:37, Rev. 22:17). But most men who hear the Gospel invitation to eternal life somehow decline to accept. Like the men invited to the great supper (Luke

---

[7]Kuyper, *op. cit.*, p. 279.

14:16-24), they have other interests. Many, aware of a desperate hunger of heart and soul, seem unwilling to believe that Christ alone can satisfy. They "will not come to [Him] that they might have life" (John 5:40). They spend their days and strength carefully gathering to themselves all the little fads and devices which flatter the flesh and leave the soul in despair.

Sometime ago, the body of a prospector who evidently had died of thirst was found in a desert in California. He had died clutching a bag of copper pyrites, "fool's gold." In his pocket was a piece of paper on which he had written, "I died rich." Millions there are who clasp to themselves a bag of fool's gold for which they spend their lives unto death—to awaken miserable paupers in hell!

We who know Christ as Saviour and Lord may well ask, Have we failed to demonstrate convincingly that we have found One who satisfies the deepest longings and meets every need of all who trust in Him? In the lovely "Song of Songs," it is only after the bride has declared the excellencies of her Beloved—One "altogether lovely"—that the daughters of Jerusalem who first protested "What is thy beloved more than another beloved?" are moved to exclaim, "Whither is thy beloved turned aside? that we may seek him with thee!" (The Song of Solomon 5:9-6:1). Friend in Christ, except our witness for our Saviour be winsome and convincing, the lost around us will not come to know Him who said, "I am come that they might have life, and that they might have it more abundantly" (John 10:10).

> And this is life eternal, that they know thee, the only true God, and Jesus Christ whom thou hast sent.
>
> JOHN 17:3

Can Eternal Life Be Forfeited?

The words that I speak unto you, they are spirit, and they are life. . . . Verily, verily, I say unto you, If a man keep my word, he shall never see death.

* * *

Let that therefore remain in you which ye have heard from the beginning. If that which ye have heard from the beginning shall remain in you, ye also shall remain in the Son and in the Father. And this is the promise that he hath promised us, the life eternal.

* * *

This is the record, that God hath given to us eternal life, and this life is in his Son. He that hath the Son hath the life; and he that hath not the Son of God hath not the life.

JOHN 6:63; 8:51
I JOHN 2:24, 25
I JOHN 5:11, 12

CHAPTER IV

CAN ETERNAL LIFE BE FORFEITED?

CHRISTIANS LONG have been divided over the question of whether a man, once saved, can subsequently forfeit salvation. The doctrine of the perseverance of the saints popularly defined as "once in grace, always in grace" has been championed with fervor by millions of sincere Christians and devout Bible scholars. It has been opposed with equal fervor by other millions equally sincere and devout.

Unfortunately, Christian charity often has been cast aside in the fervor of contention by good men on both sides. It should not be so. Some Christian communions have demonstrated that the question need not be made a test of fellowship, and that Christian men of good will of both persuasions can unite in proclaiming the saving grace of God in Christ. Nevertheless, the question of the validity of the popular doctrine of unconditional security is of more than academic interest. One cannot lightly accept or reject a doctrine of such magnitude.

In any consideration of the question before us, our real concern must be, "What saith the scripture?" In all their teaching, our Lord and the Apostles constantly appealed to the Holy Scriptures. To them must be addressed our first and final appeal in our consideration of the doctrine of the security of the believer.

I.

In the present chapter, we shall consider four discourses of Jesus, the first of which is Luke's account of our Lord's interpretation of His Parable of the Sower (chapter 8):

11 Now the parable is this: The seed is the word of God.

12 Those by the way side are they that hear; then cometh the devil and taketh away the word out of their hearts, lest they should believe and be saved.

13 They on the rock are they which, when they hear, receive the word with joy; and these have no root, which for a while believe, and in time of temptation fall away.

14 And that which fell among thorns are they which, when they have heard, go forth and are choked with cares and riches and pleasures of this life, and bring no fruit to perfection.

15 But that on the good ground are they which in an honest and good heart, having heard the word, keep it, and bring forth fruit with patience.

Let us make two observations concerning the words of our Lord. First, it is possible for one to believe only temporarily (v. 13). We are confronted, of course, with the question of what is meant by the word *believe*. Does it here denote actual saving faith, or a "believing" which falls short of true saving faith?

The word *pisteuō* possesses latitude. In the New Testament the word is "used especially of the faith by which a man embraces Jesus, i.e., a conviction, full of joyful trust, that Jesus is the Messiah—the divinely appointed author of eternal salvation in the kingdom of God, conjoined with obedience to Christ."[1] But it is true that the word can be used with reference to a conviction that falls short of the faith that actually appropriates Christ as Saviour (cf. John 2:23-25, Jas. 2:19).

Context, necessarily a major consideration in any exegesis, must be relied upon to establish the precise meaning of *pisteuousin* in verse 13. The use of the word in verse 12 establishes its meaning as it is employed in the parable. It is clearly a believing unto salvation: ". . . lest they should believe and be saved." No warrant is present for assigning a different meaning to the word as it appears in verse 13, and any exegesis which requires it is obviously prejudiced. Those who "for a while

---

[1]Thayer, *Greek-English Lexicon of the New Testament,* p. 511.

believe" are depicted by Jesus as making a sincere beginning in the life of faith. Language and context forbid any other conclusion. Their subsequent fall does not obviate the fact that their believing, while it continued, was actual saving faith.

The second observation which we would make concerning our Saviour's parable is that those who "bring forth fruit with patience" (hupomonē, steadfastness, endurance, perseverance) are those who, "having heard the word, keep it" (v. 15) in contrast with those who believe only "for a while." "This last word [hupomonē] strikes the keynote of the parable."[2] It is essential that those who receive the word "keep it" (katechō, hold fast, keep secure, keep firm possession of).

The necessity that a man faithfully retain the saving Word once received, if he would continue in grace and eternal life, is declared by Jesus in John 8:51, "Verily, verily, I say unto you, If a man keep [tēreō, retain and observe] my word, he shall never see death." Similar are His words in Luke 11:28, "Blessed are they that hear the word of God and keep [phulassō, guard and observe] it." Context (vv. 24-28) indicates that faithfully keeping the Word, once heard and received, is the way of continued deliverance and salvation.

Warning that "some shall depart from the faith," Paul admonishes Timothy, pastor of the church at Ephesus, to "take heed unto thyself and unto the doctrine; continue in them: for in doing this thou shalt both save thyself and them that hear thee" (I Tim. 4:1, 16). He warns the Corinthians that, by means of the Gospel which they accepted when he preached to them, they are now being saved (sōzesthe, present indicative passive) "if you are holding fast [katechete, present indicative] the word which I preached to you" (I. Cor. 15:1, 2).

James urges his brethren to continue to "receive with meekness the engrafted word, which is able to save your souls" (Jas. 1:21). John warns his dear children in the faith against the efforts of apostates to lead them astray through false doc-

---

[2] W. F. Adeney, The New-Century Bible: St. Luke, p. 217.

trines, exhorting them to "let that remain in you which ye have heard from the beginning [the true Gospel]. If that which ye have heard from the beginning shall remain in you, ye also shall remain in the Son and in the Father. And this is the promise which He Himself promised us, the life eternal" (I John 2:24, 25. Cf. II Tim. 3:13-15, Col. 1:21-23).

It is the testimony of our Saviour and the New Testament writers that an initial reception of the word of the Gospel must be followed by faithful retention, if men are to continue in the saving grace of Christ and the eternal life of God.

II.

The second discourse of Jesus which we shall consider is His parable of the Lord and His Steward (Luke 12):

> 42 And the Lord said, Who then is that faithful and wise steward, whom his lord shall make ruler over his household, to give them their portion of meat in due season?
> 43 Blessed is that servant whom his lord when he cometh shall find so doing.
> 44 Of a truth I say unto you that he will make him ruler over all that he hath.
> 45 But and if that servant say in his heart, My lord delayeth his coming, and shall begin to beat the menservants and maidens, and to eat and drink, and to be drunken,
> 46 The lord of that servant will come in a day when he looketh not for him, and at an hour when he is not aware, and will cut him in sunder, and will appoint him his portion with the unbelievers.

It has been argued by some that the unfaithful steward of verses 45, 46 was never a true disciple, but only a hypocrite from the beginning, and the Lord's sudden appearance simply brings to an end his false pretension of discipleship. Such an argument rests on two false assumptions:

First, it must be assumed that two different stewards are in view in the parable, one of whom proves faithful, and the other of whom proves unfaithful. But Jesus did not speak of two stewards. Rather, He spoke only of "that servant," *ho doulos ekeinos.* The demonstrative pronoun *ekeinos* is emphatic. Language forbids any assumption that more than one servant is in view in the parable.

The second false assumption on which the argument of original hypocrisy must rest is the assumption that the lord was unaware of the true character of his steward at the time of his appointing, being deceived by his hypocrisy. This might happen in the affairs of ordinary men; but it cannot happen to our Saviour, who is the Lord in view in the parable. While it is true that many pretend to be servants of Christ who do not know and follow Him as Saviour and Lord, it is equally true that Christ Himself cannot personally entrust responsibilities in His holy service to men who are not His. And it is ever true that "the Lord knoweth them that are his" (II Tim. 2:19).

It is obvious that Jesus' parable has no application to men who do not know Him as Saviour and Lord, and who have not sincerely undertaken to follow and serve Him. His parable concerns only men who know Him and to whom He commits solemn responsibilities as His true disciples.

A correct analysis of the parable is as follows:

> The Question (v. 42): "Who is the faithful and wise steward" whom his Lord will reward at his coming?
>
> The Answer (v. 43): "That servant whom his lord when he cometh shall find so doing" as instructed.
>
> The Reward (v. 44): "He will make him ruler over all that he hath."
>
> The Peril (v. 45): "That servant" may grow careless and become unfaithful during his lord's long absence.
>
> The Penalty (v. 46): The lord will come unexpectedly and "cut him in sunder" and "appoint him his portion with the unbelievers" (or the "unfaithful").[3]

---

[3]*Apistos* may mean "unfaithful" in the sense of *unbelieving, incredulous;* or of *unreliable, untrustworthy.* The precise meaning of the word in v. 46 is of no consequence, as the Scriptures everywhere affirm that faithfulness in service is the *fruit* of which true faith is the *root.*

Some may wish to argue that the parable, after all, is only hypothetical—which, of course, may be argued with respect to *all* the parables of Jesus. But such argument is without point. Our Lord's parables were given, not as entertainment, but to convey solemn spiritual verities. Whatever else our Lord's parable may teach, it cannot be denied that it clearly teaches that one who is a true disciple of Christ, known of Him and entrusted with solemn responsibilities, through carelessness and presumption can depart from the path of faithfulness and finally inherit everlasting shame and ruin.

The thesis that there are two possible courses open to the disciple during his Lord's long absence is substantiated in Luke 12:39. Jesus declared that the goodman of the house who "suffered his house to be broken through" *could* have watched, had he chosen to do so. The thesis is frequently affirmed in the New Testament, perhaps nowhere more concisely than in Hebrews 10:38, "Now the just shall live by faith: but if he[4] draw back, my soul shall have no pleasure in him."

---

[4]There is no warrant in the Greek text for the words *any man* supplied in AV. The introduction of *tis* into the text of Heb. 10:38 is ascribed to Beza. Bloomfield comments: "[Beza's] ostensible reason for introducing *tis* [is] that, by this rendering, another version was avoided, by no means agreeable to Beza's theological opinions. . . . [In Bp. Pearson's opinion] when Beza translated, 'But the just shall live by faith; but if *any man* draw back, my soul shall have no pleasure in *it*,' his two methods of excluding the 'just man' from being the subject of the latter clause—1. by introducing the words 'any man;' and, 2. by transferring God's displeasure from the *person* who draws back (him) to the act of withdrawing (it)—indicate either a want of good faith, or an undue concession to theological opinions. . . . Though [Calvin] did not venture on the *change* introduced by Beza, yet he strove to *suppress* the sense naturally resulting from the words, by rendering, *ean huposteilētai,* 'si subductus fuerit;' though such is evidently at variance with the usus loquendi both of the Classical and the Scriptural writers. And, as it would not have been convenient to attempt any justification of this version, he chose (contrary to his usual custom) to be silent upon these verses. Nothing is plainer than that all the above methods were (to use the words of Dr. A. Clarke) 'intended to save the doctrine of *final and unconditional* perseverance; which doctrine this text destroys." —S. T. Bloomfield, *The Greek Testament with English Notes, Critical, Philological, and Exegetical,* Vol. II, p. 457.

Paul recognized the fearful possibility of ultimately finding himself rejected, should he allow himself to become careless and indulgent toward sin. In I Corinthians 9:27, he declares his purpose to continually subdue his body, with its fleshly appetites, "lest that by any means, when I have preached to others, I myself should be rejected."

Many have contended that Paul's fear was not that he might fail of salvation, but rather that he might find himself disqualified for further service as an apostle and that he might fail to receive the full reward which faithfulness secures. Appeal is made to the earlier part of chapter 9 as context, especially verses 16-18. But such an appeal ignores the significance of the *immediate* context, 9:23-10:14. Robertson writes: "Paul appeals to the experience of the Israelites in the wilderness in confirmation of his statement concerning himself in 9:26 f. and as a powerful warning to the Corinthians who may be tempted to flirt with the idolatrous practices of their neighbors. It is a real, not an imaginary peril."[5] Influence of the immediate context establishes the fact that Paul's fear was the possibility of losing, not opportunities or rewards for service, but the salvation of his own soul.

It is noteworthy that Paul uses the same adjective *(adokimos)* in his warning to the Corinthians (II Cor. 13:5) to examine themselves to determine whether they are actually in the faith and indwelt by Jesus Christ. He declares that Christ does not dwell in any who are *adokimoi*. Such cannot be in grace, for "he that hath not the Son of God hath not the life." Paul's fear that he might become *adokimos* was not merely a fear that he might lose some of his opportunity and reward for service as an apostle. Commenting on I Corinthians 9:27, Robertson writes:

Most writers take Paul to refer to the possibility of his rejection in his personal salvation at the end of the race. He does not claim absolute perfection (Phil. 3:12) and so he presses on. At the end he has serene con-

---

[5]A. T. Robertson, *Word Pictures in the New Testament*, Vol. IV, p. 151.

fidence (II Tim. 4:7) with the race run and won. It is a humbling thought for us all to see this wholesome fear instead of smug complacency in this greatest of all heralds of Christ.[6]

III.

The third discourse of Jesus which we shall consider is the Parable of the Law of Forgiveness (Matthew 18):

21 Then came Peter to him and said, Lord, how oft shall my brother sin against me, and I forgive him? till seven times?

22 Jesus saith unto him, I say not unto thee, until seven times; but until seventy times seven.

23 Therefore is the kingdom of heaven likened unto a certain king which would take account of his servants.

24 And when he had begun to reckon, one was brought unto him which owed him ten thousand talents.

25 But forasmuch as he had not to pay, his lord commanded him to be sold, and his wife and children and all that he had, and payment to be made.

26 The servant therefore fell down and worshipped him, saying, Lord, have patience with me, and I will pay thee all.

27 Then the lord of that servant was moved with compassion, and loosed him, and forgave him the debt.

28 But the same servant went out and found one of his fellow servants, which owed him an hundred pence: and he laid hands on him, and took him by the throat, saying, Pay me that thou owest.

29 And his fellow servant fell down at his feet and besought him, saying, Have patience with me, and I will pay thee all.

30 And he would not, but went and cast him into prison till he should pay the debt.

31 So when his fellow servants saw what was done, they were very sorry and came and told their lord all that was done.

32 Then his lord, after that he had called him, said unto him, O thou wicked servant, I forgave thee all that debt because thou desiredst me:

33 Shouldest not thou also have had compassion on thy fellow servant, even as I had pity on thee?

34 And his lord was wroth, and delivered him to the tormentors till he should pay all that was due unto him.

---

[6]*Ibid.*, p. 150.

35 So likewise shall my heavenly Father do also unto you, if ye from your hearts forgive not every one his brother their trespasses.

Jesus here teaches that the forgiveness of God, though fully and freely granted in pure mercy and grace to undeserving sinners, nevertheless remains conditional, according to the individual's subsequent response to the gracious forgiveness which he has received. This is the point of His parable. To deny this is to deny that the parable has meaning.

Some attempt to evade the issue by insisting that the teaching belongs to another dispensation.[7] Let it be observed that such objection constitutes tacit admission that the doctrine of unconditional security cannot be established in the pre-Christian era. It also constitutes a contention that saving faith in the present era differs essentially from saving faith in former eras. Furthermore, it seems strange that men should forbid Jesus the privilege of teaching, during His earthly ministry, any great principles governing man's relation to God—not only during the few remaining days of His brief earthly ministry, but throughout the age to follow, for which He was even then preparing His disciples. It seems even stranger that men who so easily reject much of our Lord's later teaching as "not applicable to the present dispensation" do not hesitate to accept much of His earliest teaching (to Nicodemus, for example) as being fully applicable to the present age. (One friend, in conversation with the author, even denied that our Lord's words in John 15 have any bearing on the question of our relation to Christ today, since they were spoken "before Calvary"—a few hours! What delicate, fragile hairs skilled "rightly dividers" can sometimes neatly split with one swift, sure stroke of their hermeneutical broadaxe!)

It is true that Jesus made reference to certain legal and ceremonial aspects of the Mosaic economy which are not applicable today. But it is also true that He enunciated cardinal

---

[7] Cf. Lewis Sperry Chafer, *Systematic Theology*, Vol. III, p. 292.

principles governing man's spiritual relation to God which are as valid today as at the moment of utterance. One of these principles, according to His teaching in the Parable of the Law of Forgiveness, is that true repentance toward God is inseparably associated with our attitude toward our fellow men and cannot exist apart from a charitable, forgiving spirit toward others.

Such true repentance, like sincere faith and the faithful retention of the saving word of the Gospel, is necessary—not merely for a fleeting moment at the occasion of one's conversion, but continually and habitually, as an essential condition of forgiveness and salvation. "So likewise shall my heavenly Father do also unto you," warned Jesus, "if ye from your hearts forgive not every one his brother their trespasses." It is possible, warned Jesus, that Peter and others who have known the forgiving grace of God might forfeit that forgiveness. The forgiving grace of God cannot dwell in bitter, unforgiving hearts. He who refuses to forgive his brother has no real sense of need for the forgiveness of God and no just claim on His gracious forgiveness. "Forgive us our debts, as we forgive our debtors."

IV.

The fourth discourse which we shall consider contains some of the most solemn and intimate words ever uttered by our Saviour concerning the nature of the relation between Himself and all who would be His. The words were spoken on the eve of His betrayal shortly after He had instituted the simple supper which is to serve as a memorial of His death until He comes again, and which is the symbol of our partaking, by faith, of the body and blood of Him who is our life (John 15):

1 I am the true vine, and my Father is the husbandman.

2 Every branch in me that beareth not fruit he taketh away: and every branch that beareth fruit, he cleanseth it, that it may bear more fruit.

3 Already ye are clean because of the word which I have spoken unto you.

4 Abide in me, and I in you. As the branch cannot bear fruit of itself, except it abide in the vine, so neither can ye, except ye abide in me.

5 I am the vine, ye are the branches: He that abideth in me, and I in him, the same beareth much fruit: for apart from me ye can do nothing.

6 If a man abide not in me, he is cast forth as a branch, and is withered; and they gather them and cast them into the fire, and they are burned.

These words of our Lord contain a cardinal axiom of the Christian life—indeed, the foundation principle governing the relation of Christ and the individual throughout his earthly sojourn in a moral and spiritual universe. Every pertinent Bible passage and every consideration of the question of the individual's relation to the Saviour must be equated and evaluated in the light of this foundation principle enunciated by our Lord.

Before examining the principle in its setting in our passage, let us consider two verses from Jesus' discourse in John 6 in which the principle is vividly portrayed: "He that eateth my flesh and drinketh my blood dwelleth in me, and I in him. As the living Father hath sent me, and I live by the Father, so he that eateth me, even he shall live by me" (John 6:56, 57).

Jesus here declares that, just as He derives life from the Father who sent Him, in like manner all who partake of Him by faith will live by Him, and He will dwell in them and they in Him. Commenting on verse 57, Robertson writes:

The Father is the source of life and so "I live because of the Father" (kágō zō dia ton patera). He that eateth me (ho trōgōn me). Still bolder putting of the mystical appropriation of Christ (51, 53, 54, 56). Because of me (di' eme). The same idea appears in 14:19: "Because I live ye shall live also." See 11:25. Jesus Christ is our ground of hope and guarantee of immortality. Life is in Christ. . . . As the Father is the fount of life to Christ, so Christ is the fount of life to us.[3]

What Robertson speaks of as "the mystical appropriation of Christ" is more than a punctiliar once-for-all appropriation—

---

[3]Robertson, op. cit., Vol. V, p. 112 f.

the act of a moment; it is a continual process of appropriating.
This fact is conveyed by the present participles *ho trōgōn* and
pinōn. It is true that "the participle with the article sometimes
loses much of its verbal force."[9] But the present participles
under consideration cannot be deemed to have lost the durative
aspect customary in present participles, because of the influence of context. *Menō* (dwell) and *zaō* (live) are necessarily
durative from the standpoint of both *Aktionsart* and intrinsic
meaning, and their influence imposes a durative quality upon
the present participles which, under other circumstances, they
might possibly lack because of the presence of the article.
Virtually all contemporary translators have recognized this
fact. Consider, for example:

Williams: "Whoever continues to eat my flesh and drink my blood
continues to live in union with me and I in union with him. Just as
the living Father has sent me and I live because of the Father, so whoever keeps on eating me will live because of me."[10]

Montgomery: "He who feeds upon my flesh and drinks my blood
abides in me, and I in him. Just as the living Father has sent me, and
I live by the Father, so also that man who feeds on me shall live by me."[11]

Verkuyl: "He who eats My flesh and drinks My blood remains in Me
and I in him. Just as the life-giving Father sent Me and I live through
the Father, so he who nourishes on Me shall live through Me."[12]

Let us now state the foundation principle governing the relation of Christ and the individual, as implied in the words of
Jesus in John 15:1-6:

Throughout his earthly sojourn, the relation of the
individual to Christ is never a *static* relationship exist-

[9]A. T. Robertson, *A Grammar of the Greek New Testament in the Light of Historical Research*, p. 892.

[10]From *The New Testament: A Translation in the Language of the People*, by Charles B. Williams, Moody Press, Chicago. Used by permission.

[11]From *The New Testament in Modern English*, by Helen Barrett Mont-gomery, copyright 1924, 1952, by The American Baptist Publication Society, Philadelphia. Used by permission.

[12]From *The Berkeley Version of The New Testament*, by Gerrit Verkuyl, Zondervan Publishing House, Grand Rapids, Michigan. Used by permission.

ing as the irrevocable consequence of a past decision, act, or experience. Rather, it is a present mutual indwelling of the believer and the Saviour, the sharing of a common life which emanates from Him "who is our life" (Col. 3:4). For the believer, it is a living participation proceeding upon a living faith in a living Saviour. The principle is reduced to its simplest statement in the words of Jesus, "Abide in me, and I in you" (John 15:4).

Let us observe three essential truths in our Lord's teaching in John 15:1-6. First, the mutual indwelling of the disciples and the Saviour is dependent upon the volition of the disciples. "Abide [*menō*, dwell, remain, continue] in me, and I in you" (v. 4). The indwelling of Christ within the disciples is presented as the corollary of their abiding in Him.

(Some have asserted that, despite John 15:4, verse 16 indicates that the choice really lies with Christ, rather than with the disciples. They have erred in assuming that the choice in verse 16 is with respect to salvation. The choice is rather to the Apostolate, as indicated by context (vv. 15-27). Luke 6:13, Mark 3:14, John 6:70; 13:18, and Acts 1:2 all have reference to Christ's same act of choosing: the choice of certain ones of His disciples to be His Apostles.)

The second truth to observe is that the consequences of continuing to abide in Christ are His continued indwelling (v. 4a), and the consequent fruitfulness of the disciple: "I am the vine, ye are the branches: He that abideth in me, and I in him, the same bringeth forth much fruit" (v. 5).

The third important truth is that the consequences of failure to abide in Christ are (1) fruitlessness: "As the branch cannot bear fruit of itself, except it abide in the vine, no more can ye, except ye abide in me . . . for apart from me ye can do nothing" (vv. 4b, 5c); and (2) removal: "Every branch in me that beareth not fruit he taketh away . . . If a man abide not in me, he is cast forth as a branch, and is withered; and they[13] gather them and cast them into the fire, and they are burned" (vv. 2a, 6). Robertson comments:

The only way to continue "clean" (pruned) and to bear fruit is to maintain vital spiritual connexion with Christ (the vine). Judas is gone and Satan will sift the rest of them like wheat (Luke 22:31 f.). Blind complacency is a peril to the preacher. . . . There is nothing for a broken off branch to do but wither and die. . . . The apostles are thus vividly warned against presumption. Jesus as the vine will fulfil his part of the relation as long as the branches keep in vital union with him.[14]

Advocates of the doctrine of unconditional security invariably have found themselves hard pressed to interpret John 15:1-6. Reading their comments on this brief passage, one is continually reminded of the words on the sign over the old ironsmith's shop: "All kinds of fancy twistings and turnings done here."

Bishop Ryle urges us to "always remember that the passage before us is a parable, and as a parable it must be interpreted. We must be careful not to press each word and sentence in it too far . . . we must look at the main scope and the great lesson which it contains, rather than at each clause."[15] Having urged us not to examine each clause and sentence too closely, Bishop Ryle proceeds to declare of all who are cast forth from the Vine, "Doubtless there are those who seem to depart from grace, and to go back from union with Christ; but we need not doubt in such cases that the grace was not real, but seeming, and the union was not true, but fictitious."[16] This, of course, is a necessary assumption for the advocates of unconditional security. Its necessary corollary, furthermore, is the contention that the "branches in Me" of which Jesus spoke are not necessarily true believers. Unable to deny that "branches" defect and are cast forth, the proponents of unconditional security find

[13]"Men" supplied by AV is not in the Greek text.
[14]A. T. Robertson, *Word Pictures in the New Testament,* Vol. V, p. 258.
[15]J. C. Ryle, *Expository Thoughts on the Gospels,* Vol. IV, p. 331 f.
[16]*Ibid.,* p. 337.

themselves under the necessity of "defining" the branches. Bishop Ryle therefore contends that ". . . it cannot be shown that a 'branch in Me' must mean a believer in Me. It means nothing more than 'a professing member of my Church, a man joined to the company of my people, but not joined to Me.' "[17] Such a contention is necessary, of course, if one is to defend the doctrine of unconditional security. But some of us find it difficult to conceive of Jesus as saying to His Apostles, "I am the vine, and all who are professing members of my Church and joined to the company of my people, though not necessarily joined to Me, are the branches in Me."

Similarly, Hengstenberg quotes Lampe as saying, "In a certain sense, even hypocrites may be said to be in Christ, partly because, in the external fellowship of the Church, they partake of the sacrament of union with Christ, and therefore *boast themselves* of being in Christ; partly because they are *esteemed by others* to be such as belong to the mystical body, or at least are *tolerated* in the external communion of the disciples."[18] But again, it is difficult to conceive of Jesus as saying, "I am the vine, and all who partake of the sacrament in the external fellowship of the Church and who therefore boast themselves of being in Me and are esteemed by others to be such as belong to my mystical body, or at least are tolerated in the external communion of my disciples, are the branches."

Similarly, in an attempt to reconcile the passage with his theology, Calvin declares that ". . . many are supposed to be in the vine, according to the opinion of men, who actually have no root in the vine."[19] True; but irrelevant. For Jesus was not speaking about the opinions of men, but about solemn realities—about things as they are, not as men may imagine them to be. We must protest that any definition of the branches that cannot easily be inserted into our Saviour's discourse without a

---

[17]*Ibid.*, p. 334.

[18]E. W. Hengstenberg, *Commentary on the Gospel of St. John*, Vol. II, p. 244 f., italics his.

[19]John Calvin, *Commentary on the Gospel According to John*, Vol. II, p. 108.

sense of glaring incongruity is obviously inadmissible. And again, it is unthinkable that Christ should say, "I am the vine, and all who are supposed to be in the vine according to the opinion of men, some of whom do not actually have root in the vine, are the branches." Such arbitrary definitions of the branches, ridiculous as they are, are nevertheless unavoidable for all who deny that Jesus taught that men who are true believers can ultimately abandon faith and fail to abide in Him, thus to be cast forth and withered and, in the end, burned.

Again, all who would define the branches as mere professors outwardly associated with the visible church must require Jesus to refer, not to Himself, but to the church as "the vine." But Jesus did not say, "The church is the vine," but rather, "I am the vine." Nor did He speak of "branches in the church," but of "branches in Me." All manner of artifices and absurdities must be resorted to by those who would reduce our Lord's grave, heart-searching discourse to the level of the mere external by insisting that He had reference to nothing more than outward affiliation with the visible church by professed Christians. Let it be observed that only what has first been alive can become withered.

Let us be done with "all kinds of fancy twistings and turnings done here" in the futile attempts of misguided men to reconcile John 15:1-6 with what they sincerely, but mistakenly, believe to be the total message of the Holy Scriptures with respect to the way of salvation and eternal life. Let us recognize the union of Vine and branches to be what it is—the living union of Christ and all true believers, who derive life from Him as they eat His flesh and drink His blood, so simply and beautifully portrayed in the Holy Supper which Jesus had instituted just before His solemn discourse in which He said, "I am the vine, ye are the branches." Let us accept at face value our Saviour's grave and loving warning that it is indeed possible for us to forfeit eternal life by failing to abide in Him "who is our life."

In his sermon "The True Branches of the True Vine," Alexander Maclaren, the peer of British Baptist expositors, said:

. . . even at that moment, our Lord, in all His tenderness and pity, could not but let words of warning—grave, solemn, tragical—drop from His lips. This generation does not like to hear them, for its conception of the Gospel is a thing with no minor notes in it, with no threatenings. . . . But Jesus Christ could not speak about the blessedness of fruitfulness and the joy of life in Himself without speaking about its necessary converse, the awfulness of separation from Him, of barrenness, of withering, and of destruction.

Separation is withering. Did you ever see a hawthorn bough that children bring home from the woods and stick in the grate; how in a day or two the little fresh green leaves all shrivel up and the white blossoms become brown and smell foul, and the only thing to be done with it is to fling it into the fire and get rid of it? "And so," says Jesus Christ, "as long as a man holds on to Me and the sap comes into him, he will flourish; and as soon as the connection is broken, all that was so fair will begin to shrivel, and all that was green will grow brown and turn to dust, and all that was blossom will droop, and there will be no more fruit any more for ever."

Withering means destruction. The language of our text is a description of what befalls the actual branches of the literal vine; but it is made a representation of what befalls the individuals whom these branches represent, by that added clause, "like a branch." Look at the mysteriousness of the language. "They gather them." Who? "They cast them into the fire." Who have the tragic task of flinging the withered branches into some mysterious fire? All is left vague with unexplained awfulness. The solemn fact that the withering of manhood by separation from Jesus Christ requires and ends in the consuming of the withered is all that we have here. We have to speak of it pityingly, with reticence, with terror, with tenderness, with awe lest it should be our fate.

But O, dear brethren! be on your guard against the tendency of the thinking of this generation to paste a bit of blank paper over all the threatenings of the Bible, and to blot out from its consciousness the grave issues that it holds forth. One of two things must befall the branch, either it is in the Vine or it gets into the fire. If we would avoid the fire, let us see to it that we are in the Vine.[20]

---

[20]Alexander Maclaren, *Expositions of Holy Scripture: St. John*, Vol. II, pp. 15-17.

How blest are they who still abide
Close shelter'd in Thy bleeding side!
Who life and strength from Thee derive,
And by Thee move, and in Thee live.
Firstborn of many brethren Thou!
To Thee, lo, all our souls we bow;
To Thee our hearts and hands we give;
Thine may we die, Thine may we live.

ZINZENDORF (tr. Wesley)

"What Saith the Scripture?"

Verily, verily, I say unto you, He that heareth my word and believeth on him that sent me hath everlasting life, and shall not come into condemnation, but is passed from death unto life.

JOHN 5:24

And I give unto them eternal life; and they shall never perish, neither shall any man pluck them out of my hand. My Father, which gave them me, is greater than all; and no man is able to pluck them out of my Father's hand.

JOHN 10:28, 29

Chapter V

WHAT SAITH THE SCRIPTURE?

There is a solemn finality about the words of John: "This is the record, that God hath given to us eternal life, and this life is in his Son. He that hath the Son hath the life, and he that hath not the Son of God hath not the life" (I John 5:11, 12).

What are the conditions whereby men may have the Son of God and life in Him? Believers of the Scriptures all agree: "repentance toward God and faith toward our Lord Jesus Christ" (Acts 20:21). But not all agree as to the essential *circumstance* of repentance and saving faith. Many believe that saving faith is the act of a moment—one great moment in which the sinner humbly acknowledges his sin in repentance toward God and accepts Jesus Christ as his personal Saviour. They believe that one grand and holy moment of decision ushers one into an irrevocable state of grace in which he is unconditionally secure. But others are persuaded that the moment of holy decision is but the beginning, and that the state of grace is not irrevocable in our present earthly sojourn in God's moral universe in which "the just shall live by faith." They are persuaded that saving faith is not the act of a moment, but the attitude of a life; the initial decision must be perpetually implemented throughout the life of the believer, and such is not inevitable. Who is right? Serious arguments have been advanced by able advocates of the doctrine of unconditional security, arguments which demand answers from those who refuse to embrace their doctrine.

51

Many devout Christians and Bible scholars sincerely believe that it is the teaching of the Scriptures that, once a person truly experiences saving grace, his status as a child of God is irrevocable. "Once in grace, always in grace"—despite any and all eventualities. Without doubt, many of God's noblest saints are of such persuasion. But the question before us is not, Who believes what? The question of sole concern is "What saith the scripture?" Let it be remembered as we proceed in the development of our treatise that to disagree with good men is not to dishonor them, and that we are not concerned with personalities.

A popular argument of advocates of the doctrine of unconditional security, an argument from reason, is couched in the question, If eternal life can be terminated, how then is it eternal? Such a question proceeds from a fundamental misapprehension. It rests upon the erroneous assumption that, at conversion, God somehow implants a bit of eternal life within the soul of the individual in such a way that it becomes his inalienable personal possession *ipso facto*. Certainly eternal life is *eternal*. But the Bible declares that eternal life—the very life of God Himself—can only be *shared* with men. It cannot be possessed by men apart from a living union with Christ, in and through whom that life is available to men. Maclaren has well said:

Union with Christ by faith is the condition of a real communication of life. "In Him was life," says John's Gospel, meaning thereby to assert, in the language of [Col. 1:16, 17], that "in Him were all things created, and in Him all things consist." Life in all its forms is dependent on union in varying manner with the Divine, and upheld only by His continual energy. The creature must touch God or perish. Of that energy the Uncreated Word of God is the channel—"with Thee is the fountain of life." As the life of the body, so the higher self-conscious life of the thinking, feeling, striving soul is also fed and kept alight by the perpetual operation of a higher Divine energy, imparted in like manner by the Divine Word. Therefore, with deep truth, the psalm just quoted goes on to say, "In Thy light shall we see light"—and therefore, too, John's Gospel continues: "And the life was the light of men."

But there is a still higher plane on which life may be manifested, and nobler energies which may accompany it. The body may live, and mind and heart be dead. Therefore Scripture speaks of a threefold life: that of the animal nature, that of the intellectual and emotional nature, and that of the spirit, which lives when it is conscious of God and touches Him by aspiration, hope, and love. This is the loftiest life. Without it, a man is dead while he lives. With it, he lives though he dies. And like the others, it depends on union with the Divine life as it is stored in Jesus Christ; but in this case, the union is a conscious union by faith. If I trust to Him, and am thereby holding firmly by Him, my union with Him is so real that, in the measure of my faith, His fulness passes over into my emptiness, His righteousness into my sinfulness, His life into my death, as surely as the electric shock thrills my nerves when I grasp the poles of the battery.

No man can breathe into another's nostrils the breath of life. But Christ can and does breathe His life into us; and this true miracle of a communication of spiritual life takes place in every man who humbly trusts himself to Him.[1]

Maclaren's thesis is fully substantiated in the Holy Scriptures. Consider the following passages:

He that eateth my flesh and drinketh my blood dwelleth in me, and I in him. As the living Father hath sent me, and I live by the Father, so he that eateth me, even he shall live by me (John 6:56, 57).

I am the way, the truth, and the life: no man cometh unto the Father but by me (John 14:6).

I am the resurrection and the life: he that believeth in me, though he were dead, yet shall he live: and whosoever liveth and believeth in me shall never die (John 11:25, 26).

. . . Christ, who is our life . . . (Col. 3:4).

The gift of God is eternal life in Jesus Christ our Lord (Rom. 6:23 ASV).

That which was from the beginning, which we have heard, which we have seen with our eyes, which we have looked upon and our hands have handled, of the Word of life: For the life was manifested, and we have seen it, and bear witness and show unto you that eternal life which was with the Father, and was manifested unto us. . . . And this is the record,

---

[1]Alexander Maclaren, *The Epistles of St. Paul to the Colossians and Philemon (The Expositor's Bible,* ed. W. Robertson Nicoll), p. 259 f.

that God hath given to us eternal life, and this life is in his Son. He that hath the Son hath the life; and he that hath not the Son of God hath not the life. . . . Let that therefore remain in you which ye have heard from the beginning. If that which ye have heard from the beginning shall remain in you, ye also shall remain in the Son and in the Father. And this is the promise that he hath promised us, even the eternal life (I John 1:1, 2; 5:11, 12; 2:24, 25).

There can be no question whether eternal life will endure. It cannot cease. But the point of many solemn warnings in the New Testament is that our privilege of *participating* in that eternal life is directly dependent on our continuing to abide in Him in whom, alone, that life is available to men. If we fail to abide in Him, the eternal life continues; but our participation in that life ceases. We share that life only as we continue to abide in Him "who is our life."

The New Testament is filled with warnings against failing to continue in faith and in the saving grace of Christ. But unfortunately, the true import of the warning passages, despite their clarity and simplicity, has been rejected by many earnest Bible scholars. Why? We need not search far to discover the reason—which, furthermore, is quite understandable. As Westcott well says, "We are all so familiar with certain lessons which the Bible contains that we come to regard them, perhaps unconsciously, as the complete sum of its teaching. Special words, phrases, incidents, inspire our own souls and mould our own faith . . . [so] that we pass over large sections of Scripture unstudied, or force them into unison with what we hear most easily."[2]

In his popular book *Major Bible Themes*, Dr. Lewis Sperry Chafer declares:

While the great body of New Testament Scriptures which bear directly or indirectly on this question declare the believer to be secure, there are upwards of twenty-five passages which have been cited in evi-

[2]B. F. Westcott, *The Epistles of St. John*, p. vii.

dence by those who maintain that the believer is insecure.³ It is certain that an individual could not be at the same time both secure and insecure. Therefore, of these two bodies of Scripture, one body of Scripture must of necessity conform to the other.⁴

Because of their conviction that "the great body of New Testament Scriptures" teaches unconditional security, sincere men of God have been convinced that the warning passages must somehow be found to "conform" to the "great body of New Testament Scriptures which declare the believer to be secure." Proceeding on their earnest conviction, they have sought interpretations of the warning passages which allow them to "conform."

Their sincerity is not to be questioned. But unfortunately their first premise has been wrong. They have misconstrued the passages which they have regarded as establishing the doctrine of unconditional security. Uniformity in the Scriptures is to be found, not by accepting the warning passages at less than face value by assigning them unwarranted and ingenious interpretations, but through a re-examination of the proof passages of the doctrine of unconditional security. There is no lack of conformity between the warning passages and the proof passages of the advocates of the doctrine of unconditional security; the lack of conformity has been between the warning passages and men's misconstruction of their supposed proof passages of unconditional security.

---

³Please excuse me from the company of any who "maintain that the believer is insecure." It is abundantly evident from the Scriptures that the believer is secure. But *only* the believer. Many who have debated "the security of the believer" have missed the issue. The question is not, Is the believer secure? but rather, What is a *believer?*

Chafer cites 27 passages "which have been cited in evidence by those who maintain that the believer is insecure." In his *Systematic Theology,* Vol. III, pp. 290-312, he cites 51 passages. For a list of 85 New Testament passages which establish the doctrine of conditional security, and a comparison of Chafer's list of passages, see Appendix A.

⁴Lewis Sperry Chafer, *Major Bible Themes,* p. 187.

It is our intention to examine the important proof passages commonly cited in the defense of the doctrine of unconditional security. In the present chapter we shall examine two important passages from the Gospel of John, both of which are gracious promises of eternal life. First, however, let us observe that Melanchthon was correct in insisting that the Scriptures must be understood grammatically before they can be understood theologically.

I.

In the tenth chapter of John's Gospel is found a precious promise of our Saviour which has brought blessed comfort and assurance to His own through all the many centuries since He dwelt among us, full of grace and truth. Jesus said, "I give unto them eternal life: and they shall never perish, neither shall any man pluck them out of my hand. My Father, which gave them me, is greater than all; and no man is able to pluck them out of my Father's hand" (John 10:28, 29).

Thank God for such a precious promise from our Saviour! Our quotation of His promise, however, was incomplete. Unfortunately, thus it is usually quoted, and many seem hardly conscious of the fact that this is not the whole of our Lord's statement. We must not overlook verse 27, which is an integral part of the statement and quite essential. It sets forth the specific condition governing our Saviour's promise.

Jesus said, "My sheep hear my voice, and I know them, and they follow me: and I give unto them eternal life. . . ." All the verbs thus far are present indicatives. "The most constant characteristic of the [Greek] Present Indicative is that it denotes action in progress."[5] While the present indicative does not invariably denote progressive action, it generally does. Robertson says, ". . . the durative sense does not monopolize the 'present' tense, though it more frequently denotes linear ac-

---

[5]Ernest De Witt Burton, *Syntax of the Moods and Tenses in New Testament Greek*, Sec. 9.

tion. The verb and the context must decide."[6] The *Aktionsart* of the verbs in question is durative, rather than punctiliar. And certainly the context (cf. vv. 2-5, 14) ascribes progressive action to the present indicatives under consideration.

Montgomery adopts the progressive form "I am giving" for *didōmi* (v. 28) reading: "My sheep listen to my voice, and I know them and they follow me. I am giving them eternal life. . . ."[7] Her use of the word *listen* is noteworthy. The English word *listen* possesses a durative connotation that is lacking in the word *hear,* and the simple present form *listen* conveys a progressive sense. Numerous contemporary translators (including Goodspeed, Moffatt, Weymouth, Williams, Verkuyl, and Knox) have rendered *akouousin* as "listen" in John 10:27, imparting a progressive quality to Jesus' statement.

True to his purpose in his *Expanded Translation,* Wuest forcefully emphasizes the durative quality of the first three of the four present indicatives: "The sheep which are mine are in the habit of listening to my voice, and I know them by experience, and they take the same road that I take with me, and I give to them life eternal."[8]

Unlike Montgomery, Wuest does not give the progressive form for *didōmi.* But it is obvious that Christ's giving of eternal life to His sheep is commensurate with their habitual listening and following. This is an essential truth affirmed many times in the New Testament; but a truth, alas, which many somehow have failed to observe.

The use in verse 28 of the strong double negative *ou mē* together with the phrase *eis ton aiōna* (perhaps best rendered

---

[6]A. T. Robertson, *A Grammar of the Greek New Testament in the Light of Historical Research,* p. 879.

[7]From *The New Testament in Modern English,* by Helen Barrett Montgomery, copyright 1924, 1952, by The American Baptist Publication Society, Philadelphia. Used by permission.

[8]From *The Gospels: An Expanded Translation,* by Kenneth S. Wuest, copyright 1956 by Wm. B. Eerdmans Publishing Company, Grand Rapids, Michigan. Used by permission.

"not at all for ever") has doubtless led many to ignore the significance of the condition (*hear* and *follow*, v. 27) which governs the promise of not perishing forever. But precisely the
same words, *ou mē . . . eis ton aiōna*, appear in our Lord's
promise in John 8:51, where the condition governing the
promise is especially obvious: "Verily, verily, I say unto you,
If a man keep my word, he shall never see death." The necessity of following Him in order to share His life is vividly declared by our Saviour in John 8:12, "I am the light of the
world: he that followeth me shall not walk in darkness, but
shall have the light of life." Commenting on John 10:27-29,
Tholuck declares:

The Reformed Church (the Calvinistic) bases on v. 28 the doctrine that
the regenerate can never apostatize. Christ undoubtedly says that no
power can snatch away his sheep from him, (Romans viii. 37-39); but
he furnishes also the *marks* of his sheep, and only so far as the stipula-
tions contained in v. 27 and 28 are fulfilled, so far consequently as the
disciple of Christ *continues* with Christ, (John viii. 31), is he invincible.[9]

Hengstenberg protests:

It is a cold consolation to say, 'If and so long as they remain My sheep,
they are secure.' The whole strength of our soul's desire is for a guarantee
against ourselves! That there is such a guarantee is [here] assured. . . .[10]

Hengstenberg bases his contention upon a strange argument
in which he identifies the thieves and robbers (v. 8) as "the
Pharisees, or the Judaism opposed to Christ." He also identifies
the wolf (v. 12) as "the Pharisee." From the fact that the Pharisees failed "to detach from Christ" the man healed of blindness
(chapter 9), the "situation of things which the Lord had before
His eyes when He spoke," Hengstenberg somehow manages to
conclude that ". . . it becomes very plain that 'the guarantee
against ourselves' is not to be excluded, but rather that it is
the main thing here."[11]

---

[9]August Tholuck, *Commentary on the Gospel of St. John*, p. 266.
[10]E. W. Hengstenberg, *Commentary on the Gospel of St. John*, Vol. I, p. 532.
[11]*Ibid.*

But where, may we inquire, is such a "guarantee against ourselves"? Instead of offering us a guarantee against ourselves, Jesus plainly confronts us with the fact that only such as deliberately hear and follow Him are His sheep, and thus secure in Him and in the Father's hand. Godet comments:

. . . [God's] power remains the safeguard of the property of the Son which is common to Him with the Father. Can this guaranty insure believers against the consequences of their own unfaithfulness, as Hengstenberg asserts? The text says nothing like this. The question is of enemies from without who seek to carry off the sheep, but not of unfaithfulness through which the sheep would themselves cease to be sheep.[12]

The promise of Christ to safeguard His followers does not relieve them of the necessity of *following* Him. Meyer declares:

The lost sheep, *i.e.* the sheep which has been separated, and wandered away from the flock (Matt. x. 6; Luke xv. 4), typifies him who is separated from the protection and gracious leading of Christ, and has fallen into unbelief. . . . Liberty and the possibility of apostasy are not thus excluded (in answer to Augustine and the teaching of the Reformed Church); he who has fallen away is no longer a [sheep]. . . .[13]

Westcott comments:

The doctrine of "final perseverance" has been found in this passage. But we must carefully distinguish between the certainty of God's promises and His infinite power on the one hand, and the weakness and variableness of man's will on the other. If man falls at any stage in his spiritual life, it is not from want of divine grace, nor from the overwhelming power of adversaries, but from his neglect to use that which he may or may not use. We cannot be protected against ourselves in spite of ourselves.[14]

"I give unto them eternal life, and they shall never perish, neither shall any man pluck them out of my hand. My Father, which gave them me, is greater than all, and no man is able to pluck them out of my Father's hand." What a blessed promise!

---

[12]Frederick Louis Godet, *Commentary on the Gospel of John*, Vol. II, p. 162.
[13]H. A. W. Meyer, *Critical and Exegetical Handbook to the Gospel of John*, p. 329.
[14]B. F. Westcott, *The Gospel According to St. John*, p. 158.

But it is a promise only for those of whom Jesus can say, "My sheep listen to my voice, and they follow me." He can share His life only with those who follow Him. They, alone, will know the saving, keeping grace of God in Christ.

II.

Perhaps no verse has been more often cited in evidence by the advocates of the doctrine of unconditional security than has John 5:24, "Verily, verily, I say unto you, He that heareth my word and believeth on him that sent me hath everlasting life, and shall not come into condemnation, but is passed from death unto life."

"Please underscore the words 'hath everlasting life,' " say the advocates of unconditional security. Indeed! But please underscore also the words "he that heareth . . . and believeth," for they denote the condition governing the promise of everlasting life and deliverance from condemnation and death. And the *hearing* and *believing* of which Jesus spoke are not the act of a moment. The durative quality of the hearing and believing by which men share the eternal life of God, through Christ, is fully apparent in the translation of Young, who takes into account the durative quality of the present participles *akouōn* and *pisteuōn* and submits the following starkly precise rendering: "Verily, verily, I say to you—He who is hearing my word, and is believing Him who sent me, hath life age-during, and to judgment he doth not come, but hath passed out of the death to the life."[15]

Many have laid much emphasis on the the words "shall not come into condemnation" (AV). But the Greek text reads *erchetai*—present indicative, rather than future, and accurate translation must retain the present tense, as the majority of

---

[15] Robert Young, *Young's Literal Translation of the Holy Bible*. Young's rendering of the last clause is not wholly accurate. The English perfect is by no means the equivalent of the Greek perfect. More accurate than "*hath* passed out of the death" would be "*stands* passed out of the death."

translators have done. It is true that the present tense may
serve the function of the future tense. (Obviously, any "coming
into judgment" must necessarily be future, as related to the
present moment.) But the use of the present tense, rather than
the future, refutes the emphasis which many have placed upon
the words as they appear in the Authorized Version, and also
the renderings which a few translators have arbitrarily adopted.
(Williams' unfortunate rendering, "will never come under condemnation," seems to have been dictated by theology. There is
no warrant for it in the text.) The point of Jesus' statement is
that, on the basis of their present faith, all who hear and believe
are delivered from present condemnation occasioned by unbelief (cf. John 3:18, 19) and stand passed (*metabebēken,* perfect active indicative) out of spiritual death into life.

Contrary to the assumption of many, John 5:24 does not
present a privileged position which, once attained, is forever
irrevocable. Quite to the contrary, our Saviour's words depict a
privileged position directly governed by the specific condition
of habitually hearing and believing. Jesus declares that the
happy circumstance of deliverance from present condemnation and of standing passed out of death into life is the privilege only of such as habitually hear His word and believe the
Father. It is only on the basis of a present hearing and believing that one shares the eternal life of God and enjoys deliverance from present condemnation and spiritual death. Alford
declares, "The *pisteuōn* [believing] and the *echei z. ai.* [hav-
ing everlasting life] are *commensurate;* where the faith is, the
possession of eternal life is; and when the one remits, the other
is forfeited."[16]

Wuest's translation of John 5:24, except for the last clause,
is excellent. Notice the vigorous emphasis he gives to the present participles and his correct retention of the present tense for
erchetai: "Most assuredly, I am saying to you, He who habitually hears my word and is believing the One who sent me has

---

[16]Henry Alford, *The Greek Testament,* p. 747.

life eternal, and into judgment he does not come. . . ." But his
rendering of the final clause is extremely unfortunate: ". . . but
has been permanently transferred out from the sphere of death
into the life."[17]

Wuest's rendering of the final clause is completely without
warrant. First, the perfect indicative *metabebēken* is active,
rather than passive as Wuest has rendered it. But much more
serious is Wuest's insertion of the word *permanently*, which
constitutes an affirmation concerning the future—an assertion
that the *status quo* resulting from the past transition cannot be
altered in the future. But the Greek perfect tense makes no
affirmation concerning the future. It affirms two things: the fact
of an action in the past, and the fact of the continued existence
of the results of the action, as of the present moment (the
moment of speaking). It makes no affirmation whatever with
respect to the future.

In its most frequent use the Perfect Indicative represents an action as
standing at the time of speaking complete. The reference of the tense is
thus double; it implies a past action and affirms an existing result. . . .
It is important to observe that the term "complete" or "completed" as a
grammatical term does not mean *ended,* but *accomplished,* i.e., *brought
to its appropriate result, which result remains at the time denoted by the
verb.* "The Perfect, although it implies the performance of the action in
past time, yet states only that it stands completed at the present time."[18]

It is true that the perfect tense is the tense to use if a past
act is known to have permanent consequences. But it is equally
true that the perfect tense does not in any way *affirm* the fact
of permanency; it only affirms the fact of the present existence
of the consequences of the past act, as of the moment of
speaking. The fact of actual permanency must be established
by supplementary comment. There is nothing in the language
of John 5:24 to affirm that the transition from death to life is
irrevocable. Wuest's insertion of the the word *permanently* is

[17]Wuest, *op. cit.*
[18]Burton, *op. cit.*, Sec. 74, 85, italics his.

not translation, but is rather unwarranted embellishment, interpretation, and commentary dictated by theology rather than by the language of the text. Contrary to Wuest's unfortunate rendering, *metabebēken* in John 5:24 means no more than "has passed and, as of this moment of speaking, still remains passed" (out of death into life).

Wuest's insertion of the word *permanently* is not only totally without warrant from the standpoint of the Greek text; it is also completely contrary to the context of the whole New Testament. We shudder to think how many times advocates of the fallacious doctrine of unconditional security may innocently cite Wuest's rendering, "has been permanently transferred out from the sphere of death into the life," in opposition to the obvious meaning of the solemn and explicit warning passages. Because it is in perfect accord with their doctrine, many will confidently assume that it is an accurate translation. But it is completely unwarranted. There is always the danger that godly, sincere men may inadvertently bend their Greek to the pattern of their theology.

Contrary to the translations of some and the opinions of many, the New Testament affirms that eternal life in Christ is our present possession only on the condition of a present living faith, rather than as the irrevocable consequence of a moment's act of faith sometime in the past. Consider John 1:12, "But as many as received him, to them gave he power to become the sons of God, to them that believe on his name." It is significant that, in the Greek text, three successive aorists are followed, not by an aorist participle, but by a present participle. Robertson quotes Broadus as pointing out that the Greek is "an aorist-loving language," especially the *koinē* of the New Testament.[19] It is therefore reasonable to assume that, when a New Testament writer adopts a more precise tense instead of the customary indefinite aorist, he does so for precision and emphasis.

---

[19] A. T. Robertson, *A Grammar of the Greek New Testament in the Light of Historical Research*, p. 831.

The switch from a succession of aorists to the present tense in
John 1:12 may be considered deliberate for emphasis of the
durative quality of the faith that makes men sons of God. That
emphasis is especially vivid in Weymouth's translation: "But
to all who have received Him—that is, to those who trust in His
name—He has given the privilege of becoming children of
God."[20]

John 1:12 depicts clearly how saving faith is both punctiliar
and durative. There is a moment of decision when the soul consciously and deliberately exercises faith, receiving Jesus Christ
as Saviour. In that moment, the individual is accepted of God
in Christ and becomes born of the Spirit. But he must continue
in faith if he is to continue in grace and eternal life. Westcott
declares that in John 1:12, "the effective reception of Christ is
explained to be the continuous energy of faith which relies
upon Him as being for the believer that which He has made
Himself known to be."[21] Dr. Edwin Charles Dargan writes:

Men sometimes make the mistake of taking this initial act of repentance
and faith as if that completed all that man had to do in order to be saved;
and in a sense this is true, provided that faith and repentance be continued; but the Scriptures show that there must be this continuance, and
this is what we call perseverance. Our Lord tells us, "He that endureth
to the end, the same shall be saved" (Matt. 10:22).[22]

There is no warrant in the New Testament for that strange
at-ease-in-Zion definition of perseverance which assures Christians that perseverance is inevitable and relieves them of the
necessity of deliberately persevering in faith, encouraging them
to place confidence in some past act or experience. James Denney has well said:

. . . there is nothing superficial in what the New Testament calls faith
. . . It is not simply the act of an instant, it is the attitude of a life; it
is the one right thing at the moment when a man abandons himself to

---

[20]From *Weymouth's New Testament in Modern Speech*, Harper & Brothers,
New York. Used by permission.

[21]Westcott, *op. cit.*, p. 9.

[22]Edwin Charles Dargan, *The Doctrines of Our Faith*, p. 134.

Christ, and it is the one thing which keeps him right with God for ever. It is just as truly the whole of Christianity subjectively as Christ is the whole of it objectively.

· ·

Nothing can by any possibility go beyond faith, and the whole promise and potency of Christianity are present in it. The sinner who through faith is right with God is certainly not made perfect in holiness, but the power which alone can make him perfect is already really and vitally operative in him. And it is operative in him only in and through his faith.

· ·

Grace is not a thing which can be infused [and] there are no gifts of grace which, so to speak, can be lodged bodily in the soul. Grace is the attitude of God to man which is revealed and made sure in Christ, and the only way in which it becomes effective in us for new life is when it wins [from] us the response of faith. And just as grace is the whole attitude of God in Christ to sinful men, so faith is the whole attitude of the sinful soul as it surrenders itself to that grace. Whether we call it the life of the justified, or the life of the reconciled, or the life of the regenerate, or the life of grace or of love, the new life is the life of faith and nothing else. To maintain the original attitude of welcoming God's love as it is revealed in Christ bearing our sins—not only to trust it, but to go on trusting—not merely to believe in it as a mode of transition from the old to the new, but to keep on believing—to say with every breath we draw, "Thou, O Christ, art all I want; more than all in Thee I find"— is not a part of the Christian life, but the whole of it.

· ·

"I have been crucified with Christ, and it is no more I that live, but Christ liveth in me." On the basis of such expressions as these the doctrine of a union—sometimes it is called a mystical union—of Christ and the Christian has been supported; and either justification or reconciliation itself, or the life of the justified and reconciled, is explained by reference to this union. The objective atonement, the finished work of Christ on the cross, is viewed with impatience if it is not denied, and union with Christ, participation in His death and resurrection, is regarded as something far higher and finer and containing far surer guarantees for a new and holy life than mere trust in one who died for our sins. Such a mode of thought, however, involves a complete departure from New Testament lines. Certainly the New Testament is full of the idea that the Christian is united to Christ, that in a real sense he is one with his Lord. But he is one with Him simply and solely through faith.[23]

---

[23]James Denney, *The Christian Doctrine of Reconciliation*, pp. 291-303.

"Abide [*menō*, remain] in me, and I in you." The faith on which our union with Christ depends is not the act of some past moment. It is a present living faith in a living Saviour. Peter declares that we are "kept by the power of God *through faith* unto salvation ready to be revealed in the last time," and that it is on the basis of our *present believing* in Him whom we have not seen that we are now "receiving the end of [our] faith, even the salvation of [our] souls" (I Pet. 1:5, 8, 9).

"This is the record," writes John, "that God hath given to us eternal life, and this life is in his Son. He that hath the Son hath the life, and he that hath not the Son of God hath not the life." It is impossible to overemphasize the truth which John declares. And it is essential that we heed John's exhortation: "Let that therefore abide in you which ye have heard from the beginning [the true Gospel, in contrast to the "gospel" of the "antichrists" who endeavor to "seduce" the believers—v. 26]. If that which ye have heard from the beginning shall remain in you, ye also shall continue in the Son and in the Father. And this is the promise that he hath promised us, even the life eternal" (I John 2:24, 25). John's words are an echo of our Saviour's promise (and implied warning): "Verily, verily, I say unto you, If a man keep my word, he shall never see death" (John 8:51).

The warnings of John and of Jesus find numerous echoes in the words of other New Testament writers, including Paul: "Now the Spirit speaketh expressly that in the latter times some shall depart from the faith. . . . Take heed unto thyself, and unto the doctrine; continue in them: for in doing this thou shalt both save thyself, and them that hear thee" (I Tim. 4:1, 16). "Evil men and seducers shall wax worse and worse, deceiving, and being deceived. But continue thou in the things which thou hast learned and hast been assured of, knowing of whom thou hast learned them; and that from a child thou hast known the holy scriptures, which are able to make thee wise unto salvation through faith which is in Christ Jesus" (II Tim. 3:13-15). "Now I make known unto you, brethren, the gospel which I preached unto you, which also ye received, wherein also ye stand, by which also ye are saved, if ye hold fast the word which I preached unto you, except ye believed in vain" (I Cor. 15:1, 2 ASV).

One urgent warning of Paul merits special consideration at this time. To the Colossians, he writes, "And you, who were in time past alienated and enemies in your mind by wicked works, yet now hath he reconciled in the body of his flesh though death, to present you holy and unblameable and unreproveable in his sight: if ye continue in the faith grounded and settled, and be not moved away from the hope of the gospel which ye have heard" (Col. 1:21-23).

The above passage has been a source of much embarrassment to men whose theology requires them to seek some interpretation which allows them to avoid the frank acceptance of the passage for what it says. The efforts of some to rescue their "Pauline theology" from the words of Paul have led to some ingenious interpretations and "arrangements" by sincere, godly men whose motives were honest and noble. Colossians 1:21-23 is another passage over which we might well hang the sign from the old ironsmith's shop: "All kinds of fancy twistings and turnings done here." Chafer writes:

Two issues appear in this context: that of God's work for man and that of man's work for God. In fact, the contrast between divine responsibility and human responsibility appears many times in the Colossian Epistle. No end of doctrinal disorder has been engendered by the disarrangement of these so widely different ideas. A worthy student will not rest until he can trace his way through, and separate, these two lines of truth.[24]

It is interesting to observe how Chafer manages to "trace his way through and separate these two lines of truth" in Colossians 1:21-23:

Because of a misleading punctuation which introduces only a comma after the word *death*, the two lines of thought have been not only con-

---

[24]Chafer, *Systematic Theology*, Vol. III, p. 307.

nected, but the work of God for man has been supposed to depend on man's work for God. That would be acceptable Arminian interpretation of doctrine, but it is not the meaning of the passage.[25] With no punctuation in the original text, it is allowable to place a full stop after the word *death* (vs. 22) and to begin a new part of the sentence with the next word *to.* This arrangement, without changing any words, divides properly between the two aspects of truth which are wholly unrelated in the sense that they are not interdependent. Thus the text is rescued from implying what it does not, that the work of God depends on the work of man.[26]

It is true that ancient writers customarily joined words and sentences together in unbroken lines, and the earliest Greek uncials extant reveal that punctuation marks were few and were used most sparingly by copyists, if at all. We must therefore assume that this was the circumstance of the original autographs of the New Testament. While, in the nature of the case, it has been necessary for textual critics to insert punctuation marks as the text seems to require, such procedure must be done with all possible caution and restraint, for it inevitably constitutes interpretation. Justification must be found for every insertion of punctuation, especially of a mark as critically significant as a full stop. And justification must be sought in the language of the text, rather than in one's theology. It is at this point that we must reject Chafer's assumption (which is not shared, to our knowledge, by any textual critic) that "it is allowable to place a full stop after the word *death* (vs. 22) and to begin a new part of the sentence with the next word *to.*" Even as his argument frankly discloses, Chafer's assumption stems from the requirements of his theology; and it is com-

---

[25]Chafer's charge is unfair. It cannot be established from the writings of Arminius that he believed or taught that "the work of God for man depends on man's work for God." He did deny that the Scriptures teach that salvation is thrust upon some and denied to others *unconditionally.* He rejected Calvin's doctrines of limited atonement, unconditional election, and irresistible grace. He believed that the Bible teaches that men, as responsible moral agents, must appropriate what God in mercy and grace has provided for undeserving sinners. But that is quite a different matter from teaching that "the work of God for man depends on man's work for God."

[26]Chafer, *op. cit.,* p. 307 f.

pletely contrary to the requirements of the language of the
text. While his "arrangement" does not "change any words,"
it divides a coherent sentence into two parts, the first of which
remains an acceptable sentence, but the second of which is
merely a dangling, incoherent conglomeration of words beginning with an infinitive and lacking any subject. We must insist that it is not at all allowable to insert periods in the text
of the Holy Scriptures merely because we find that dividing a
sentence will "rescue" a text from negating our theology.

Chafer's "arrangement" involves him in a serious erroneous
assumption. He asserts that "holy and unblameable and unreproveable in his sight" are

. . . words which imply human responsibility and faithfulness. It naturally follows that, in the light of this responsibility, all depends upon
those believers. This feature of the context is augmented by the further
declaration: "if ye continue in the faith [Christian doctrine] grounded
and settled, and be not moved away from the hope of the gospel, which
ye have heard" (vs. 23).[π]

Chafer's argument demands that we assume that the blessed
circumstance of appearing before God "holy and unblameable
and unreproveable" is actually a matter of personal endeavor
and attainment, a matter of spiritual growth and development,
a personal achievement in which "all depends upon the believers." But we cannot so assume; for Paul speaks of an absolute condition, whereas the believer's personal spiritual attainment is only relative. Experimentally, we cannot attain perfection. We shall appear before Christ to be judged just as we
are at the end of our pilgrim way—which certainly will be far
short of the absolute condition of "holy and unblameable and
unreproveable." There will be much for which we shall be
called to account and for which we must justly be reproved (cf.
II Cor. 5:10, I Cor. 4:5, Rom. 14:10, 12).

Contrary to Chafer's assumption, the blessed circumstance of
appearing before God "holy and unblameable and unreprove-

[π]*Ibid.*, p. 307, brackets his.

able" is not a matter of human achievement; it is the exalted privilege of believers "by grace, through faith." It is the gracious consequence of the imputation of that "righteousness of God which is through faith in Jesus Christ unto all and upon all who believe" (Rom. 3:21).[28] The happy circumstance of appearing before God "holy and unblameable and unreproveable" is part of God's gracious salvation for undeserving sinners saved "not by works of righteousness which we have done [or could do], but according to his mercy." Chafer has woefully misconstrued the work of God as being the work of man. His assumption is erroneous, and his whole contention is without foundation.

Chafer concludes his discussion of Col. 1:21-23 by declaring, "No more complete statement of God's work for man will be found than Colossians 2:10: 'And ye are complete in him, which is the head of all principality and power.' "[29] Chafer, of course, regards Paul's words as descriptive of a static relationship between Christ and the believer which is irrevocable, despite any and all eventualities. He apparently ignores the significance of the grave warnings which surround verse 10: "This I say, lest any man should beguile [paralogizomai, delude, deceive by false reasoning] you with enticing words" (v. 4), influencing them to abandon "the stedfastness of your faith in Christ" (v. 5). "Beware lest any man spoil [sulagōgeō, make a prey of] you through philosophy and vain deceit" (v. 8) by leading them astray from the true Gospel and simple faith in

---

[28]Let us observe that identical words appear in Col. 1:22, hagious kai amōmous . . . katenōpion autou, and Eph. 1:4, hagious kai amōmous katenōpion autou. Cf. Eph. 5:27, Paul's affirmation that Christ will present the Church to Himself hagia kai amōmos. (Westcott, ad loc.: "Her fitness and her beauty are alike due to His sacrifice of Himself.") It is altogether unlikely that Chafer would have asserted of the words, as they appear in the Ephesian passages, that they are "words which imply human responsibility and faithfulness." On the contrary, in the Ephesian passages they doubtless would be construed as words which imply only sovereign (unconditional) election, to the exclusion of all thought of "human responsibility and faithfulness" and of "all depending upon the believers." Such are the vagaries of theology.

[29]Ibid., p. 308.

Christ in whom, alone, we are spiritually "complete" (v. 10). Those who sought to persuade them to become preoccupied with "shadows" rather than with Christ Himself (vv. 16, 17) would, if successful, thereby "beguile" them (*katabrabeuō*, deprive them of their prize) by causing them, like themselves, to turn to the worship of angels, no longer holding fast the Head, Christ (vv. 18, 19). The warnings are indeed urgent.

In Christ, alone, is all we need for time and for eternity. We are complete in Him. Let us, then, heed the many warnings against the peril of turning aside from Him who is our hope, our peace, and our life. We dare not ignore the fateful contingency with which Paul confronts us: God, who has reconciled us to Himself through the death of His Son, will ultimately present us (cf. II Cor. 4:14) "holy and unblameable and unreproveable before him" in His own holy presence—*if* we continue in the faith grounded and settled, and be not moved away from the hope of the Gospel which we have heard.

Is it not time to stop trying to force the plain, explicit warning passages to "conform" to an incomplete comprehension of the supposed proof passages of the erroneous doctrine of unconditional security? Is it not time to begin heeding the many solemn warnings of our Saviour and the Apostles, instead of "explaining" them into total irrelevance through ingenious interpretations or deftly circumventing them by theological hypothesis? And some of us may well ask ourselves, Shall we continue to avoid preaching to our congregations the urgent warnings which Paul and others so faithfully sounded to believers in their day?

> And when they had preached the gospel to [Derbe] and had taught many, they returned again to Lystra, and to Iconium and Antioch, confirming the souls of the disciples and exhorting them to continue [*emmenō*, remain, persevere, hold fast] in the faith, and that we must through much tribulation enter into the kingdom of God.
>
> ACTS 14:21, 22

"*Shall Never Thirst*"

Whosoever drinketh of the water that I shall give him shall never thirst; but the water that I shall give him shall be in him a well of water springing up into everlasting life.

*　　*　　*

If any man thirst, let him come unto me and drink. He that believeth on me, as the scripture hath said, out of his inmost being shall flow rivers of living water.

JOHN 4:14; 7:37, 38

CHAPTER VI

SHALL NEVER THIRST

To TIMOTHY at Ephesus, the Apostle Paul wrote, "Let the elders that rule well be counted worthy of double honor, especially they who labor in the word and doctrine."

The saints are much in debt to the men of God who diligently labor in the Word and doctrines of the holy faith. Great are their responsibilities, for their task is fraught with grave eternal consequences. To expound the saving Word to immortal souls, who according to their understanding and response to that Word will forever dwell in the light of life eternal or in the shades of second death, is not a task to be lightly assumed. "My brethren," cautions James, "be not many of you teachers, knowing that we shall receive severer judgment."

For the exacting task of the exegete, a knowledge of grammar is an essential tool. But grammar, alone, is not a sufficient guide. There are other important considerations, especially the matter of context. And there is a sense in which the entire canon of Holy Scripture must be regarded as "context." No verse or passage of Scripture may possess a meaning contrary to the total revelation of all of Holy Writ. Overlooking the implications of the fact that all the Bible is "context,"many capable scholars have erred in their interpretation of important passages.

In his book *Treasures From the Greek New Testament for the English Reader,* Dr. Kenneth S. Wuest writes:

"Whosoever drinketh of this water shall thirst again: but whosoever drinketh of the water that I shall give him shall never thirst; but the water that I shall give him shall be in him a well of water springing up into everlasting life." (John 4:13,14).

The first occurrence of the word "drinketh" is in a construction in the Greek which refers to continuous action, and the second use of the word in the original presents the mere fact of the action without reference to the progress of the action. The fuller translation therefore reads, "Every one who keeps on constantly drinking of this water shall thirst again. But whosoever takes a drink of the water which I shall give him shall never thirst." . . . The person who keeps on drinking of the wells of the world, lifeless, dull, brackish, polluted, stale, will thirst again. The world with all its sin does not satisfy, never can. But the person who takes one drink of the spring of eternal life never thirsts again.

The reason why one drink satisfies is that when the sinner takes one drink of eternal life, that one drink becomes in him a spring of water leaping up into a fountain of eternal life. . . . The one drink itself is a spring that ever keeps bubbling up, ever refreshing and satisfying the one who takes a drink of the water of life.[1]

Dr. Wuest's interpretation implies that a moment's act of faith in Christ effects a state of grace which is self-perpetuating and irrevocable. The total context of Scripture, however, affirms that while the divine provision of grace is constant and perpetual, man's appropriation can only be progressive rather than once-for-all as the act of a moment. The initial act of appropriation is essential; but it must subsequently be continually implemented, and such is not inevitable. Dr. Wuest's interpretation rests on an assumed significance of the juxtaposition of the present participle *pinōn* (v. 13) and the aorist subjunctive *piēi* (v. 14). Such a construction is sometimes significant; but not always, and certainly not in the present instance. (Any significance must derive, not from the aorist, but from the linear tense.)

Dr. Wuest's interpretation is permissible from the standpoint of grammar. But while it is permissible, it is not authorized;

---

[1]Kenneth S. Wuest, *Treasures From the Greek New Testament for the English Reader*, p. 29 f.

for there is another interpretation equally warranted by grammar. Furthermore, the other interpretation is positively required by a consideration of other Scriptures. We shall establish two facts: (1) that there is nothing in the language of verse 14 to limit the drinking to a single once-for-all act; and (2) that a consideration of other Scriptures requires that the drinking be viewed as an extended, progressive action.

1. As Dr. Wuest rightly asserts, an aorist "presents the mere fact of [an] action without reference to the progress of the action." The action represented by a given aorist may indeed be point-action; but as far as language is concerned, it may quite as well be linear. Robertson declares:

The "constative" aorist just *treats* the act as a single whole entirely irrespective of the parts or time involved. If the act is a point in itself, well and good. But the aorist can be used also of an act which is not a point. This is the advance that the tense makes on the verb-root. All aorists are punctiliar in statement (cf. Moulton, *Prol.*, p. 109). The "constative" aorist treats an act as punctiliar which is not in itself point-action.[2]

This latitude of the aorist is found in the dependent moods, as well as in the indicative:

The aorist of the dependent moods represents the action expressed by the verb as a simple event or fact, without reference either to its progress or to the existence of its result. As in the Indicative the verb may be indefinite, inceptive, or resultative, and when indefinite may refer to a momentary or extended action or to a series of events.[3]

Robertson[4] cites numerous examples of aorists used to represent action requiring extended periods of time, among which is John 2:20 in which the building of Herod's temple, requiring forty-six years, is represented by the aorist *oikodomēthē*. In John 1:14, the aorist *eskēnōsen* (dwelt) covers the entire

---

[2] A. T. Robertson, *A Grammar of the Greek New Testament in the Light of Historical Research*, p. 832, italics his.

[3] Ernest De Witt Burton, *Syntax of the Moods and Tenses in New Testament Greek*, Sec. 98.

[4] Robertson, *op. cit.*, p. 833.

earthly life of Jesus. In John 1:18, the aorist *exēgēsato* (declared) refers to Christ's entire manifestation of God throughout His earthly life and ministry.

Obviously, aorists may represent actions requiring extended periods of time. It is therefore unwise in any instance to assume, without corroborative evidence, that the action represented by an aorist is necessarily point-action. Unfortunately, translators and exegetes have sometimes allowed the distinction between aorists and linear tenses to impose requirements upon aorists which are unwarranted. They have sometimes assumed that the contrast between aorists and linear tenses requires aorists to specify point-action. But aorists only constitute mere assertions of fact without precise definition. True to the name, aorists simply declare the fact of an action without specifying whether the action is punctiliar or linear. All aorists are punctiliar in *statement;* but not necessarily in *fact.* The concept conveyed by any aorist, therefore, requires definition by context, logic, and analogy.

The use of both an aorist and a durative tense may indicate no contrast whatever, even when used in immediate proximity. In I Corinthians 10:4 we find an aorist and an imperfect used interchangeably. The aorist *epion* declares the fact that the Israelites drank of the water of life from the Rock (Christ) which followed them, without specifying whether the drinking was a single act or a durative process. But the imperfect *epinon* specifies that the drinking was not a momentary act, but an extended process. Both the aorist and the imperfect have reference to the same act of drinking from the Rock. Obviously, therefore, the aorist *epion* has reference to an extended process, rather than to a single momentary act.

It is thus evident that, while the aorist subjunctive *piēi* in John 4:14 does not *specify* durative action, neither does it in any wise *proscribe* it. There is nothing in the language of John 4:14 to limit the drinking to a momentary once-for-all act.

2. A consideration of other Scriptures requires that the act of drinking in John 4:14 be viewed as progressive, rather than

as a momentary once-for-all act. Reference has just been made to the fact that the drinking from the spiritual Rock, Christ, as depicted in I Corinthians 10:4, is clearly a progressive action, rather than a momentary once-for-all act. The entire force of Paul's analogy in I Corinthians 10 is destroyed if one assumes that our drinking of the water of life in the present era, unlike Israel's drinking in the wilderness, is a momentary once-for-all act, rather than progressive.

Let us consider another invitation of Jesus, virtually identical with His invitation to the woman of Sychar: "In the last day, that great day of the feast, Jesus stood and cried, saying, If any man thirst, let him come unto me and drink. He that believeth on me, as the scripture hath said, out of his inmost being shall flow rivers of living water" (John 7:37, 38).

The use of the present imperative *pinetō* in verse 37 is significant, especially in view of the prevalence of the aorist imperative in the New Testament. Concerning the distinction between aorist and present imperatives, Robertson affirms that "in the positive imperative we are free to consider the significance of the aorist (and present) tense in the essential meaning. Here the distinction between the punctiliar (aorist) and the durative (present) is quite marked."[5] Burton affirms that "the present of the dependent moods is used to represent an action as in progress or as repeated."[6] The present imperative is regularly durative.

It is obvious that the "drinking" to which Jesus invited men in John 7:37 is not a momentary once-for-all act, but an action in progress, or repeated. Language permits no other interpretation. We submit that if Wuest's inference from the aorist in John 4:14 were correct, and a single momentary once-for-all act of drinking sufficed for all time to come, then the aorist should appear also in John 7:37 and in all kindred passages. This, however, is not the case.

---

[5]*Ibid.*, p. 855.
[6]Burton, *op. cit.*, Sec. 96.

Let us summarize. In John 4:14, we are confronted with an act of drinking which, according to language, may be either punctiliar or durative. In John 7:37, we are confronted with an act of drinking which, according to language, is definitely durative. We submit that the construction of John 7:37 necessarily governs the interpretation of John 4:14. The drinking of the water of life of which Jesus taught in John 4:14 and elsewhere is a continual, progressive action, rather than a momentary once-for-all act as Wuest and numerous others have interpreted it to be.

The supply of water drawn from Jacob's well is soon exhausted, and one thirsts again and must return to draw a fresh supply. Thus it is with all temporal satisfactions. But the living water that Jesus gives is inexhaustible. It is a living well within, springing up into everlasting life. The living presence of the Saviour in the hearts of all who trust in Him continually satisfies the thirst and longings of the soul. But drinking the precious water of life which the Saviour bestows is not the act of a moment. It is the habitual communion of all who trust in Him and share the eternal life of God through living faith in the living Saviour.

> On the last day, the great day of the feast, Jesus stood and cried aloud, "If anyone is thirsty, let him come to me and drink. Whoever continues to believe in me will have, as the Scripture says, rivers of living water continuously flowing from within him."
>
> JOHN 7:37, 38 WILLIAMS

Let us not close the chapter without considering briefly the Source of the water of life. The promise of Jesus is that, to all who believe in Him, *as the scripture hath said,* out of his inmost being shall flow rivers of living water." As Vincent points out, although "there is no exactly corresponding passage . . . the quotation harmonizes with the general tenor of several passages."[7] It is possible that Jesus had in mind Isaiah 58:11,

---

[7]Marvin R. Vincent, *Word Studies in the New Testament,* Vol. II, p. 163.

"And the Lord shall guide thee continually, and satisfy thy soul in drought, and make fat thy bones: and thou shalt be like a watered garden, and like a spring of water, whose waters fail not."

There is another important possibility. Robertson points out that some ancient Western writers held that *ek tēs koilias autou* (out of his belly) refers to Christ, rather than to the believer. "It is a difficult question and Westcott finally changed his view and held *autou* to refer to Christ."[8] Scriptures substantiating Westcott's view are more numerous than those substantiating the alternate view. Prominent among them is the precious promise of Isaiah 12:3, "Therefore with joy shall ye draw water out of the wells of salvation." The Douay-Challoner Text is especially appealing: "You shall draw waters with joy out of the saviour's fountains."

The words of our Saviour in John 7:37, 38 were

. . . probably suggested by the libations of water drawn from the Pool of Siloam each morning of the feast (while Isa. xii 3 was sung), and carried in a golden vessel by a procession of priests who poured it over the altar at the morning sacrifice. If it was discontinued on the eighth day, as seems probable, in token of their having come into "a land of springs of water," the proclamation of Jesus in the temple would be none the less impressive as the offer of satisfaction for the soul whose thirst no Jewish ritual could quench.[9]

Consider the following kindred passages: "For with thee is the fountain of life: in thy light shall we see light" (Psalm 36:9). "All my springs are in thee" (Psalm 87:7). "For my people have committed two evils; they have forsaken me, the fountain of living waters, and hewed them out cisterns, broken cisterns, that can hold no water. . . . O Lord, the hope of Israel, all that forsake thee shall be ashamed, and they that depart from me shall be written in the earth, because they have for-

[8]A. T. Robertson, *Word Pictures in the New Testament*, Vol. V, p. 131.

[9]J. A. McClymont, *The Gospel of St. John* (The New Century Bible, ed. W. F. Adeney), p. 197.

saken the Lord, the fountain of living waters" (Jer. 2:13; 17:13).

To the woman of Sychar, Jesus promised that "the water that I shall give [you] shall be in [you] a well of water springing up into everlasting life." But a spring of water is only a surface manifestation. Every spring, or "living well," must have its source within the hidden recesses of the earth. The "living water" is indeed "a spring of water that keeps on bubbling up within [the believer] for eternal life" (Williams); but its Source is ever "that spiritual Rock, Christ," of whom we continue to drink by faith. The living water is ever "the water that I shall give him."

Peter declares of apostates who "have left the straight road and gone astray" that "such men are dried-up springs" (II Pet. 2:15, 17 Williams). We cannot continue to drink of the water of life if we become severed from its blessed Source.

Amidst the parched wilderness of a perishing world, ever let us dwell beside the Fountain of Life. All our springs are in Him. From "streams of mercy, never ceasing," ever let us drink, that we thirst not. And, drinking, let us summon others to the Fount whose living waters cannot fail.

> Ho, every one that thirsteth, come ye to the waters. . . .
> And let him who is athirst come. And whosoever will, let him take the water of life freely.
>
> ISAIAH 55:1, REVELATION 22:17

"Born of God"

Verily, verily, I say unto thee, Except a man be born again, he cannot see the kingdom of God. . . . Except a man be born of water and of the Spirit, he cannot enter into the kingdom of God. That which is born of the flesh is flesh, and that which is born of the Spirit is spirit.

JOHN 3:3, 5, 6

Of his own will begat he us with the word of truth, that we should be a kind of firstfruits of his creatures. . . . Wherefore lay aside all filthiness and prevailing wickedness, and receive with meekness the implanted word which is able to save your souls.

JAMES 1:18, 21

CHAPTER VII

BORN OF GOD

IT WAS NIGHT. No prudent man went about the dark streets of Jerusalem alone at night unless his mission was urgent. There were perils of robbers lying in wait in darkened doorways along the narrow streets, and of Roman soldiers who often were suspicious and impatient with men who ventured out at night.

But Nicodemus the Pharisee, a member of the Sanhedrin and a man of position in Jerusalem, had come to Jesus by night. Perhaps, more than robbers or Roman soldiers, he feared embarrassment in the eyes of his colleagues, should he be seen sitting as a learner before the strange young rabbi from Nazareth. Or perhaps the burning questions in his mind and heart would not allow him to rest until morning: Who is this Jesus who has such courageous zeal for the sanctity of the temple—this doer of miracles who speaks with such evident authority? Can it be possible that he is actually the long awaited Messiah of Israel? At least it seems evident that he is a prophet—a teacher come from God! What can he tell us about the promised kingdom?

To his surprise, Jesus began to answer his questions before he had opportunity to frame them in words. But to Nicodemus, the words of Jesus seemed strange and mysterious:

Jesus answered and said unto him, Verily, verily, I say unto thee, Except a man be born again, he cannot see the kingdom of God. Nicodemus saith unto him, How can a man be born when he is old? Can he enter a second time into his mother's womb and be born? Jesus answered,

85

Verily, verily, I say unto thee, Except a man be born of water and of
the Spirit, he cannot enter into the kingdom of God. That which is
born of the flesh is flesh, and that which is born of the Spirit is spirit.
Marvel not that I said unto thee, Ye must be born again. The wind blow-
eth where it listeth, and thou hearest the sound thereof, but canst not tell
whence it cometh, and whither it goeth: so is every one that is born
of the Spirit (John 3:3-8).

Thus did Jesus disclose to a solitary inquirer the essential
nature of the relation to God made possible for men through
the redemption to be accomplished in Himself. There is another birth possible for man who enters this world born of a
woman—a birth from above, of the Spirit of God; a birth that
enables man to be a part of the kingdom and family of God and
to share His eternal life.

"How can these things be?" asked Nicodemus. Gently, but
firmly, Jesus reproved him for his apparent ignorance of the
nature of the spiritual relationship of God and men who walk
with Him by faith. "Art thou the teacher of Israel, and knowest
not these things?"

Although somewhat obscurely, the doctrine of a spiritual
birth from above does appear in embryonic form in the Old
Testament. Numerous passages disclose the nature of the spiritual relation between God and the faithful as being that of a
father and sons and daughters, and certain passages imply a
spiritual birth from above. (Cf. Deut. 14:1; 32:6, 19, I Chron.
29:10, Ps. 82:6; 103:13, Isa. 1:2; 30:1, 9; 43:6; 45:11; 63:8, 16;
64:8, Jer. 3:4, 19; 31:9, Hos. 1:10, Mal. 1:6; 2:10, Ezek. 36:25-
27—cf. John 3:5). Paul's words in II Corinthians 6:17 f. seem to
be, not a quotation from a specific passage or passages, but
rather a sort of mosaic which gathers together the essence of
much that was said by the prophets which indicates that the
spiritual relation between God and believers is that of a father
and sons.

Again Paul's words in Galatians 3:23-4:7 disclose that believers under Law were as much the children of God as are
believers in the present era. The distinction Paul makes is not

one of relationship, but only of position: believers under Law were in the position of minor children subject to the supervision of the paedagogue (the law), whereas believers now enjoy the position of mature sons who have attained their legal majority. The Old Testament faithful were children and heirs of God, and the New Testament concept of the filial relation of believers to God, while more vivid, is not at all new. The fact of a spiritual birth in Zion, by the grace of God, for men born sinners, is beautifully portrayed in Psalm 87.

As "the teacher of Israel," Nicodemus was justly rebuked for his apparent ignorance of the new birth. But the rebuke of Jesus did not imply that Nicodemus should have understood just how the Spirit effects the spiritual birth of men. The birth of the Spirit involves "heavenly things" which lie hidden in the wisdom and power of God, things which are not intelligible for finite man.

Beneath all definitions [of the work of the Holy Spirit in regeneration] there remains the mystery of life, and the mystery of the action of Spirit upon spirit. What this spiritually vivifying touch of God is, no man will ever know. Probably regeneration itself is never a matter of actual consciousness to a man. It is apparent in its consequences, but is not discerned in itself; hence we have no opportunity of examining it. The region lies deep in us, and the agent, the Holy Spirit, acts unseen, not calling attention to himself, and apparently not desiring to be seen in his inner working. Thus we have no material for a definition of regeneration from within. But this obscurity need not trouble us, for it is only the obscurity that hangs over all inner spiritual processes: we may trace their preparations, and follow out their consequences, but they lie too deep to be examined in themselves.[1]

"Ye must be born again," said Jesus. But the second birth is not something which men must or can accomplish of themselves—something which men can achieve and offer to God for His inspection and approval. Rather, it is a holy relationship

---

[1] William Newton Clarke, *An Outline of Christian Theology*, p. 397. We must reject many of Clarke's views; but the above paragraph is excellent, and true to our Lord's teaching in John 3:5-8.

with God wrought within the souls of men by the power of the Spirit, as men submit to the will of God through repentance and faith. And it is the essential circumstance in which men share the eternal life of God. Without it, there is only spiritual death.

A corpse may be embalmed, stuffed with herbs, and encased as a mummy. Its corruption is invisible, all unsightliness carefully concealed. So do many men embalm the dead soul, fill it with fragrant herbs, and wrap it like a mummy in a shroud of self-righteousness so that, of the indwelling corruption, scarcely anything appears. But as the Egyptians by their embalming never could restore life unto their dead, so can these soul-mummies with all their Egyptian arts never kindle one spark of life in their dead souls.[2]

"Ye must be born again!" The necessity of the new birth for the salvation of men is a powerful keynote of evangelism which we dare not neglect. But let us take care that our preaching and teaching be Scriptural, lest our emphasis be merely upon an overt experience rather than upon a holy relationship. Let us beware lest we convey the impression that the new birth is somehow an *agent* of salvation, rather than merely a *circumstance*. It is Jesus who saves, rather than the new birth. Let us observe that the teaching of the New Testament concerning the new birth was given, not to evangelize the lost, but to instruct believers concerning the nature of their spiritual relationship with God through faith in Jesus Christ.[3] The doctrine of the

---

[2]Abraham Kuyper, *The Work of the Holy Spirit,* p. 280 f.

[3]To insist that Nicodemus was not under saving grace at the time of his conference with Jesus is to assert that men could not experience salvation under the old dispensation, or that Nicodemus was impenitent toward God and an unbeliever with respect to the way of salvation under the old economy (which remained valid until the sacrifice of Jesus on the cross). Such an assertion is contrary to John's brief account of Nicodemus (3:1 ff.; 7:50 f.; 19:39-42), which indicates that he was a godly Jew of unfeigned faith whose heart was open to the truth. Jesus' rebuke, "ye receive not our witness . . . ye believe not" (v. 11 f.), is couched in the plural, indicating that the charge was directed, not against Nicodemus personally, but against the Pharisees and the Sanhedrin collectively and perhaps the Jews as a whole (cf. John 1:11). The

new birth does not appear in any of the discourses in the Book of Acts, nor does it figure prominently in the Epistles, with the exception of I John. All that is said concerning it is directed to believers who already have come into such holy circumstance.

Our Lord's brief discourse to Nicodemus is sufficient to establish the doctrine as of paramount importance as a divine ultimatum to all men: "Except a man be born again, he cannot see the kingdom of God." Let us never be guilty of neglecting to preach the necessity of the new birth as the essential circumstance of salvation. But let us take care that our emphasis remain true to the Scriptures. While the doctrine cannot be overemphasized, unfortunately it can be misconstrued.

A popular and serious error is the assumption that an equation somehow exists between physical birth and spiritual birth: whatever is intrinsic in physical birth is equally intrinsic in spiritual birth; whatever may be predicated of one may likewise be predicated of the other. Laboring under such erroneous assumption, many have concluded that spiritual birth, like physical birth, is necessarily irrevocable. "If one has been born," they ask, "how can he possibly become unborn?" "I may be a wayward, disobedient son," say they, "but I must forever remain my father's own son." In defense of what seems to them to be an obviously logical conclusion, they have proceeded in good conscience to impose unwarranted and fanci-

---

fact that Nicodemus had come to Jesus as an earnest inquirer marked him as an exception to the prevailing attitude.

Despite the many sermons which have portrayed Nicodemus as a man "religious, but lost," there is no warrant for assuming that Nicodemus was not in the circumstance of Zacharias and Elisabeth, who were "both righteous before God, walking in all the commandments and ordinances of the Lord blameless" (Luke 1:6). But his understanding of the nature of the spiritual relationship of God and the faithful was quite imperfect (vv. 3-13), and he had urgent need for instruction concerning the role of Jesus as the true sacrifice for sins and the sole object of faith for believers in the new economy so soon to supersede the era of Law (v. 14 f.), lest he stumble and fall through offense at Christ (Luke 2:34, Rom. 9:32 f.) and, rejecting the Messiah at His appearing, become a "branch broken off because of unbelief" (Rom. 11:20).

ful interpretations upon many simple discourses of Jesus and upon many plain, explicit warning passages in the New Testament. After all, the Scriptures must agree! But consider three essential differences between physical birth and spiritual birth:

1. Physical birth effects the inception of the life of the subject *in toto,* whereas spiritual birth involves only a transition from one mode of life to another.

(It may be objected that spiritual birth is not a transition from an old life to a new life on the grounds that, when one is born of the Spirit, he passes "out of death into life," becoming "a new creation in Christ." This is true; but only within the limits of the total definition of the Scriptures. For it is also true that the man who is "dead in trespasses and in sins" is nevertheless a rational spiritual being who is personally accountable for his life and his sins and who, except he repent, must answer before God in solemn judgment. What is depicted as "death," for the reason that the sinner is "alienated from the life of God," is neverthless *spiritual life* on a degenerate plane—a spiritual life for which the lost must answer to God in judgment. The New Testament contains many references to the old life of Christians before conversion, which references have to do with the *spiritual* lives of men in an unregenerate state.)

2. In physical birth, the subject has no prior knowledge and gives no consent, whereas in spiritual birth, the subject must have a prior knowledge of the Gospel and must give consent.

(It may be objected that, in view of John 1:13 and James 1:18, the spiritual birth of men is by the will of God, rather than by the will of men. Such an objection proceeds from the old fallacy of "either . . . or," a ridiculous assumption unwittingly entertained by many sincere Bible scholars. Actually, the spiritual birth of men is by the will of *both* God and man. "Of his own will begat he us with the word of truth." Yes, but not apart from the consent of our wills. Of his own will, the groom takes a bride; but not apart from the will and consent of the bride. God was under no constraint to bestow spiritual birth upon men, at such frightful cost to Himself, other than the constraint of His own love and grace. "Of his own will," therefore, the Father of lights gives good gifts to men and begets as His own dear children all who believe His word of truth. The initiative is with God. But God's initiative demands a response from man. Men are not born of the Spirit apart from a prior knowledge of the Gospel [Rom. 10:8-17] nor apart from their own consent [John 5:40].[4])

3. In physical birth, the individual receives a life independent of his parents. They may die, but he lives on. But in spiritual birth, the subject receives no independent life. He becomes a partaker of the life and nature of Him who begets—a participant, by faith, in the eternal life of God in Christ "who is our life."

In view of obvious essential differences, it cannot be considered strange that spiritual birth, unlike physical birth, is not irrevocable. It is folly to assume that an equation exists between physical birth and spiritual birth, and that whatever is intrinsic in physical birth is equally so in spiritual birth. Physical birth and spiritual birth are equally real, but essentially different. While an analogy exists between the two, there is no equation whatever.

---

[4]With respect to John 1:13, let us note that numerous important early Fathers reject the reading, *hoi . . . egennēthēsan,* which Tertullian declared a corruption of the text by the Valentinian Gnostics who denied the virgin birth of Jesus, in favor of a singular verb (cf. Blass, *Philology of the Gospels,* p. 234 ff.). If the Greek uncials are correct as we have them, the reference is to the spiritual birth of believers. If Tertullian, Irenaeus, and other early Fathers are correct, John's reference is to the physical birth of Jesus. The following arguments may be advanced for the latter view: (1). The opinion of important early Fathers, as indicated. (2). Language implies that the reference is to physical birth: "born not of bloods [so Greek text], nor of the will [*thelēma,* Thayer: inclination, desire] of the flesh, nor of the [desire] of man." (3). An assertion of the obvious fact that the spiritual birth of belivers is not effected by bloods nor by the inclination or desire of the flesh would be completely without necessity or purpose. (4). The fact of the Incarnation, whereby the Word entered the stream of humanity, is the theme of John's Prologue, and is under immediate consideration (v. 14).

"That which is born of the flesh is flesh, and that which is born of the Spirit is spirit." Jesus doubtless sensed in Nicodemus the presence of a serious misapprehension common among the Jews: the assumption that to have been born a descendant of Abraham after the flesh somehow ensured spiritual kinship with Abraham and with God Himself (cf. John 8:33-42). But the relationship of God and the faithful is a matter of spirit rather than flesh. While the physical relationship of fathers and sons cannot be annulled, the spiritual union and accord of earthly fathers and sons can be destroyed (and, tragically, sometimes is). The relationship of men and God, as their Creator, cannot be annulled; but the truly sublime and holy relationship which God desires to enjoy with men is of the spirit, rather than the flesh, and is voluntary and not indissoluble during man's probationary sojourn on earth in God's moral universe.

Many are accustomed to think of the new birth exclusively in terms of an immediate transformation wrought by the Spirit when the conditions of repentance and faith are present in an individual. This, of course, is a concept true to the Scriptures. But although true, it is not the *whole* of the truth. The new birth is a spiritual relationship between God and man which begins with a quickening by the Spirit when man yields to the will of God through repentance and faith in Jesus Christ, and which is sustained by the Holy Spirit as the individual continues in repentance and faith. The beginning is essential; but it is not the whole.

Consider John 1:12: "As many as received him [*elabon,* aorist indicative, a definite act in past time—conversion] to them gave he [*edōken,* aorist indicative, a definite act in past time—conversion] power to become [or, to be] children of God, to those who believe [*pisteuousin,* present participle, present progressive action—perseverance in faith] in his name." John depicts both aspects—the initial act of faith at the reception of Christ, whereby the relationship is effected, and the persevering faith in Him whereby the relationship is sustained. The distinction is vivid in Verkuyl's translation: "But to those who did accept

Him, He granted ability to become God's children, that is, to those who believe in His name." Westcott comments on John 1:12:

As far as we can conceive of "this right to become children," it lies in the potential union with the Son, whereby those who receive Him are enabled to realize their divine fellowship. . . . It is important to observe how throughout the passage the divine and human sides of the realisation of Sonship are harmoniously united. The initial act is at once a "begetting" (*egennēthēsan*) and a "reception" (*elabon*). . . . The issue is complete on the part of God, but man must bring it to pass by continuous exertion (*genesthai tekna, tois pisteuousin*). . . . The words [to them that believe] are in apposition with the preceeding *them*. The effective reception of Christ is explained to be the continuous energy of faith which relies upon Him as being for the believer that which He has made Himself known to be.[5]

To think of the new birth exclusively as a transformation wrought by the Spirit at the moment of conversion is to have an inadequate concept of the doctrine as defined in the Holy Scriptures. There are two aspects of the new birth: the initial experience (conversion), and sustained relationship (perseverance). Of the twenty times in which the New Testament refers to the fact of being born of God (*gennaō* and *anagennaō*)[6] seven instances are perfect participles and three are perfect indicatives, emphasizing the *sustained relationship* aspect of the new birth. (The perfect tense affirms not only the fact of a past event, but also the continued existence of the results of that event, as of the moment of speaking.) Of the other ten instances, one is almost certainly a reference to Jesus (I John 5:18, *gennētheis*)[7] and another is very possibly a reference to Jesus (John 1:13), leaving eight, nine, or possibly ten instances which emphasize the *initial experience* aspect of the new birth.

---

[5]B. F. Westcott, *The Gospel According to St. John*, p. 9.

[6]John 1:13; 3:3, 5, 6, 7, 8, I Cor. 4:15, Phm. 10, Jas. 1:18, I Pet. 1:3, 23, I John 2:29; 3:9; 4:7; 5:1 (three times) 4, 18 (two times).

[7]The Vatican Manuscript reads *tērei auton* in place of *tērei heauton* (which most scholars regard as correct) making the aorist passive participle *gennētheis* a reference to Jesus, rather than to the believer. Cf. Williams, Verkuyl, Weymouth, RSV, Moffatt.

The noun *anakainōsis* (renewal, renovation) is associated with a punctiliar verb form in Titus 3:5, referring to the *initial experience* aspect of the new birth, and with a durative verb form in Romans 12:2, emphasizing the *sustained relationship* aspect. The verb *anakainoō* (make new) is durative in both II Corinthians 4:16 and Colossians 3:10, emphasizing the *sustained relationship* aspect of the new birth.

The new birth must have a beginning. It must begin with a definite conversion experience (which, according to circumstances, may or may not be spectacular) wherein the individual, repenting and receiving Christ as Saviour, is made a new creation in Christ by act of the Holy Spirit. But from the moment of inception, the new birth stands as a present relationship to be sustained by the Holy Spirit.

Of eight references in I John to the fact of the believer's being born of God (considering that *gennētheis* in 5:18 refers to Jesus), four are perfect participles and three are perfect indicatives. John's emphasis is on the new birth as a present relationship, rather than as a past event. But there are specific conditions essential to the sustaining of the relationship.

An important truth concerning the conditional aspect of the new birth is found in I John 3:9, "Whosoever is born of God doth not commit sin; for his seed remaineth in him: and he cannot sin, because he is born of God." First, what is the meaning of "cannot sin?" Certainly it does not mean "cannot commit a sin," for this would contradict John's own statements (I John 1:8-2:2) and the consistent testimony of the Scriptures. As Robertson affirms, "the present active infinitive *hamartanein* can only mean 'and he cannot go on sinning.'"[8] This is consistent, not only with grammar, but with the uniform teaching of the New Testament. He who is born of God "cannot practice sinning" (Williams).

But how is it true that one who is born of God "cannot practice sinning?" Is it an *absolute* impossibility that he should be-

[8]A. T. Robertson, *Word Pictures in the New Testament*, Vol. VI, p. 223.

gin to practice sinning? Obviously not, for there are many warnings directed to believers against so doing (e.g., Rom. 6, 8:12-
14, Eph. 4:17 ff., Heb. 10:26, Jas. 1:12-16, Gal. 6:7-9, and many
others). Therefore, since it is not an *absolute* impossibility, it
is only a *relative* impossibility. Thus, for one to "stand begotten
of God" (a literal rendering of the perfect participle *gegen-
nēmenos*) and to "practice sinning" is a moral and spiritual in-
compatibility. The two conditions cannot co-exist.

It is evident therefore that the circumstance, "cannot practice sinning," is not presented as an inevitable *consequence* of
the new birth, but as an essential *condition* governing the continued realization of the new birth in the individual. A major
thesis of I John is the Apostle's insistence that there are specific
conditions under which the new birth *can* exist, and other specific conditions under which it *cannot* exist (cf. 1:5-7; 2:3-11,
15-17, 24-29; 3:6-24; 4:7, 8, 20-5:1). John insists that, apart from
a sincere intention and endeavor to do good and to avoid evil,
one cannot "stand begotten of God." No man whose allegiance
is to the world, the flesh, and the devil can "stand begotten
of God," sharing His divine nature and eternal life through
His saving grace in Christ. (Recognition of this truth would
"rescue" many simple teachings of Jesus which advocates of
unconditional security have discarded as "not applicable to the
present dispensation.")

Chafer objects, ". . . to make sonship, which by its nature is
interminable and is a position before God which rests wholly
on the merit of Christ, to be conditioned by and dependent
upon human worthiness is to contradict the whole order of divine grace and to make impotent man to be, in the end, his own
savior."[9]

First, let us observe that Chafer reasons from the erroneous
assumption that an equation exists between physical and spiritual birth: ". . . sonship, by its nature is interminable. . . ."

---

[9] Lewis Sperry Chafer, *Systematic Theology*, Vol. III, p. 225 f.

Again, there definitely is a sense in which man is "his own savior." (Cf. I Tim. 4:16, Acts 2:40, etc.) The Saviour who came "that the world through him might be saved" is of no benefit except to "as many as receive him" and "believe in his name." By complying with the Gospel invitation to trust in the Saviour whom God has provided, a man does in one sense (a Scriptural sense) become "his own savior." Furthermore, it cannot be altogether wrong to speak of "human worthiness," in view of such statements as these:

Thou hast a few names even in Sardis which have not defiled their garments; and they shall walk with me in white: for they are worthy. He that overcometh, the same shall be clothed in white raiment; and I will not blot out his name out of the book of life, but I will confess his name before my Father, and before his angels (Rev. 3:4, 5).

. . . exhorting them to continue in the faith, and that we must through much tribulation enter into the kingdom of God. . . . We glory in you in the churches of God for your patience and faith in all your persecutions and tribulations that ye endure: which is a manifest token of the righteous judgment of God, that ye may be counted worthy of the kingdom of God, for which ye also suffer (Acts 14:22, II Thess. 1:4, 5).

He that overcometh shall inherit all things; and I will be his God, and he shall be my son (Rev. 21:7).

Despite the objections of Chafer and other sincere advocates of the doctrine of unconditional security, our sonship remains conditional throughout our earthly sojourn in God's moral universe. Consider Paul's warning: "Therefore, brethren, we are debtors, not to the flesh, to live after the flesh. For if ye live after the flesh, ye shall die: but if ye through the Spirit do mortify the deeds of the body, ye shall live. For as many as are led by the Spirit of God, they are sons of God" (Rom. 8:12-14). He further declares (v. 17) that we are children and heirs of God with Christ only "if so be that we suffer with him." (Cf. II Tim. 2:12, "If we endure (hupomenō), we shall also reign with him: if we deny him, he also will deny us.") Liddon comments on Rom. 8.14, "This huiotēs [sonship], although a product of God's grace, depends for its continuance on man's passive obedience to the leading of the Holy Spirit of God (v. 14)."[10]

The conditional aspect of the new birth is apparent in a comparison of the first clauses of verses 6 and 9 of I John 3:

> "Whosoever abideth in him sinneth not."
> "Whosoever is born of God doth not commit sin."

What John attributes in verse 6 to "abiding in him" he attributes in verse 9 to being "born of God." John thus implies that "abiding in him" and being "born of God" are equivalent. Thus we see that "abiding in Christ" is infinitely more than a matter of "fellowship" and "consecration." It is nothing less than continuing "born of God." To "stand begotten of God," then, is a present relationship proceeding from the present condition of "abiding in Christ." This is in full accord with our Lord's teaching in John 15.

Many contend that "abiding in Christ" is a privilege of "fellowship" which is important, but optional, for all who enjoy the "relationship" of being born of God. They declare that it is the key to spiritual power and victory over sin in the life of the Christian. They contend, however, that one can remain born of God without abiding in Christ. Much of their difficulty stems from the fact that they assign their own particular meaning to the word "abide." Its meaning, to them, has become quite foreign to the actual meaning of *menō* which, in addition to *abide*, is commonly rendered *remain, continue, endure, tarry, dwell*, etc. Doubtless they would not so easily have adopted their particular interpretation of our Lord's solemn words concerning "abiding" in Him, as found in John 15, if the translators of the Authorized Version had rendered *menō* as "remain" (as they did in many other passages, and as numerous contemporary translators do in John 15) instead of as "abide."

Some appeal to the second clause of I John 3:6, "whoever sinneth hath not seen him, neither known him," to contend that

---

[10]H. P. Liddon, *Explanatory Analysis of St. Paul's Epistle to the Romans*, p. 132.

"Christians" whose lives do not accord with their profession are not men who have departed from Christ, but men who never have truly known Him as Saviour. Certainly there are many whose professions of faith are false from the beginning. But there are others who depart from Christ after having truly known Him as Saviour and Lord. Those who cite I John 3:6b as evidence that all "Christians" whose lives contradict their profession necessarily are men who never have known Christ in a true saving relationship rest their argument, of course, on the English translation. But the English perfect is by no means the equivalent of the Greek perfect tense (heōraken and egnōken). The English perfect has but a single aspect, whereas the Greek perfect possesses two aspects. It is concerned, not only with the fact of an act in the past, but also with the fact that the results of that act continue to exist at the present moment. An act in the past, when considered entirely apart from the question of the continued existence of the results of that act, as of the moment of speaking, is affirmed by either the aorist or the imperfect. An expanded rendering of John's words is, "whoever deliberately practices sin has not seen Him and continued seeing Him, nor known Him and continued knowing Him." John's statement is applicable to men whose professions of faith have been false from the beginning, and it is equally applicable to apostates who have departed from true saving faith in Christ.[11]

Westcott asserts that John's statement has no bearing on ". . . the question of the indefectibility of grace. It deals with the

---

[11]Many have appealed to Matt. 7:23 to contend that all false prophets (vv. 15 ff.) and impostors are men whom Christ never has known, according to His statement, "I never knew you." Let us observe that Jesus declared only that He would *profess* to them (*homologeō*) that He never knew them. Cf. Luke 13:25, 27, where Jesus warned His hearers that He would say of them, "I know you not whence ye are"—which obviously could be true only figuratively, rather than literally (cf. John 8:23, 44). With respect to the men in view in Matt. 7:23, Jesus will deny acquaintance with all of them alike. But while His relationship with many of them never shall have been more than merely pretended and fictitious, His relationship with others shall have once been real. Cf. II Tim. 2:12, Rev. 3:5, 8-12.

actual state of the man. Past sight and past knowledge cease to be unless they go forward."[12] Lange considers that John has reference specifically to apostasy: "John's idea therefore is this: Every one that sinneth, and that while he is sinning, is one in whom seeing and knowing Christ is a fact of the past, but without continuing to act and to last to the present."[13] There is nothing about I John 3:6b that affirms that "Christians" whose lives contradict their profession of faith are necessarily men who never have known Christ in a true saving relationship.

The First Epistle of John depicts clearly the continuing conditional aspect of the new birth. Let us consider a logical syllogism derived from John's assertions in 2:29-3:10:

Major Premise: Only those who abide in Christ avoid habitual deliberate sinning (v. 6).

Minor Premise: All who stand begotten of God avoid habitual deliberate sinning (v. 9).

Conclusion: Only those who abide in Christ stand begotten of God.

"Abiding in Christ" is more than a matter of fellowship, consecration, and "the victorious life." It is life itself. It is remaining in Him "who is our life," and thus continuing to stand begotten of God. Surely, these considerations impart a deep sense of the awful solemnity of our Saviour's words in John 15, "Abide [remain] in me, and I in you. If a man remain not in me, he is cast forth as a branch and is withered; and they gather them and cast them into the fire, and they are burned."

Before concluding the chapter, let us consider the meaning of the words, "his seed remaineth in him" (I John 3:9). Various definitions of the "seed" are offered by commentators. We believe that the most satisfactory interpretation is that "the seed is the word of God" (Luke 8:11). This harmonizes perfectly with our Lord's Parable of the Sower and many other passages.

---

[12]B. F. Westcott, *The Epistles of St. John,* p. 104.

[13]J. P. Lange, *Commentary on the Holy Scriptures, ad loc.*

Some have objected to this interpretation on the ground that John uses *sperma* rather than *sporos*. But the objection is seen to be invalid when one considers that *sperma* and *sporos* are used interchangeably in II Corinthians 9:10, and that *sperma* is used with respect to the sowing of plant seeds in Mark 4:31, I Corinthians 15:38, and Matthew 13:24 ff.

It is altogether possible, of course, that "his seed" has reference to Jesus. Certainly Jesus, the "seed of the woman" and of Abraham and David, is also the seed of God, "the only begotten of the Father." "His seed" which remains in him who stands begotten of God may indeed refer to Jesus, who said, "Remain in me, and I in you."

It may be considered certain that the "seed" which remains in the faithful is the Word of God, considered either as the spoken Word which, hidden in our hearts, keeps us from sinning against God (Ps. 119:11), or as the "Word made flesh" in the Person of Jesus, who remains in all who remain in Him. It is probably impossible to establish a more precise definition. But none is needed. For the closest possible affinity exists between the spoken Word and the Word Incarnate. Many things attributed by the Scriptures to the one are equally attributed to the other.

In any event, it is imperative that we continue to hide in our hearts both the spoken Word of God, which will keep us from sinning against Him, and the Incarnate Word who said, "Remain in me, and I in you. . . . If a man keep my word, he shall never see death." Apart from the indwelling Word, we cannot stand begotten of God.

Men who would see the kingdom of God will do well to ponder and heed *all* that the Holy Scriptures declare concerning the new birth which God, in mercy and love, has made possible for the children of men, that they may be part of His everlasting kingdom and forever share His own eternal life.

"The Earnest of the Spirit"

Now he which stablisheth us with you in Christ and hath anointed us is God, who hath also sealed us and given the earnest of the Spirit in our hearts.

II CORINTHIANS 1:21, 22

In whom ye also trusted, after ye heard the word of truth, the gospel of your salvation: in whom also, having believed, ye were sealed with that Holy Spirit of promise, which is the earnest of our inheritance until the redemption of the purchased possession, unto the praise of his glory.

EPHESIANS 1:13, 14

And grieve not the Holy Spirit of God, whereby ye are sealed unto the day of redemption.

EPHESIANS 4:30

CHAPTER VIII

THE EARNEST OF THE SPIRIT

HAVE YOU EVER thanked God for Himself? Have you thanked Him that it is in *Him* we live and move and have our very being? Have you thanked Him for the kind of God He is? "God is faithful," writes Paul, "by whom ye were called unto the fellowship of his Son Jesus Christ our Lord" (I Cor. 1:6).

Long ago, Augustine said, "Thou hast made man for Thyself, and he is restless until he rests in Thee." Not only is it true that man is never really satisfied until he rests in God; it is also true that God Himself will not be satisfied until He is in the midst of all His own in a perfect everlasting fellowship which can never be marred in any way. "Behold, the tabernacle of God is with men, and he will dwell with them and they shall be his people, and God himself shall be with them and be their God" (Rev. 21:3).

Never will God be satisfied until, in His eternal day, He dwells among His people, forever showing "the exceeding riches of his grace in his kindness toward us through Christ Jesus" (Eph. 2:7). Ever moving toward the fulfillment of the longing of His heart and of all His purposes in grace, God is constantly at work among His own who are yet pilgrims on earth, drawing them onward toward the ultimate realization of the privileges of their holy sonship.

"[I am] confident of this very thing," writes Paul to the Philippians, "that he which hath begun a good work in you will go on completing it until the day of Jesus Christ" (1:6). To the Corinthians, he writes that Christ "shall also confirm you unto

103

the end, that ye may be blameless in the day of our Lord Jesus Christ" (I Cor. 1:8). "The Lord is faithful," he assures the Thessalonians, "who shall establish you and keep you from the evil one" (II Thess. 3:3). For them he prays, "And the very God of peace sanctify you wholly; and I pray God your whole spirit and soul and body be preserved blameless unto the coming of our Lord Jesus Christ" (I Thess. 5:23). He prays in confidence that "faithful is he that calleth you, who also will do it" (v. 24).

For himself, Paul is confident that "the Lord shall deliver me from every evil work, and will preserve me unto his heavenly kingdom" (II Tim. 4:18). "We who are in this tabernacle do groan, being burdened," writes Paul to the Corinthians. "Not that we desire to be unclothed, but clothed upon, that mortality might be swallowed up by life. Now he who has fashioned us for this very thing is God, who has given unto us the earnest of the Spirit" (II Cor. 5:4, 5).

God is at work in His children. He has given them a pledge of His faithfulness and an earnest of the ultimate fulfillment of His purpose in their redemption: His own Spirit, sent to dwell in the hearts of His pilgrim sons. Paul declares that the Holy Spirit is both the seal and the earnest of our final redemption:

> God "has sealed [*sphragizō,* set an official mark upon] us and given the earnest of the Spirit [*ton arrabōna tou pneumatos,* genitive of apposition: the Spirit is Himself the earnest] in our hearts" (II Cor. 1:22).

> "Ye were sealed with the promised Holy Spirit [*tōi pneumati,* instrumental case: the Spirit is the instrument of sealing] who is the earnest of our inheritance until the redemption of the purchased possession" (Eph. 1:13, 14).

> "Grieve not the Holy Spirit of God, in whom [*en hōi,* the Spirit is the element in which we are sealed]

ye were sealed unto the day of redemption" (Eph.
4:30).

The Holy Spirit is the official seal of God's ownership, and
the believer's God-given earnest of his promised inheritance as
a son and heir of God. Wonderful! But there is more: the Spirit
is continually at work in the believer to bring to consummation
all that is within the perfect will of God for all His sons in
Christ. The gracious Comforter, our Paraclete on earth even as
is Christ in heaven, has been sent by the Father to dwell within
us and to abide with us for ever, instructing, encouraging, and
guiding us along our pilgrim way to the Father's house.

Blessed and manifold are His ministries in our behalf. He
has come to teach us all things (John 14:26); to empower us in
our witness for Christ (John 15:26, 27, Acts 1:8); to guide us
into all truth and show us things to come and the things of
Christ (John 16:13); to direct us in our service (Acts 13:2); to
fulfill the righteousness of the law in us (Rom. 8:4); to bear
witness to our sonship (8:16); to help our infirmities and to
make intercession for us (8:26); to reveal to us something of
the glory of the things which God has prepared for those who
love Him (I Cor. 2:9 ff.); to impart His gifts to empower us
for effective service (12:1 ff.); to bring forth in us His gracious fruit of Christ-likeness (Gal. 5:22 ff.); and ultimately, to
quicken our mortal bodies at the coming of Jesus (Rom. 8:11).
Gracious are all His many ministries in our behalf.

But the Holy Spirit can do nothing for those who refuse His
ministry. Therefore, we are exhorted to "be filled with the
Spirit" (Eph. 5:18); to walk after the Spirit rather than after
the flesh (Gal. 5:16 ff.); to sow to the Spirit rather than to the
flesh (6:7-9); to live after the Spirit rather than after the flesh
(Rom. 8:1-13); and to be led of the Spirit, that we may be sons
of God (v. 14). We are further warned against grieving the
Spirit (Eph. 4:30), against quenching the Spirit (I Thess.
5:19), and against ultimately doing despite unto the Spirit of
grace (Heb. 10:29). All these solemn exhortations and warn-

ings affirm that the believer has a definite personal responsibility with respect to the ministry of the Holy Spirit which he dare not ignore.

"God is faithful," declared Paul. Constant and faithful are the Father, Son, and Spirit. But the faithfulness of God cannot avail for unfaithful men. Paul's confidence for the Philippians that "he which hath begun a good work in you will go on perfecting it until the day of Jesus Christ" was not based on some inexorable divine law which must continue operative regardless of the conduct of the Philippians. Quite to the contrary, his confidence stemmed from his observation of the personal conduct of the Philippians themselves.

Many who have appealed to Philippians 1:6 in defense of the doctrine of unconditional security seem completely to have ignored the immediate context (and the larger context, as well). Consider verse 7: "It is right for me to think this of you all" (i.e., that God's perfecting work in them would continue until the day of Christ) because they were standing fast with Paul in the defense and confirmation of the Gospel in the face of growing persecution which, even then, left Paul in bonds. Again, the stedfastness of their fellowship in the Gospel in the past (v. 5), as Meyer declares

. . . forms also the ground of [Paul's] just confidence for the future. . . . [Their fellowship in the Gospel], from the first day until now, is that which alone can warrant and justify [Paul's] confidence for the future. . . . That which [God] has begun He will complete, namely by the further operations of His grace. The idea of resistance to this grace, as a human possibility, is not thereby excluded; but Paul has not to fear this on the part of his Philippian converts, as he formerly had in the case of the Galatians (Gal. i. 6, iii. 3).[1]

The faithfulness of God is beyond question. But the faith and faithfulness of men (the two are inseparably involved, according to the Scriptures) is quite another matter. In the

---

[1]H. A. W. Meyer, *Critical and Exegetical Hand-Book to the Epistles to the Philippians and Colossians, and to Philemon,* p. 13 f.

case of the Philippians, Paul's assumption that God's gracious work in them would continue until the day of Jesus Christ seemed fully warranted by their evident zeal in the faith. On the ground of their stedfastness, Paul felt that his confidence was fully justified. There was every reason to assume that the faithfulness of God would continue to meet with a corresponding faithfulness on the part of the Philippians themselves.

Paul's confidence for the Philippians was not one which he could necessarily entertain with respect to some others of his converts—some of the Corinthians, for example. Consider, too, the case of the Galatians. The Galatians "began in the Spirit" (3:3); but some of them later came to believe that they were somehow to be "made perfect by the flesh." As the ground of their justification and hope, some of them turned from Christ to the works of the flesh. Christ therefore became of no profit to them; they became "severed from Christ" (ASV; cf. Thayer on *katargeō*) and "fallen from grace" (5:2-4). "Sowing to the flesh," even those things which seem good in themselves, brings destruction; but "sowing to the Spirit" brings life everlasting (6:7-9).

Paul's confidence that the Philippians would continue stedfast in the faith and Gospel was the ground of his confidence that, in their case, God would continue to perform His gracious work in them until the day of Jesus Christ. Commenting on Philippians 1:6, Robertson writes, "God began and God will consummate it . . . but not without their cooperation and partnership."[2] God was at work in the Philippians to bring them to perfection in the day of Jesus Christ. But His work, far from obviating the necessity of effort on their part, demanded their cooperation and perseverance. This Paul urges upon them: "But whatever be the point that we have already reached, let us persevere in the same course" (3:16 Weymouth).

Paul (3:3-17) bids them follow his example as one who perseveres in simple faith in Christ alone, to the exclusion of all

---

[2]A. T. Robertson, *Word Pictures in the New Testament*, Vol. IV, p. 436.

confidence in the flesh, "pressing onward toward the goal, to win the prize to which God through Jesus Christ is calling us upward" (3:14 Williams). He reminds them (vv. 18, 19) that he had repeatedly warned them against the example of apostates whose god was the satisfaction of carnal appetites, as indeed he now warns them, "even weeping" ("Deep emotion as he dictated the letter and recalled these recreant followers of Christ."[3]). He exhorts them, in contrast to these sensual apostates, to continue to look heavenward in anticipation of the coming of the Saviour (vv. 20, 21), in view of which certain prospect he warns them to "stand fast in the Lord" (5:1).

Elsewhere in his epistle, Paul admonishes them to "work out your own salvation with fear and trembling" (2:12). For their encouragement, he reminds them that "it is God which worketh in you both to will and to do of his good pleasure" (v. 13). Many have appealed to verse 13 to deny that verse 12 imposes any responsibility upon men with respect to their actual salvation. The initiative rests entirely with God, say they. God works within us to cause us both to will and to do His good pleasure. Therefore, say they, our working out of salvation is not our work, but God's; and He cannot fail.

But they overlook the fact that God's work in men is not one of compulsion and constraint. The Scriptures bear abundant testimony that, despite God's gracious work, men do depart from His will and good pleasure, and the warnings against so doing are many and urgent. God is at work in His children. But His faithfulness in His work does not obviate the essential importance and necessity of their cooperation, nor does it in any manner coerce them or compel their compliance.

"God is faithful, who will not suffer you to be tempted above that ye are able, but will with the temptation also make a way to escape, that ye may be able to bear it" (I Cor. 10:13). Let us observe that God's faithfulness does not relieve us of our responsibility. Rather, it only ensures that we shall be able to

---

[3]*Ibid.*, p. 456.

"bear" every temptation and to "escape"—if we will. We remain under the necessity of continuing to "flee from idolatry" (v. 14), to avoid "tempting Christ" (v. 9), and to "take heed lest we fall" through presumption (v. 12). The faithfulness of God is of no avail for unfaithful men.

The will of God for men is not necessarily the will of men toward Him. Paul affirms (Rom. 2:4) that God, in His goodness, is leading toward repentance even obdurate men who, with "hardness and impenitent hearts," continue to treasure up wrath against the day of judgment. God is commanding all men everywhere to repent (Acts 17:30); but few men wish to heed His command. Jesus declared that the Pharisees and lawyers, in their refusal to submit to the baptism of John, rejected God's counsel (*boulē*, purpose) for them (Luke 7:30). The will of God for men is not necessarily the will of men toward Him.

Christ is eternally faithful. "If we disbelieve, yet he remaineth faithful: for he cannot deny himself" (II Tim. 2:13 Alford). Our hope for salvation rests upon the faithfulness of Him who is "the same yesterday, today, and for ever." But His faithfulness cannot avail for men who disown Him. Paul's urgent warning to Timothy, the pastor of the church at Ephesus, is especially vivid in Verkuyl's translation: "If we endure, then we shall also reign with Him. If we go back on Him, then He will also personally go back on us. If we play Him false, He will Himself remain faithful; for He cannot play false to Himself." Our treachery to Christ cannot alter His constant faithfulness; but neither can it leave undisturbed our relation to Him. He cannot deny Himself; but He *will* deny us, if we deny Him. "Remain in me, and I in you."

While the faithlessness of many in Israel did not nullify the faithfulness of God in keeping His promises, neither did the faithfulness of God prevent the faithlessness of many of His covenant people (Rom. 3:3-8). The faithfulness of God toward Israel did not prevent "some of the branches" from becoming severed from Him: "Because of unbelief, they were broken off" (Rom. 11:20). Paul warns the Gentile believers not to be presumptious, but to recognize that the same tragedy could befall them, for they only stand by faith (vv. 20-22). To assume that Christians cannot become lost because of the faithfulness of God is to ignore an essential part of the truth. The faithfulness of God cannot avail for men who become unfaithful. "Let us hold fast the confession of our hope without wavering: for he is faithful who promised" (Heb. 10:23).

Abraham was "fully persuaded that, what God had promised, he was able also to perform" (Rom. 4:21). But the faith which was "imputed to him for righteousness" (v. 22) was not merely the persuasion of one grand and holy moment; it was his *enduring* persuasion. No lesser faith could have inherited the promise of God. The enduring faith of Abraham which was reckoned as righteousness, and which made him an heir of God, is vividly portrayed in Hebrews 6:11-15, an urgent exhortation to believers: "We desire that every one of you show the same diligence to the full assurance of hope unto the end: that ye be not slothful, but followers of them who through faith and patience inherit the promises. For when God made promise to Abraham, because he could swear by no greater, he sware by himself, saying, Surely blessing I will bless thee, and multiplying I will multiply thee. And so, after [Abraham] had patiently endured, he obtained the promise."

The great promises of the faithfulness of God in performing His work of grace in our hearts by His Spirit until the day of Jesus Christ (such as Phil. 1:6, I Cor. 1:8, II Thess. 3:3, I Thess. 5:24, and II Tim. 4:18) all assume a corresponding faithfulness on the part of man. To suppose that there are no qualifications attached to such promises, simply because they are not expressly stated in the verses themselves, is as unwarranted as to assume that all the world must be saved because John 3:17 declares that "God sent not his Son into the world to condemn the world, but that the world through him might be saved." We are not at liberty to accept John 3:17, while ignoring verse 18 and a multitude of other passages of Holy Scripture. Let us not insist that the whole of God's revelation be compressed into a single verse. Philippians 1:6 and kindred verses do not stand alone. "God is faithful." But what is our response to His faithfulness? Maclaren writes:

. . . what attitude in us corresponds to the faithfulness of God? I need only quote one of the expressions in the Epistle to the Hebrews to give the answer, "Hold fast the profession of your faith without wavering, for He is faithful that promised." Our faith corresponds with and is the answer to God's faithfulness. As with two instruments tuned to the same pitch, when a note is struck on the one, the chords of the other vibrate it back again, so God's faithfulness should awake the music of answering faith in our responsive and vibrating hearts. If He is worth trusting, let us trust Him.

. . . .

The progressive perfecting of the Christian life is guaranteed by the thought of the faithfulness of God. He does not begin a work and then get disgusted with it, or turn to something else, or find that His resources will not avail to work it out to completion.

. . . .

None that look on God's work will ever have the right to say, "This man began to build, and was not able to finish." There are no half-completed failures in God's workshop. Only you have to keep yourself under His influences. It is useless to talk about the "final perseverance of the saints" unless you remember that only they who continuously yield themselves to God are continuously the subjects of His cleansing and hallowing grace. If they do, the progressive perfecting of those upon whom He has begun to work is sure.[4]

Commenting on Hebrews 7:22 ("Jesus was made a surety of a better covenant"), Westcott declares, "Christ is not said to be a surety for man to God, but a surety of a covenant of God with man."[5] In like manner, while the Holy Spirit is the earnest of our inheritance and the pledge of God's faithfulness, He is no surety of our corresponding faithfulness. The coming of the Spirit of grace into our hearts at conversion is no guarantee that we shall not subsequently grieve, quench, and finally do despite

---

[4]Alexander Maclaren, *Expositions of Holy Scripture: Second Timothy, Titus, Philemon, and Hebrews*, pp. 66, 64 f.

[5]B. F. Westcott, *The Epistle to the Hebrews*, p. 189.

to Him who comes to guide our steps toward the Jerusalem which is above.

"Brethren, we are debtors, not to the flesh, to live after the flesh," warns Paul. "For if ye live after the flesh, ye shall die: but if ye through the Spirit do mortify the deeds of the body, ye shall live. For as many as are led by the Spirit of God, they are sons of God" (Rom. 8:12-14). Men who have no concern to live after the Spirit of God cannot remain His sons. "This [sonship], although a product of God's grace, depends for its continuance on man's passive obedience to the leading of the Holy Spirit of God."[6] The faithful ministry of the Holy Spirit avails nothing for men who become indifferent toward His nurture and guidance and who despise His reproof. Preaching from Ephesians 4:30 ("Grieve not the Holy Spirit of God, whereby ye are sealed unto the day of redemption"), Maclaren said:

We have here a plain warning as to the possibility of thwarting [the Holy Spirit's] influences. Nothing here about irresistible grace; nothing here about a power that lays hold upon a man and makes him good, he lying passive in its hands like clay in the hands of the potter! You will not be made holy without the Divine Spirit; but you will not be made holy without your working along with it. There is a possibility of resisting, and there is a possibility of co-operating. Man is left free. God does not lay hold of anyone by the hair of his head and drag him into paths of righteousness whether he will or no. . . . We have to work with God, and we can resist. Ay, and there is a deeper and a sadder word than that applied by the same Apostle in another letter to the same subject. We can "quench" the light and extinguish the fire.

What extinguishes it? Look at the catalogue of sins that lie side by side with this exhortation of my text. They are all small matters—bitterness, wrath, anger, clamour, evil-speaking, malice, stealing, lying, and the like; very "homely" transgressions, if I may so say. Yes, and if you pile enough of them upon the spark that is in your hearts you will smother it out. Sin, the wrenching of myself away from [the Holy Spirit's] influences, not attending to [His] whispers and suggestions,

---

[6]H. P. Liddon, *Explanatory Analysis of St. Paul's Epistle to the Romans*, p. 132.

being blind to the teaching of the Spirit through the Word and through Providence: these are the things that "grieve the Holy Spirit of God."

. . . .

"Grieve not the Holy Spirit of God." A father feels a pang if he sees that his child makes no account of some precious gift that he has bestowed upon him, and leaves it lying about anywhere. A loving friend, standing on the margin of the stream and calling to his friends in a boat when they are drifting to the rapids, turns away sad if they do not attend to his voice. That Divine Spirit pleads with us and proffers [His] gifts to us, and turns away . . . sick at heart, not because of wounded authority, but because of wounded love and baffled desire to help, when we, in spite of [Him], will take our own way, neglect the call that warns us of our peril, and leave untouched the gifts that would have made us safe.[7]

Many contend that, although believers may offend and grieve the Holy Spirit, He will never depart from one in whom He has come to dwell. The quenching of the Spirit against which Paul warned can never become total or final, they believe. In evidence, they cite the promise of Jesus, "And I will pray the Father, and he shall give you another Comforter, that he may abide with you for ever" (John 14:16).

The Spirit's indwelling within the believer is a blessed fact. A precious intimate relationship between the Spirit and believers was implemented after Jesus, through His death, secured access into Heaven's Holy of Holies through Himself for all who abide in Him. But our Lord's words, "that he may abide with you for ever," do not constitute a promise that apostasy has somehow become impossible, and that the Holy Spirit can never withdraw from one in whom He once has taken up residence, regardless of his subsequent response to His ministry of guidance and reproof. Many have missed the meaning and significance of Christ's promise.

Our Saviour's promise of another Comforter (like Himself) to abide with His disciples was given at what, for the Apostles,

---

[7]Maclaren, *Expositions of Holy Scripture: Ephesians,* pp. 267-270.

was a moment of profound despair. They were facing the immediate prospect of the Master's departure from their midst. It was an awesome prospect which they had failed to anticipate. They felt a desperate need for reassurance.

Despite their limited understanding, the eleven of them had remained stedfast in their faith in Him in past months, in the face of growing opposition and the distressing fact that many had turned back to walk no more with Him. But their firm persuasion that He had words of eternal life and their constant anticipation of His eventual triumph and the restoration of Israel (Acts 1:6), with Jesus enthroned as king, had sustained their hope. His presence among them had been their constant inspiration and strength. Such dismal prospect as His departure from their midst had not so much as entered their minds.

But now: "Little children, yet a little while I am with you. Ye shall seek me: and as I have said unto the Jews, Whither I go ye cannot come, so now I say to you." It was a bleak prospect which seemed to blight all fond hopes, plunging them into gloom and despair. What need they had for reassurance! Their grave misgivings and uncertainties were reflected in their anxious questions:

"Lord, where are you going?" asked Peter. "Why can't I fol-you now?" "Lord, we don't know where you are going; how can we know the way?" asked Thomas. "Lord, before you go away," entreated Philip, "just show us the Father, and that will sustain us." What pangs of loneliness and uncertainty they felt as they faced the Master's departure. They had depended upon Him for everything!

But Jesus had two wonderful promises for them. One was a promise concerning Himself. He would return and they would see Him again, though the world would not (no unbeliever saw Jesus after His burial and resurrection); and they would know His spiritual presence and abide in His love, even while He was bodily with the Father in Heaven:

I will not leave you helpless orphans. I am coming back to you. In just a little while the world will not see me any more, but you will be seeing me. Because I am to live on, you too will live on. At that time you will know that I am in union with my Father and you are in union with me and I am in union with you. Whoever continues to hold and keep my commands is the one who really loves me, and whoever really loves me will be loved by my Father; yes, I will love him Myself and will make Myself real to him. . . . If anyone really loves me, he will observe my teaching, and my Father will love him, and both of us will come in face to face fellowship with him; yes, we will make our special dwelling-place with him. . . . I have loved you just as the Father has loved me. You must remain in my love. If you continue to keep my commands, you will remain in my love, just as I have kept my Father's commands and remain in His love (John 14:18-21, 23; 15:9, 10 Williams).

Although He was to be absent from them bodily, He would still be with them spiritually. They could remain in His love, if they would, and know intimate fellowship with Him and with the Father. If they would but continue in His word and teaching, He and the Father would make their spiritual dwelling-place within their hearts. What a precious promise!

The other reassuring word of the Master was His promise of the coming of the Holy Spirit to abide with them during the time of His own bodily absence: "And I will ask the Father and He will give you another Helper, to remain with you to the end of the age" (14:16 Williams). The abiding presence of the Comforter, however, cannot be dissociated from the spiritual presence of Jesus Himself, which He promised to His disciples for "all the days until the consummation of the age" (Matt. 28:20). Meyer affirms:

In the Paraclete . . . Christ Himself is present with His own (Matt. xxviii. 20); for in the mission of the Spirit, who is the Spirit of Christ (Rom. viii. 9; Gal. iv. 6), the self-communication of the exalted Christ takes place (Rom. viii. 10; Gal. ii. 20), without, however, the Paraclete ceasing to be an *allos*, another [subject than He, although dependent on the Son]. . . .[3]

---

[3]H. A. W. Meyer, *Critical and Exegetical Hand-Book to the Gospel of John*, p. 415.

Westcott comments:

Christ's historical Presence was only for a time. His spiritual Presence was "for all the days until the consummation of the age" (Matt. xxviii. 20). This Presence [is] fulfilled through the Spirit.[9]

Christ's promise of the presence of the Holy Spirit to abide "for ever" (*eis ton aiōna*, unto the age) during His own bodily absence from the earth has been fulfilled thus far, and will continue to be fulfilled throughout all the days of the age, until Jesus comes again. But to assume that the promise of Jesus constitutes a pledge that the Holy Spirit must remain in every person in whom He once takes up residence, regardless of how that person subsequently responds to His ministry of guidance and reproof, is to ignore many grave warnings in the Scriptures, including our Saviour's solemn warning spoken on the same occasion, "Remain in me, and I in you."

We have earlier declared that throughout his earthly sojourn, the relation of the believer to Christ is never a *static* relationship existing as the irrevocable consequence of a past decision, act, or experience. Rather, it is a living relationship—a present mutual indwelling of the believer and the Saviour, the sharing of a common life which emanates from Him "who is our life." For the believer, it is a living participation proceeding upon a living faith in a living Saviour. The foundation principle governing the relationship is reduced to its simplest statement in our Saviour's words, "Remain in me, and I in you." The believer's relation to the Holy Spirit cannot be dissociated from his relation to Christ; it is one and the same. The relationship between the Holy Spirit and the Christian is not static and indissoluble.

"If we live by the Spirit," writes Paul to the Galatians, "then[10]

---

[9]B. F. Westcott, *The Gospel According to St. John*, p. 205.

[10]For the inferential use of *kai*, cf. Mark 10:26 and Jas. 2:4 (Text. Rec.). *Kai* possesses great latitude, and context must determine its precise meaning in any passage (cf. Robertson, *Grammar*, p. 1182). Context here indicates the inferential use.

let us walk by the Spirit" (5:25). If our very life in Christ depends on the Spirit, as Paul has shown them, then by all means let us walk in the Spirit! We cannot *live* by the Spirit if we refuse to *walk* in the Spirit. Paul's admonition follows his warning that we cannot live after both the flesh and the Spirit (v. 17), and it is only as we walk after the Spirit that we avoid living after the flesh (v. 16). There is a terrible penalty attached to living after the flesh: "I warn you again, even as I have warned you in the past, that they who practice such things [the works of the flesh] shall not inherit the kingdom of God" (vv. 19-21). "Be not deceived," he warns them, "God is not to be mocked: for whatsoever a man soweth, that shall he also reap. For he that soweth to his flesh shall of the flesh reap destruction [*phthora*, Thayer: perishing, loss of salvation, eternal misery]; but he that soweth to the Spirit shall of the Spirit reap life everlasting. And let us not be weary in well doing: for in due season we shall reap, if we faint not" (6:7-9).

Paul warns the Romans that "to be carnally minded—death, but to be spiritually minded—life and peace" (8:6). "Brethren," he writes, "we are debtors, not to the flesh, to live after the flesh. For if ye live after the flesh, ye shall die: but if ye through the Spirit do mortify the deeds of the body, ye shall live. For as many as are led by the Spirit of God, they are sons of God" (Rom. 8:12-14). Godet comments:

The life of the Spirit is not realized in the believer without his concurrence merely from the fact that the Spirit has once been communicated to him. There is needed on man's part a persevering decision, an active docility in giving himself over to the guidance of the Spirit. For the guidance of the Spirit tends constantly to the sacrifice of the flesh; and if the believer refuses to follow it on this path, he renounces the life of the Spirit and its glorious privileges.[11]

The Blessed Spirit of God has come to abide for ever and to guide the steps of pilgrims toward the Father's house and the everlasting inheritance of the faithful. But his gracious ministry

---

[11]F. L. Godet, *Commentary on the Epistle to the Romans*, p. 307.

cannot avail for men who despise His guidance and reproof, and who turn from sowing to the Spirit to sow to the flesh. Such men cannot remain in Christ and His Spirit. The Holy Comforter cannot continue to dwell in men who close their hearts against His loving ministry.

> Our blest Redeemer, ere He breathed
>   His tender last farewell,
> A Guide, a Comforter bequeathed,
>   That He might with us dwell.
>
> He came sweet influence to impart,
>   A gracious, willing Guest,
> When He can find an humble heart
>   Where, welcome, He can rest.
>
> And His that gentle voice we hear,
>   Soft as the breath of even,
> That checks each fault, that calms our fear.
>   And speaks to us of Heaven.
>
> Spirit of Purity and Grace,
>   Our weakness pitying see;
> Still make our hearts Thy dwelling-place,
>   And worthier of Thee.

HARRIETT AUBER (adapted)

"Once for All"

Then said he, Lo, I come to do thy will, O God. He taketh away the first, that he may establish the second. By the which will we are sanctified through the offering of the body of Jesus Christ once for all. And every priest standeth daily ministering and offering oftentimes the same sacrifices, which can never take away sins. But this man, after he had offered one sacrifice for sins for ever, sat down on the right hand of God, from henceforth expecting till his enemies be made his footstool. For by one offering he hath perfected for ever them that are sanctified.

* * *

By so much was Jesus made a surety of a better covenant. And they truly were many priests, because they were not suffered to continue by reason of death. But this man, because he continueth ever, hath an unchangeable priesthood. Wherefore he is able also to save them to the uttermost that come unto God by him, seeing he ever liveth to make intercession for them.

* * *

Having therefore, brethren, boldness to enter into the holiest by the blood of Jesus, by a new and living way which he hath consecrated for us through the veil, that is to say, his flesh; and having an high priest over the house of God, let us draw near with a true heart in full assurance of faith, having our hearts sprinkled from an evil conscience, and our bodies washed with pure water. Let us hold fast the confession of hope without wavering, for he is faithful who promised.

HEBREWS 10:9-14; 7:22-25; 10:19-23

Chapter IX

ONCE FOR ALL

To His critics, Jesus once said, "You search the scriptures, for in them you think to have eternal life; and these are they which testify of me; and yet you will not come to me that you might have life" (John 5:39, 40). With what diligence they pored over the Scriptures! Yet they failed to see Him who is the Alpha and Omega, the center and circumference of Holy Writ, and therefore failed to come to Him for life when He appeared visibly among them. Their study of the Scriptures, despite their zeal, was tragically impaired by preconception and prejudice.

It is an unfortunate fact that many today, some of whom are completely sincere, are seriously hindered in their study of the Scriptures through their failure to suppress preconceptions. At best, such can be done only imperfectly; and it is true for all of us that, subjectively, the meaning of what we read and hear is conditioned to some extent by our preconceptions, from which it is impossible to be wholly free. It is therefore helpful in our study of any passage of Scripture to consult the original text and as many good translations as possible. Too many preconceptions can lodge undisturbed among the old familiar words of our favorite translation—which, for many of us, is still the beloved Authorized Version.

Many advocates of the doctrine of unconditional security have appealed to two verses in the tenth chapter of the Epistle to the Hebrews: "By the which will we are sanctified through the offering of the body of Jesus Christ once for all. . . . For

121

by one offering he hath perfected for ever them that are sanctified" (Heb. 10:10, 14). A casual reading does seem to warrant
the conclusion that the sanctification[1] of a believer, once effected, is "once for all . . . for ever," and therefore irrevocable.
But let us examine the passage carefully.

Two great truths are in view in Hebrews 10:10-14 and context: Christ's offering of Himself as the eternally efficacious
"one sacrifice for sins for ever," and the consequent sanctification and perfection of all who trust in Him. We shall establish
two facts: (1) The circumstance, "once for all," is associated
primarily with our Saviour's offering of Himself as the eternal
sacrifice for sin, and only secondarily with men; and (2) individual men participate in the benefit of Christ's once-for-all
atonement for the sins of mankind, not by virtue of a single
once-for-all act of faith, but as they continually rely upon Him.

1. It is Christ's offering of Himself as the propitiatory sacrifice for the sins of all men, rather than the actual sanctification
of specific persons, which is said to be "once for all . . . for ever."
The contrast between the oft-repeated sacrifices of the old
economy, which could "never take away sins," and Christ's
effectual "one sacrifice for sins for ever" is a prominent theme
of the Epistle to the Hebrews. Consider the following passages:

[Jesus] needeth not daily, as those high priests, to offer up sacrifice . . .
for this he did once, when he offered up himself (7:27).

By his own blood he entered in once into the holy place, having obtained
eternal redemption for us (9:12).

Nor yet that he should offer himself often, as the high priest entereth into
the holy place every year with blood of others. For then must he often
have suffered since the foundation of the world: but now once in the
consummation of the ages hath he appeared to put away sin by the sacrifice of himself. And as it is appointed unto men once to die, and after
this, judgment, so Christ was once offered for the sins of many (9:25-28).
And every priest standeth daily ministering and offering repeatedly the
same sacrifices, which can never take away sins. But this man, after he

---

[1]"Sanctification" in the present chapter is positional, rather than experimental.

had offered one sacrifice for sins for ever, sat down on the right hand of God (10:11, 12).

The sacrifice of Jesus on the Cross of Golgotha occurred at a specific time in a specific place. It was "once in the consummation of the ages . . . in the fulness of the time" that Jesus died on a hill outside Jerusalem. But what occurred at a precise time and place is independent of time and location. It is eternally contemporary. Its value and efficacy extend from the moment of the intrusion of sin in Eden until the time when he who is unjust must be unjust still, and he who is righteous shall be righteous still (Rev. 22:11). What Jesus accomplished through the one offering of Himself is "once for all . . . for ever!"

While the circumstance, "once for all," has reference to Christ's offering of Himself as the one eternal sacrifice for sin, there is a secondary application to believers, as they trust in Him. It is secondary because it is a consequence of Christ's once-for-all act of sacrifice, and because it avails for men progressively, as they meet necessary conditions. "The work is complete on the divine side (*hēgiasmenoi, teteleiōken*) and gradually appropriated on man's side (*hagiazomenous*)."[2]

It may be objected that we are overlooking the significance of Hebrews 10:1, 2: "For the law having a shadow of good things to come, and not the very image of the things, can never with those sacrifices which they offered year by year continually make the comers thereunto perfect. For then would they not have ceased to be offered? because the worshippers once purged should have had no more conscience of sins." Some may wish to contend that, by contrast with the ineffectual Levitical sacrifices, it must be assumed that Christ's sacrifice does actually bestow an irrevocable once-for-all cleansing from all sins—past, present, and future—upon the man who once believes, whereby for him there shall be "no more conscience of sins." This, indeed, many good men believe and teach. But the writer of the Epistle to the Hebrews is not among them.

---

[2]B. F. Westcott, *The Epistle to the Hebrews*, p. 345.

The writer's point is not that, had one of the Levitical sacrifices somehow proved to be actually efficacious, the worshippers immediately would have experienced an irrevocable once-for-all cleansing from all sins—past, present, and future. His point is that, had a single sacrifice ever proved efficacious, for *once*[3] the worshippers would have been cleansed from sin—actually, rather than merely ceremonially. Henceforth, instead of offering additional sacrifices, they would have appealed to the validity of the one sacrifice which had proved efficacious. The evidence of the efficacy of that particular sacrifice would have been the complete appeasement of the worshippers' "conscience of sins"—a circumstance which neither people nor high priest (9:9) ever experienced through the offering of the Levitical sacrifices, because of their lack of any intrinsic value (10:4). Far from removing their consciousness of sins and guilt, the sacrifices served rather to remind them of their sins (10:3). Furthermore, the continual repetition testified to their lack of any true efficacy.

The writer's point in Hebrews 10:1-4 is only that the Levitical sacrifices, being ineffectual and merely ceremonial, could accomplish no more than to anticipate a superior sacrifice which, by contrast, could actually expiate the sins of the people and remain perpetually efficacious. The "once-for-all" sacrifice of Jesus is the substance of which the Levitical sacrifices were but shadows.

2. That Hebrews 10:10-14 does not teach that men enter irrevocably into a state of sanctification before God through a single once-for-all experience of grace in Christ is indicated by

---

[3]Numerous translators render *hapax* as "once for all" in Heb. 10:2. But they are in error, in the light of context. The word itself may mean either *once for all*, or *once, one time*. It is rendered simply as *once* in Heb. 9:7, II Cor. 11:25, Phil. 4:16, I Thess. 2:18, and Jude 5, in none of which instances could it retain any sensible meaning if rendered as *once for all*. Thus, *hapax* may sometimes be rendered *once for all*, and at other times must be rendered simply as *once*. Context must determine. The total message of Hebrews indicates that it must be rendered as *once* in 10:2.

two important considerations. First, it is implied through the use of the perfect participle *hēgiasmenoi* in v. 10 and the present passive participle *hagiazomenous* in v. 14, both of which possess a linear aspect and are concerned with the present moment. Their significance is fully apparent in Verkuyl's excellent rendering (italics mine): "By which divine will we are *being made holy* by means of the offering up once for all of the body of Jesus Christ. . . . For with a single offering He has forever perfected those who *are being made holy.*" Thus, while the efficacy of Christ's sacrifice stands eternally irrevocable, the benefit of His once-for-all sacrifice is progressively imparted to men as they draw near to God through Him and are thereby made holy before God, in Christ.

Consider Montgomery's translation of Hebrews 7:24, 25 (which properly reckons with the verb tenses): "But [Christ], because of his abiding forever, holds his priesthood inviolable. Hence he is able to continue saving to the uttermost those who are ever drawing near to God through him, seeing that he is ever living to intercede for them." Maclaren writes:

In [Christ's] great offering, considered as including [His] life as well as His death . . . you have folded up in indissoluble unity the pattern, the motive, and the power for all righteousness of character; and he reaches the end for which God created him who, laying his hand on the head of that offering, not only transfers his sins to it, but receives its righteousness into him. By one offering that dealt with guilt and wiped it all out, and that deals with the tyranny of evil and emancipates us from it, and that communicates to us a new life formed in righteousness after the image of Him who created us, we are delivered from the burden of our sins and perfected, in so far as we lay hold of the power that is meant to cleanse us.[4]

A second important evidence that Hebrews 10:10-14 does not teach that men enter irrevocably into a state of grace through a single once-for-all act is the significance of immediate

---

[4]Alexander Maclaren, *Expositions of Holy Scripture: Hebrews and the Epistle of James*, p. 89.

context. Having declared the fact of the perpetual efficacy of Christ's once-for-all sacrifice, the writer immediately proceeds to exhort his readers "therefore" diligently to persevere: "Therefore, brethren, having boldness to enter into the holiest by the blood of Jesus . . . [our] high priest over the house of God, let us keep on drawing near[5] with a true heart in full assurance of faith. . . . Let us keep on holding fast[5] the confession of hope without wavering, for he is faithful who promised. And let us keep on considering[5] one another to incite to love and good works, not forsaking the assembling of ourselves together, as the manner of some is, but encouraging one another; and so much the more as ye see the day [of His coming, v. 37] approaching. For if we sin wilfully. . . ." The writer immediately launches one of the sternest of his numerous warnings against the peril of apostatizing—warnings which are addressed to "holy brethren, partakers of the heavenly calling," for whom Jesus Christ is "the Apostle and High Priest of our confession" (3:1).

In view of the exhortations and warnings which immediately follow, it is obvious that the writer does not teach in Hebrews 10:10-14 that a single once-for-all act of faith ushers one into an irrevocable state of grace. Christ's offering of Himself constitutes a once-for-all sacrifice for sin which remains eternally efficacious; but our participation in the benefit of His one sacrifice is progressive and wholly governed by our continuing in faith and submission to Him.

Consider Hebrews 13:12-17: "Wherefore Jesus also, that he might sanctify the people with his own blood, suffered [once] outside the gate. Therefore, let us keep on going forth[5] unto him outside the camp, bearing his reproach. For here we have no enduring city, but we seek one to come. By him, therefore, let us keep on offering[5] the sacrifice of praise to God continually. . . . Keep on obeying[6] your leaders and submitting:[6] for

---

[5]Greek present subjunctive, durative.
[6]Greek present imperative, durative.

they watch vigilantly for your souls as they that shall give account."[7]

James Denney declares that the writer to the Hebrews, like Paul and other New Testament writers, has

. . . the conception of a *finished work* of Christ, a work finished in His death, something done in regard to sin once for all, whether any given soul responds to it or not.

. . . .

[He], like other New Testament writers, makes the death of Christ the very thing by which sin is annulled as a power barring man's approach to God. His idea is not that Christ by His death, or in virtue of it, acts immediately upon the sinful soul, turning it into a righteous one, and in that sense annulling sin; it is rather that sin is annulled and, in its character as that which shuts man out from God's presence and makes worship impossible, ceases to be, through the once for all accomplished sacrifice of Christ.

. . . .

[In taking upon Himself in His death the sins of the world, Jesus] does perfectly, and therefore finally and once for all, something through which sinful men can enter into fellowship with God. He lays the basis of the new covenant; He does what sinners can look to as a finished work; He makes an objective atonement for sin—exactly what St. Paul describes as *katallagē* or reconciliation. There is peace now between God and man; we can draw near to the Holy One.

The Epistle to the Hebrews does not make as clear to us as the Pauline epistles how it is that Christ's death becomes effective for men. The author was not an evangelist so much as a pastor, and it is not the initiation of Christianity, but its conservation, with which he deals throughout. But the answer to the question is involved in the conception of Christ as Priest. The priest is a person who acts as the representative of a people: he does something which it properly falls to them to do, but which they cannot do for themselves; by God's grace he does it, and on the strength of it they draw near to God. The epistle lays great stress on the fact that Christ has identified Himself with man; in substance, therefore, it may be

---

[7]It may be questioned whether pastors who are persuaded that the security of Christians is unconditional can properly watch for the souls of their flock. We would question, not their sincerity, but an essential aspect of their pastoral orientation. Cf. Acts 14:22; 11:23, Rom. 11:20-22, I Cor. 15:1, 2, II Cor. 1:24, Col. 1:23, I Tim. 4:16, Gal. 5:21; 6:7-9, Jas. 1:12-16; 5:19, 20, Heb. 3:12-14, I John 2:24, 25, Jude 20, 21, II Pet. 1:8-12. Cf. John 21:15-17 ("feed my sheep") with Jas. 1:21 and John 6:63c and 8:51.

said, His work must be appropriated by men's identifying themselves with Him.

. . . .

He is the object of the Christian confession, both as Apostle and High Priest (iii. 1); it is to those who obey Him that He is the author of eternal salvation (v. 9); and He is the centre to which the eyes and hearts of Christians are steadily directed. [In His death, He has achieved] something to which we can look as a finished work, and in which we can find the basis of a sure confidence toward God.[8]

Having a High Priest over the house of God whose own blood secures our access into the Holy of Holies, let us continue to draw near with true hearts in full assurance of faith, holding fast the confession of hope without wavering. He was once offered to bear our sins; and unto all who look for Him shall He appear again, apart from sin, unto the consummation of salvation.

> O Thou eternal Victim, slain
> A sacrifice for guilty man,
> By the eternal Spirit made
> An offering in the sinner's stead;
> Our everlasting Priest art thou,
> Pleading thy death for sinners now.
>
> Thy offering still continues new;
> Thy vesture keeps its crimson hue;
> Thou art the ever-slaughtered Lamb,
> Thy priesthood still remains the same;
> Thy years, O Lord, can never fail;
> Thy goodness is unchangeable.
>
> O that my faith may never move,
> But stand unshaken as thy love!
> Sure evidence of things unseen,
> Passing the years that intervene,
> Now let it view upon the tree
> My Lord, who bleeds and dies for me.
>
> CHARLES WESLEY

"Looking unto Jesus. . . ."

---

[8]James Denney, *The Death of Christ*, pp. 225-236.

"An Advocate with the Father"

My little children, these things write I unto you, that ye sin not. And if any man sin, we have an advocate with the Father, Jesus Christ the righteous: and he is the propitiation for our sins: and not for our's only, but also for the sins of the whole world.

I JOHN 2:1, 2

Seeing then that we have a great high priest that is passed into the heavens, Jesus the Son of God, let us hold fast our profession. For we have not an high priest which cannot be touched with the feeling of our infirmities, but was in all points tempted like as we are, yet without sin. Let us therefore come boldly unto the throne of grace, that we may obtain mercy, and find grace to help in time of need.

HEBREWS 4:14-16

CHAPTER X

AN ADVOCATE WITH THE FATHER

"AND DEAR GOD, please bless Tippy, and help him not to make any sins." Thus did our three-year-old son, in his evening prayer, entreat for his puppy. It was a good prayer. "My dear children," wrote the aged John, "these things write I unto you that you sin not."

But Christians do sin. And the fact of our sin confronts us with two perils. First, we may deny that we sin. To do so is to practice self-deception (I John 1:8) and to presume to be without need of a saviour from sin. It is to deny our need for an advocate with the Father. It is to fail to confess our sins and to find forgiveness, cleansing, and continued fellowship with the God who is light, in whom is no darkness at all. The doctrine of eradication and sinless perfection is not only contrary to the plain statement of the Holy Scriptures; it is a deadly snare and delusion which robs its adherents of any sense of need for an advocate with the Father and constitutes a denial of Christ's intercession in their behalf. It is a short, direct route out of grace. "The truth" and "his word" are not to be found in any who deny the fact of their sin (I John 1:8, 10). He who is the Word Incarnate, and who said, "I am the truth" (John 14:6), cannot dwell in any who deny the fact of their sin and, therefore, their need for Him as Intercessor and Advocate.

A second peril inherent in the fact that we do sin is the peril of consenting to sin. Sin, we may tell ourselves, is an inevitable fact of human life and conduct, even for Christians. Therefore, it may be viewed as normal. Why be distressed about it? There is no occasion for concern. Many "Christians," in this day of

131

"easy believism," have adopted such a casual attitude toward sin. But despite the rationalizations of many, there is occasion for real concern for sin. Sin is at war against the soul (I Pet. 2:11), an all-out war of the deadliest sort.

Many sincere men believe that, while sin in the life of the Christian will mar his fellowship with Christ, it cannot affect his salvation in any way. They believe that the question of salvation is eternally and irrevocably determined in a single once-for-all act of faith in Christ. In the moment of conversion, as they believe, all the individual's sins—past, present, and future—are forever remitted. Dr. Donald Grey Barnhouse, for example, writes:

. . . do not think for a moment that all that we receive at the moment of our new birth is the remission of sins that have been committed up to the moment of salvation.

. . . .

. . . the moment a person is born again, forgiveness has been provided for all the sins he ever has committed and for all the sins that he ever will commit in the course of his life.[1]

But the truth of the matter is that long before "the moment a person is born again" complete forgiveness was provided—not only for *his* sins, "but for the sins of the whole world" (I John 2:2). There is nothing about a man's experience of conversion which adds one iota to the provisions of the Atonement. The Atonement was wrought "while we were yet sinners." Full provision for complete remission has been made—once for all and for ever! No man's conversion adds anything to the scope or the adequacy of Christ's atonement. A man's conversion does not somehow heap a few more sins upon Christ on His cross and lengthen the cords of grace, that they may extend a bit farther than before. Nothing in a man's conversion alters or enlarges the provisions of Calvary. A man's faith in Christ simply appropriates for him, personally, all the benefit which Christ secured, potentially, for *all* men through the offering of

---

[1]Donald Grey Barnhouse, *Life by the Son,* pp. 65, 67.

Himself as the eternal propitiation "for the sins of the whole world."

Paul and the Apostles went everywhere declaring—not that God would somehow *do* something about the sins of men, if only they would believe; but that God already *has done* something (all that needs to be done!) for sinful men, who need only to enter by faith into the provision of what God has accomplished for all time and eternity through the once-for-all offering of Christ. "God in Christ was reconciling *the world* unto himself . . . [therefore] be *ye* reconciled to God!" (II Cor. 5:19, 20).

There is a vast difference between God's *provision* in the Atonement and individual men's *appropriation* of what God has provided. Failure to distinguish between provision and appropriation, between what is objective and what is subjective, has caused good men to err in their appraisal of the Atonement. Such error has led to the further error of misconstruing the advocacy of Christ. For example, Dr. Chafer writes:

Through the present priestly advocacy of Christ in Heaven there is absolute safety and security for the Father's child even while he is sinning. An advocate is one who espouses and pleads the cause of another in the open courts. As Advocate, Christ is now appearing in Heaven for His own (Heb. 9:24) when they sin (I John 2:1).[2]

It would be completely contrary to fact to assume that Dr. Chafer viewed sin lightly. No one acquainted with his works and his own godly life would so assume. But while his last statement is true, we must take strong exception to his first statement in the form in which it stands. The New Testament writers do not contend that "there is absolute safety and security for the Father's child even while he is sinning." Quite to the contrary, they warn against the peril of presuming to continue in grace while consenting to deliberate sinning:

This I say then, Walk in the Spirit, and ye shall not fulfil the lust of the flesh. For the flesh lusteth against the Spirit, and the Spirit against the

---

[2]Lewis Sperry Chafer, *Major Bible Themes*, p. 54.

flesh. . . . I warn you again, as I have also warned you in time past, that they who practice such things [the works of the flesh] shall not inherit the kingdom of God. . . .They that are Christ's crucify[3] the flesh with the affections and lusts. . . . Be not deceived; God is not to be mocked: for whatsoever a man soweth, that shall he also reap. For he that soweth to his flesh shall of the flesh reap corruption [*phthora*, destruction, perishing]; but he that soweth to the Spirit shall of the Spirit reap life everlasting. And let us not be weary in well doing; for in due season we shall reap [life everlasting, final and irrevocable], if we faint not (Gal. 5:16, 17, 21, 24; 6:7-9).

For to be carnally minded—death; but to be spiritually minded—life and peace. . . . Brethren, we are debtors, not to the flesh, to live after the flesh. For if ye live after the flesh, ye shall die;[4] but if ye through the Spirit do mortify the deeds of the body, ye shall live. For as many are led by the Spirit of God, they are sons of God. . . . Shall we sin, because we are not under the law, but under grace? God forbid. Know ye not that to whom ye yield yourselves servants to obey, his servants ye are to whom ye obey; whether of sin unto death, or of obedience unto righteousness? . . . Let not sin therefore reign in your mortal body, that ye should obey it in the lusts thereof. . . . For the wages of sin is death; but the gift of God is eternal life through Jesus Christ our Lord. (Rom. 8:6, 12-14; 6:15, 16, 12, 23).

Blessed is the man that endureth temptation: for when he is tried, he shall receive the crown of life, which the Lord hath promised to them that love him. . . . But every man is tempted, when he is drawn away of his own lust, and enticed. Then when lust hath conceived, it bringeth forth sin: and sin, when it is finished [matured, full grown], bringeth forth death. Do not err, my beloved brethren (Jas. 1:12, 14-16).

---

[3]*Estaurōsan*, a gnomic aorist expressing a general truth, and timeless. Cf. Luke 7:35, *edikaiōthē*, *is justified;* John 15:6, *eblēthē*, *is cast; exēranthē*, *is withered;* John 15:8, *edoxasthē*, *is glorified.* As Robertson affirms, "The Greek aorist is translatable into almost every English tense except the imperfect" (*Grammar,* p. 848). Context is obviously a vital factor in determining the precise meaning of any aorist. Translators have rendered the aorists in Luke 7:35, John 15:6, 8, and elsewhere, by English presents because of the requirements of context. Certainly context requires that *estaurōsan* in Gal. 5:24 be considered gnomic and be rendered by the English present tense.

[4]"Death" in Rom. 8:13; 6:13; 6:16, 21, 23, Gal. 6:8, James 1:15; 5:20, and I John 5:16 is not to be construed as mere physical death. Physical death is not a contingency, but a certainty—for the godliest saint as well as for all others, in the present era. Nor is mere *physical* death the true antithesis of everlasting life (as in Gal. 6:8, Rom. 6:21, 22, etc.).

Whoever remains in Him does not practice sin: whoever practices sin has not continued seeing Him, nor continued knowing Him.[5] Little children, let no man deceive you; he who practices righteousness is righteous, even as He is righteous. He who practices sin is of the devil. Whoever continues begotten of God does not practice sin (I John 3:6-9).

Peter, Jude, and the writer to the Hebrews sound similar warnings against the peril of presuming to continue in grace while deliberately pursuing habitual sin.[6] Throughout our earthly sojourn, we are continually confronted with the necessity of choosing whether we shall have a Saviour who saves us from (not *in* or *with*) our sins, or unrestrained sin without a Saviour. We cannot have both. If Jesus is to save us, we must consent to be saved "from our sins" (Matt. 1:21).

It would be an error, of course, to suppose that the moment a Christian sins he is immediately severed from the Saviour and deprived of His saving grace. To assume that grace is immediately withdrawn from the Christian who sins is to deny the essence and meaning of grace. If grace is not for sinners, it is not *grace*. If mercy is not for the undeserving, it is not *mercy*. Thank God, grace is for *sinners*, not the sinless—of whom there is none save Jesus, our Holy Saviour. On-again, off-again "Christians" who receive so much, and lose it so soon, are a reproach to Christ and His saving grace.

Proof of the fact that men are not immediately deprived of grace by a single act of sin is seen in the fact that God reproves and chastens His children for their sin. Chastening is an evidence of sonship, not disinheritance. (The question of chastening will be considered in the following chapter.) James warns that "lust, when it conceives, brings forth sin; and sin, when it is fully matured, brings forth death" (1:15). James presents spiritual death as the consequence, not of a single act of sin, but of an extended pattern of sinning. Similarly, Paul's warnings against "sowing to the flesh" (Gal. 6:8) and "living after

---

[5]For a discussion of the perfect indicatives *heōraken and egnōken,* see p. 98.
[6]Cf. I Peter 1:13-17; 2:11; 4:1-7, II Peter 1:1-12; 3:14-18, Jude 17-21, Hebrews 3:13; 10:26 ff.

the flesh" (Rom. 8:13) are warnings against, not single acts of sin, but continued deliberate patterns of behavior. We shall be wise to observe, however, that the best safeguard against the development of a habitual pattern of deliberate sinning is a firm repudiation of every sin of which we become conscious, in humble contrition and confession before our High Priest who "is able to continue saving to the uttermost those who are ever drawing near to God through him, seeing that he is ever living to intercede for them" (Heb. 7:25 Montgomery).

"If any man sin, we have an advocate with the Father, Jesus Christ the righteous." What a precious promise! But John also warns, "Whoever remains in Him does not practice sin: whoever practices sin has not continued seeing Him, nor continued knowing Him." The renderings of the Authorized Version make John appear to contradict himself: Whoever sins has an advocate—Jesus Christ; but whoever sins is a stranger to Christ and is of the devil (2:1 and 3:6, 8). There is no contradiction, of course. The Authorized Version fails to depict the difference between the punctiliar aorist subjunctive in 2:1 and the linear aspects of the verbs in chapter 3. It is the difference between sin as an isolated act, and habitual sinning as a deliberate pattern of behavior. For the man who follows such a pattern, Jesus cannot intercede before the Father's throne of judgment. He cannot serve as Advocate for men while they deliberately consent to sin. Grace is for sinners; but not for wilful sinners who deliberately pursue sin.

"My dear children, these things write I unto you, that you sin not. But if any man sin. . . ." Despite our best intentions and holiest aspirations, we do sin. But thank God, "we have an advocate with the Father, Jesus Christ the righteous; and he is the propitiation for our sins." There is a remedy for the sins of the saints: "If we keep on confessing[7] our sins, he is faithful and righteous to forgive us our sins, and to cleanse us from all unrighteousness" (I John 1:9).

---

[7]*Homologōmen*, present subjunctive, durative.

An essential aspect of confession before our High Priest is the sincere intention of forsaking the sins we confess. We cannot ask forgiveness for sins we have no intention of forsaking. "God is light, and in Him is no darkness at all. If we claim that we have fellowship with Him, and walk in darkness, we lie and do not practice the truth. But if we walk in the light, as He is in the light, we [God and the believer—v. 6] have fellowship one with another, and the blood of Jesus Christ his Son cleanseth us from all sin" (I John 1:5-7). There is no promise of forgiveness and cleansing from sin except for men who sincerely endeavor (though, at best, imperfectly) to "walk in the light, as He is in the light." "Can two walk together, except they be agreed?" (Amos 3:3). We cannot walk with Him whose habitation is light unless we are willing to share His enmity against sin.

If we consent to His conditions, if we come before Him with contrite heart, if we forsake the sins which nailed Jesus to His cross, we may know that we have an Advocate with the Father who is, Himself, the propitiation for all our sins. We may confess our sins in full assurance that "He is faithful and righteous to forgive us our sins, and to cleanse us from all unrighteousness." He has given His word. Let us trust Him.

> What a Friend we have in Jesus,
>   All our sins and griefs to bear!
> What a privilege to carry
>   Everything to Him in prayer!
>
> Can we find a friend so faithful
>   Who will all our sorrows share?
> Jesus knows our every weakness;
>   Take it to the Lord in prayer.
>
> We are weak, and heavy-laden,
>   Bowed beneath the weight of care—
> Precious Saviour, still our Refuge,
>   Bear us up in holy prayer!
>
>   JOSEPH SCRIVEN (adapted)

"We have an Advocate. . . ."

"The Chastening of the Lord"

For if we would judge ourselves, we should not be judged. But when we are judged, we are chastened of the Lord, that we should not be condemned with the world.

I Corinthians 11:31, 32

My son, despise not thou the chastening of the Lord, nor faint when thou art rebuked of him: for whom the Lord loveth he chasteneth, and scourgeth every son whom he receiveth. If ye endure chastening, God dealeth with you as with sons; for what son is he whom the father chasteneth not? But if ye be without chastisement, whereof all are partakers, then are ye bastards, and not sons.

Furthermore, we have had fathers of our flesh which corrected us, and we gave them reverence: shall we not much rather be in subjection unto the Father of spirits, and live? For they verily for a few days chastened us after their own pleasure; but he for our profit, that we might be partakers of his holiness.

Hebrews 12:5-10

CHAPTER XI

THE CHASTENING OF THE LORD

CHRISTIANS SIN. There is no need to labor the point. "If we say that we have no sin, we deceive ourselves, and the truth is not in us;" we insinuate that God is a liar, "and his word is not in us" (I John 1:8, 10). Only men practicing self-deception and under deadly delusion refuse to confess with James, "In many things we all offend" (James 3:2).

But such is the love of the Father, He loves all His stumbling, erring children. With tender compassion beyond that of earthly fathers, He watches patiently to see whether His erring children judge themselves for their sins. "For if we would judge ourselves, we should not be judged" of the Lord. Parental discipline is not required for the child who acknowledges and abandons the error of his way.

But if we neglect to judge ourselves, "we are judged [and] chastened of the Lord, lest [*hina mē,* cf. Thayer] we should be condemned with the world." God judges and chastens His children, not because He delights to afflict them, but because He knows the ultimate tragedy awaiting them if they be not corrected. As a faithful, compassionate Father, He chastens His erring children, lest they share the final condemnation of the impenitent, rebellious world.

Three variations of the word *krinō* appear in I Corinthians 11:31, 32: *diakrinō, krinō,* and *katakrinō.* Paul's use of the three different forms requires that distinctions be made. While the Authorized Version distinguishes between *krinō* ("judge") and *katakrinō* ("condemn"), no distinction is made between *di-*

141

akrinō and *krinō*. An "expanded translation" is required to convey the full meaning of Paul's words: "For if we took discriminating inventory of ourselves for the purpose of correction, we should not be judged (by the Lord) with a view to corrective discipline. But when we are so judged, we are disciplined by the Lord for correction, lest we should be finally condemned along with the world."

God's purpose in the chastening of His sons is further defined in Hebrews 12. We are told that He chastens us "for our profit, that we may be partakers of his holiness" (v. 10) and that we may continue to "follow . . . holiness, without which no man shall see the Lord" (v. 14). His purpose is that His chastening shall "yield the peaceable fruit of righteousness unto them who are exercised thereby" (v. 11).

We may well inquire, however, whether His purpose is necessarily realized in every instance. Many, of course, assume that it cannot be otherwise; for the purpose of God can never fail. We agree that the purpose of God cannot fail—within the limitations which He Himself has imposed upon His own will.

God created man a spiritual intelligence with the capacity for worship, which is his highest function. Worship, by its very nature, can be only voluntary. It can be encouraged, but never coerced. In His sovereign act of creating man a rational spiritual intelligence with the capacity for worship (and with worship's inevitable corollary—the power and responsibility of moral and spiritual initiative and decision), God has voluntarily imposed limitations upon His own actions and, to an extent, circumscribed the latitude of His own freedom of will. Thus, though God "now commands all men everywhere to repent" (Acts 17:30), men are yet free to remain impenitent and to accept the consequence of eternal damnation, despite the fact that God "wills to have all men to be saved" (I Tim. 2:4) and "is longsuffering to usward, not willing that any should perish, but that all might come to repentance" (II Pet. 3:9).

Many have ignored the fact that, when God chastens His children, there are two possible consequences, rather than one.

This is clearly indicated in Hebrews 12:5, 9: "My son, despise not the chastening of the Lord, nor faint when thou art rebuked of him. . . . Furthermore we have had fathers of our flesh who corrected us, and we gave them reverence: shall we not much rather be in subjection unto the Father of spirits, and live?" Clearly, there are two alternatives. The Christian may submit to the Father's chastening and be exercised thereby and profit and continue to partake of His holiness and live; or he may despise His chastening and faint and give up in utter rebellion against His correction—and die! The writer reinforces his warning with the admonition: "See that ye refuse not him that speaketh. For if they escaped not who refused him that spake on earth, much more shall not we escape, if we turn away from him that speaketh from heaven" (v. 25).

Consider his words, "we had fathers of our flesh who corrected us, and we gave them reverence: shall we not much rather be in subjection unto the Father of spirits, and live?" (v. 9). The Old Testament antecedent gives cause for solemn reflection:

If a man have a stubborn and rebellious son who will not obey the voice of his father or the voice of his mother, and who, when they have chastened him, will not hearken unto them, then shall his father and his mother lay hold on him and bring him out unto the elders of his city and unto the gate of his place; and they shall say unto the elders of his city, This our son is stubborn and rebellious, he will not obey our voice; he is a glutton and a drunkard. And all the men of his city shall stone him with stones, that he die: so shalt thou put evil away from among you; and all Israel shall hear, and fear (Deut. 21:18-21).

The stern Old Testament provision for the elimination of disobedient sons who refuse correction is applied by the writer to the Hebrews, not to the prospect of mere physical death, but to the prospect of spiritual death. He is concerned with the question of our relationship, not with the fathers of our flesh, but with "the Father of spirits." We cannot refuse God's correction and continue to *live* as His spiritual sons. Only "as many as are led by the Spirit of God are sons of God" (Rom. 8:14).

The issue involved in the question of our response to the Father's chastening is nothing less than the privilege of continuing to partake of His holiness and to share His life as His spiritual sons.

Delitzsch comments: "To submit ourselves to the Father of spirits is an essential condition of our life—*hupotagēsometha kai zēsomen: zēin* here as at x:38, expresses true, abiding (not merely transient or apparent) life, *i.e.*, likeness to God and communion with Him."[1]

We have considered in the preceding chapter the fact that Jas. 1:15, Rom. 8:12-14, Gal. 6:7-9, and kindred passages declare that spiritual death is the inevitable consequence of habitual sinning as a deliberate pattern of behavior. In Eph. 5:1 ff., Paul declares that our spiritual sonship makes necessary demands upon us in the matter of our conduct—demands which are optional only as sonship, itself, remains optional:

So you must keep on following God's example, as dearly loved children of His, and practice living in love, just as Christ loved you too and gave Himself for you as a fragrant offering and sacrifice to God. But sexual vice and any form of immorality or sensual greed must not so much as be mentioned among you, as that is the only course becoming in God's people; there must be no indecency, silly talk or suggestive jesting, for they are unbecoming. There should be thanksgiving instead. For you may be absolutely sure that no one who is sexually impure, immoral, or greedy for gain (for that is idolatry) can have a part in the kingdom of Christ and God. Stop letting anyone deceive you with groundless arguments about these things, for it is because of these very sins that God's anger comes down upon the disobedient [sons. Be not therefore co-sharers] with them (Eph. 5:1-7 Williams).[2]

Certainly Paul's warning against being co-sharers with those who are disqualified from any part in the kingdom of Christ and of God is a warning against sharing in their immoral and

---

[1]Franz Delitzsch, *Commentary on the Epistle to the Hebrews*, Vol. II, p. 320.

[2]Brackets indicate departure from Williams' translation. His rendering of v. 7 ("So you must stop having anything to do with them") arbitrarily limits the meaning of Paul's words.

worldly pattern of living, which stems from impenitence toward God. But it is equally a warning against ultimately sharing
the wrath of God which must be the certain consequence of
such habitual worldliness, except they repent. "Stop letting anyone deceive you with groundless arguments about these things,"
warns Paul. Please observe that the arguments were not about
the possible fate of *outsiders*. There is no reason to assume that
the Ephesians were debating the question of whether unbelievers who made no profession of faith in Christ and who
frankly lived for carnal gratification might nevertheless, in their
present state, somehow have an inheritance in the kingdom of
Christ and escape the wrath of God. Such a question is not de-
batable. Paul's warning to the Ephesians, then, is against allowing themselves to be led astray by the specious arguments of
antinomians who "turned the grace of God into lasciviousness"
(Jude 4) and who, with "great swelling words of vanity,"
sought to "allure through the lusts of the flesh" (II Pet. 2:18)
those who imagined that they could set their affections on
the lusts of the world, the flesh, and the devil, and somehow
still retain an inheritance in the kingdom of Christ and escape
the wrath of God against the sons of disobedience.

Similarly, Paul's warning to the Galatians (5:19-21) is not
concerning the possible fate of outsiders, but of *themselves*,
should they walk after the flesh rather than after the Spirit.
The warning of Gal. 6:7-9 is directed, not to outsiders who
make no profession of faith in Christ, but to *believers* whom
Paul assumes to be already engaged in sowing to the Spirit, and
who need only to continue their present course (v. 9).

If the Ephesians prefer to have "fellowship with the unfruitful works of darkness," rather than to reprove them (v. 11),
they ultimately must find themselves to be co-sharers of the
wrath of God, together with those with whom they were co-
sharers of carnal, indulgent living. The inevitable consequence
of sowing to the flesh, except they repent, is perishing *(phthora)*
and final condemnation with the world. This is the whole point
of Paul's warning to the Corinthians that, "when we are judged,

we are chastened of the Lord, lest we should be finally condemned with the world" (I Cor. 11:32).

To save His erring children from ultimate destruction, God chastens them to awaken them to their peril, that they may confess the error of their way and continue to partake of His holiness and to live as His spiritual sons. But just as the faithfulness of God in not permitting His children to be tempted above what they are able to bear (I Cor. 10:13) does not, of itself, ensure that they necessarily will avail themselves of the way of escape and thus endure the temptation, so the Lord's chastening does not, of itself, ensure that men will profit thereby. Commenting on I Corinthians 11:31, 32, Godet writes:

The believer ought constantly *to judge himself;* such is the normal state. If he fails in this task, God reminds him of it by judging him by some chastisement which He sends on him, *he is judged;* and if he does not profit by this means, nothing remains for him but to suffer in common with the world the final judgment from which God sought to preserve him, *to be condemned.*[3]

Similarly, Westcott comments on Hebrews 12:7: "The divine purpose is unquestionable, but at the same time the efficacy of the discipline depends on the spirit with which it is received. Patient endurance alone converts suffering into a beneficent lesson."[4]

But Calvin, of course, contends that God's chastening must inevitably eventuate in the submission of the erring and can never end in ultimate rebellion and condemnation. As evidence, he appeals to the provisions of the Davidic Covenant, as many other advocates of the doctrine of unconditional security have done:

For he who cannot deceive has declared that the covenant made with us in our true Solomon stands fast and will never be broken, "If his children forsake my law, and walk not in my judgments; if they break my statutes and keep not my commandments; then will I visit their trans-

---

[3]F. L. Godet, *Commentary on the First Epistle to the Corinthians,* Vol. II, p. 169, italics his.

[4]B. F. Westcott, *The Epistle to the Hebrews,* p. 400.

gression with the rod, and their iniquity with stripes. Nevertheless, my loving-kindness will I not utterly take from him, nor suffer my faithfulness to fail." (Ps. lxxxix. 31-34).[5]

Calvin errs, first, in his appraisal of God's covenant with David; for he assumes that it involved all his descendants equally with David himself. But this is not so. God's covenant was with *David*, not his descendants; and, with the exception of one particular Person (the promised Seed), David's descendants were involved only incidentally. It cannot be said that the Davidic Covenant has the same import for the line of Solomon (which came to such a dismal terminus in Zedekiah) as for David himself and for Jesus, the promised Seed (the Son of David through Nathan, rather than Solomon—"a *righteous* Branch unto David . . . a greater than Solomon"). God's covenant with David finds its fulfillment, not in "his children" in general, but in the promised Seed (Jesus), "the Holy One of Israel, our king" (Ps. 89:18). God promised, "I will make *him* my firstborn, higher than the kings of the earth. My mercy will I keep for *him* for evermore, and my covenant shall stand fast with *him*" (vv. 27, 28).

Again, Calvin errs in equating the Davidic Covenant with the question of the personal salvation of all the Davidic kings, for which there is no warrant whatever. He obviously misconstrues the promise of verse 33, "My lovingkindness will I not utterly take from him [i.e., from David, not from *them*— "his children," as Calvin misconstrues it], nor suffer my faithfulness to fail" (in allowing His covenant with David to fail to be fulfilled in his promised Seed, Christ). Calvin wrongly applies the promise to the question of the personal salvation of all of David's descendants and, by inference, to all believers in the present era. The surety of the Davidic Covenant has no bearing whatever upon this important matter. The covenant itself is sure: "My covenant will I not break, nor alter the thing that is gone out of my lips. Once have I sworn by my holiness

---

[5]Calvin, *Institutes*, 3:4:32.

that I will not lie unto David. His seed shall endure for ever, and his throne as the sun before me" (vv. 33-36). But Calvin errs in failing to differentiate between the certainty of the covenant with David, to be fulfilled in Christ, and God's absolute freedom to deal with David's children who "forsake my law, walk not in my judgments, break my statutes, and keep not my commandments" (vv. 30, 31). Delitzsch comments:

. . . the faithlessness of David's line in relation to the covenant shall not interfere with (annul) the faithfulness of God—a thought with which one might very naturally console one's self in the reign of Rehoboam. Because God has placed the house of David in a filial relationship to Himself, He will chastise the apostate members as a father chastises his son. . . . But even if, as history shows, this means of chastisement should be ineffectual in the case of individuals, the house of David as such will nevertheless remain ever in a state of favour with Him. . . . God asserts that He will not disappoint David in reference to this one thing, viz. the perpetuity of his throne.[6]

The certainty of the fulfillment of God's covenant with David concerning the perpetuity of his throne could neither affect, nor be affected by, the outcome of God's dealings with David's "children" who forsook Him, some of whom submitted to His correction, and others of whom hardened their hearts against His chastening and suffered ultimate condemnation, according to the record of the Scriptures (cf. Jer. 22). Calvin errs, both in his interpretation and in his application of the Davidic covenant. There is nothing in God's covenant with David which determined what God must do with respect to any particular individual, other than David and his promised Seed, Jesus. The question of either the kingship or the salvation of other persons is in no way involved, the erroneous assumptions of Calvin to the contrary notwithstanding.

In like manner, the fact of God's covenant relationship with Israel did not ensure that all individuals in Israel must inevitably profit from His correction and participate in His sal-

---

[6]Franz Delitzsch, *Commentary on the Psalms*, Vol. III, p. 40 f.

vation. Jeremiah complained of Judah, "Thou hast stricken them, but they have not grieved; thou hast consumed them, but they have refused to receive correction: they have made their faces harder than a rock; they have refused to return. . . . Shall I not visit for these things? saith the Lord: shall not my soul be avenged on such a nation as this?" (Jer. 5:3, 29). Repeatedly, God charged through His prophets that He had chastened Israel and Judah to the fullest measure—without profit. There was nothing left but judgment. Nevertheless, God promised never to "make a full end" of the children of Israel (Jer. 31:35-37; 33:25, 26). For He has always His "remnant" of faithful ones in Israel who, though often they be few, yet seek His face and walk with Him. But though a faithful remnant in Israel always was spared, all who despised His correction were destroyed. The fact that God's promises with respect to Israel ultimately will be fulfilled and His covenants with Abraham and David will be fully honored is of no benefit whatever to individuals who transgress and refuse His correction. For, "I will purge out from among you the rebels, and them that transgress against me. . . . O Lord, the hope of Israel, all that forsake thee shall be ashamed, and they that depart from me shall be written in the earth, because they have forsaken the Lord, the fountain of living waters" (Ezek. 20:38, Jer. 17:13). "Zion shall be redeemed with judgment, and her converts [returning ones][7] with righteousness. And the destruction of the transgressors [rebellious][7] and of the sinners shall be together, and they that forsake the Lord shall be consumed" (Isa. 1:27 f.). Any who in the days of the prophets encouraged themselves in their evil and rebellion on the ground of an assumed "covenant benefit" were equally as foolish as the Jews of Jesus' day who excused their impenitence and unbelief on the ground that "we are Abraham's seed."

There was nothing in God's covenants with Abraham or David which rendered any man in Israel immune to the con-

[7]Franz Delitzsch, *Biblical Commentary on the Prophecies of Isaiah*, p. 106 f.

sequences of his own rebellion against the chastening rod of God. Nor is there anything in the New Covenant in the precious blood of Jesus which now renders men immune to the consequences of their folly if they "despise the chastening of the Lord and faint [give up] when they are rebuked of Him." No man who refuses to "be in subjection to the Father of spirits" can live as His spiritual son. "Whom the Lord loveth He chasteneth, and scourgeth every son whom he receiveth. . . . [But] he that being often reproved hardeneth his neck shall suddenly be destroyed, and that without remedy. . . . He that covereth his sins shall not prosper: but whoso confesseth and forsaketh them shall have mercy" (Heb. 12:6, Prov. 29:1; 28:13).

There are but two perils with respect to the Father's chastening. One is to be without it. The "Christian" who is without the evident chastening of God has urgent cause to "examine himself, whether he be in the faith" (II Cor. 13:5). All God's sons are partakers of the discipline of Him who "scourges every son whom He receives."

The only other possible peril with respect to the Father's chastening is to refuse His correction. Augustine warns: "I tell you, brethren, many Christians sin venially; many are scourged and so corrected for the sin, chastened, and cured; many turn away altogether, striving with a stiff neck against the discipline of the Father, even wholly refusing God as their Father, though they have the mark of Christ, and so fall into such sins that it can only be announced against them 'that they who do such things shall not inherit the kingdom of God.' "[8]

Let us beware the peril of dispising God's reproof and failing to profit thereby. Maclaren has well said:

. . . the sorrow that is meant to bring us nearer to Him may be in vain. The same circumstances may produce opposite effects. [People] have been made hard, and sullen, and bitter, and paralysed for good work, because they have some heavy burden or some wound that life can never heal, to be carried or to ache. Ah, brethren! we are often like shipwrecked

---

[8]Augustine, *The Nicene and Post-Nicene Fathers of the Christian Church* (Philip Schaff, edit.), Vol. VIII, p. 436.

crews, of whom some are driven by the danger to their knees, and some are driven to the spirit-casks. Take care that you do not waste your sorrows; that you do not let the precious gifts of disappointment, pain, loss, loneliness, ill-health, or similar afflictions that come into your daily life, mar you instead of mending you. See that they send you nearer to God, and not that they drive you farther from Him. See that they make you more anxious to have the durable riches and righteousness which no man can take from you, than to grasp at what may yet remain of fleeting earthly joys.

So, brethren, let us try to school ourselves into the habitual and operative conviction that life is discipline. Let us yield ourselves to the loving will of the unerring Father, the perfect love. Let us beware of getting no good from what is charged to the brim with good. And let us see to it that out of the many fleeting circumstances of life we gather and keep the eternal fruit of being partakers of His holiness. May it never have to be said of any of us that we wasted the mercies which were judgments too, and found no good in the things that our tortured hearts felt to be also evils, lest God should have to wail over any of us, 'In vain have I smitten your children; they have received no correction!'⁹

⁹Alexander Maclaren, *Expositions of Holy Scripture: Hebrews and James*, p. 226 f.

"If We Deny Him"

The disciple is not above his master, nor the servant above his lord. It is enough for the disciple that he be as his master, and the servant as his lord. If they have called the master of the house Beelzebub, how much more shall they call them of his household? Fear them not therefore: for there is nothing covered that shall not be revealed; and hid, that shall not be known.

* * *

Fear not them which kill the body, but are not able to kill the soul: but rather fear him which is able to destroy both soul and body in hell. . . . Whosoever therefore shall confess me before men, him will I confess before my Father which is in heaven. But whosoever shall deny me before men, him will I also deny before my Father which is in heaven.

MATTHEW 10:24-26, 28, 31, 32

Christ [was faithful] as a son over his own house; whose house are we, if we hold fast the confidence and the rejoicing of the hope firm unto the end. . . . For we are made partakers of Christ, if we hold the beginning of our confidence steadfast unto the end.

HEBREWS 3:6, 14

If we endure, we shall also reign with him: if we deny him, he also will deny us.

II TIMOTHY 2:12

Chapter XII

IF WE DENY HIM

WHAT DOES A MAN write who, facing the prospect of imminent death, sits down to write to a dear friend? It depends, of course, on many things. But perhaps on nothing so much as whom he knows. "I know whom I have believed," wrote Paul to Timothy, "and am fully persuaded that he is able to keep that which I have committed unto him against that day" (II Tim. 1:12).

Paul was supremely confident. "The time of my departure is at hand [and] I am now ready to be offered up. I have fought the good fight, I have finished the course, I have kept the faith. Henceforth there is laid up for me the crown of righteousness which the Lord, the righteous judge, will give me at that day; and not to me only, but unto all them also who have loved his appearing" (II Tim. 4:6-8).

Writing as one who had "fought, kept, and finished" and now was ready to depart, Paul was deeply concerned that Timothy should look well to his own faith and ministry, as he himself had done. And so he exhorts, "hold fast . . . keep . . . endure . . . flee . . . follow . . . continue . . . watch. . . ." Especially must Timothy be alert because of the certainty of the increase of apostasy as the age wears on. "Bad men and impostors will go on from bad to worse, misleading others and misled themselves. But you, on your part, must continue to abide by what you have learned and been led to rely upon, because you know from whom you learned it and that from childhood you have known the sacred Scriptures which can give you wisdom that leads to salvation through the faith that leans on Christ Jesus" (II Tim. 3:13-15 Williams).

155

That the Scriptures warn men against the peril of apostasy, no one will deny. There is serious disagreement, however, about who can become guilty of apostasy. Many have assumed that apostasy is possible only for men who never actually have entered into a saving relationship with God. Apostasy, as they believe, is the act of men who come to an apprehension of the Gospel without any sincere desire in their hearts to obey it, and who deliberately refuse to accept Christ and His Gospel after having become fully persuaded of the truth. Their thesis is unacceptable, however, for the following reasons: (1) it is contrary to a specific principle clearly enunciated in the Scriptures; (2) it is contrary to the meaning of the word itself; and (3) it is contrary to the significance of the warnings in the light of context.

1. Their erroneous thesis concerning apostasy stands in direct contradiction to a specific principle affirmed numerous times in the Scriptures, perhaps nowhere more explicitly than in our Lord's declarations to His disputants: "If any man wills to do His will, he shall know of the doctrine, whether it be of God, or whether I speak of myself" (John 7:17). "Why do ye not understand my speech? it is because ye cannot hear my word. Ye are of your father the devil, and the desires of your father ye will to do. . . . If I say the truth, why do ye not believe me? He who is of God heareth God's words: ye therefore hear them not [in the sense of understanding] because ye are not of God" (John 8:43-47. Cf. 5:46, 47; 18:37d). Westcott comments on John 7:17:

If any man will do . . . *i.e., if* it be any man's will to do His will. The force of the argument lies in the moral harmony of the man's purpose with the divine law so far as this law is known or felt. If there be no sympathy there can be no understanding. Religion is a matter of life and not of thought only. The principle is universal in its application. The *Will of God* is not to be limited to the Old Testament revelation, or to the claims of Christ, but includes every manifestation of the purpose of God.[1]

---

[1] B. F. Westcott, *The Gospel According to St. John*, p. 118.

Again, he comments on John 8:47, "For this reason, because the power of hearing (v. 43) depended on inward affinity, the Jews could not hear, because they were not of God."[2]

The Scriptures uniformly affirm that men who are not motivated by a true desire to obey the will of God cannot, under such circumstance, come to a true apprehension or sincere persuasion of divine truth. They "hear" without *hearing* and "see" without *seeing* (Matt. 13:12-15). Face to face with light, they remain in darkness—for one reason alone: they do not will to obey the truth. They may have some sort of *approximate* intellectual understanding; but they can have no real apprehension or persuasion of God's truth apart from a sincere will to obey Him. They are like the clever dog which barks the correct number of times, according to the numeral held before him by his master, but which has no perception whatever of the actual significance of numerals or of their use in the simplest arithmetic. The thesis that apostasy is the act of men who have come to a sincere apprehension and persuasion of the truth of the Gospel without a corresponding desire and intention to obey the truth is diametrically opposed to a specific principle clearly affirmed in the Scriptures.

2. Again, their thesis is contrary to the meaning of the term. The English word *apostasy* is derived from the Greek noun, *apostasia*. Thayer defines *apostasia* as "a falling away, defection, apostasy; in the Bible sc. from the true religion." The word appears twice in the New Testament (Acts 21:21, II Thess. 2:3). Its meaning is well illustrated in its use in Acts 21:21, *apostasian didaskeis apo Mōuseōs*, "you are teaching apostasy (defection) from Moses." Moulton and Milligan cite the use of *apostasia* with reference to "the burning of title-deeds by Egyptian 'rebels.' "[3]

A kindred word is the synonym *apostasion*. Thayer defines *apostasion*, as used in the Bible, as "divorce, repudiation." He

---

[2]*Ibid.*, p. 137.
[3]James Hope Moulton and George Milligan, *The Vocabulary of the Greek Testament*, p. 68.

cites Matthew 19:7 and Mark 10:4, *biblion apostasiou*, "a bill of divorce." He also cites Matthew 5:31, *dotō autei apostasion*, "let him give her a bill of divorce." He cites the use of *apostasion* by Demosthenes as "*defection*, of a freedman from his patron." Moulton and Milligan cite the use of *apostasiou sugraphē* as a "bond of relinquishing (of property sold) . . . a contract of renunciation . . . the renunciation of rights of ownership."[4] They also cite the use of *apostasion* "with reference to 'a deed of divorce.' "[4]

The meaning of the verb *aphistēmi* (2nd aorist infinitive, *apostēnai*) is, of course, consonant with the meaning of the nouns. It is used transitively in Acts 5:37, *apestēsen laon opisō autou*, "drew away people after him." Intransitively, it means *to depart, go away, desert, withdraw, fall away, become faithless*, etc.

Apostasy, according to New Testament usage, constitutes defection, revolt, withdrawal, departure, and repudiation. An apostate, according to New Testament definition, is one who has severed his union with Christ by withdrawing from an actual saving relationship with Him. Apostasy is impossible for men who have not entered into a saving relationship with God. (Cf. Luke 8:12, 13. Unbelief is found in both verses; but it is mere *unbelief* in v. 12, whereas it constitutes *apostasy* in v. 13).

3. Again, their thesis is contrary to the significance of the many warnings against apostasy, as defined both by language and by context. The warnings against succumbing to the ugly peril of apostasy are directed, not to men who have not as yet obeyed the Gospel, but to men who obviously are true believers. Consider the following passages:

Take heed that no man deceive you. For many shall come in my name, saying, I am Christ; and shall deceive many. . . . And many false prophets shall arise, and deceive many. And because iniquity shall abound, the love of many shall wax cold. But he that endureth unto the end, the same shall be saved (Matt. 24:4, 5, 11-13).

---

[4]*Ibid.*, p. 69.

(Some have interpreted v. 13 to mean only that he who survives the tribulation will be saved *physically* by the appearing of the Lord. Such interpretation completely ignores the context (cf. vv. 11, 12—clearly a spiritual peril) and amounts to no more than a declaration that he who does not perish bodily will survive physically—a meaningless statement of the obvious. Observe that in His statement that false Christs and false prophets "shall deceive many," Jesus pointedly warns His disciples, "Take heed that no man deceive *you*.")

I am the true vine, and my Father is the husbandman. Every branch in me that beareth not fruit he taketh away. . . . I am the vine, ye are the branches. . . . Remain in me, and I in you. . . . If a man remain not in me, he is cast forth as a branch, and is withered; and they gather them and cast them into the fire, and they are burned (John 15:1-6).

And a great number believed and turned unto the Lord. Then tidings of these things came unto the ears of the church which was in Jerusalem: and they sent forth Barnabas, that he should go as far as Antioch. Who, when he had come and had seen the grace of God, was glad, and exhorted them all, that with purpose of heart they should cleave unto the Lord (Acts 11:21-23).

[Paul and Barnabas] returned again to Lystra, and to Iconium and Antioch, confirming the souls of the disciples and exhorting them to continue in the faith, and that we must through much tribulation enter into the kingdom of God (Acts 14:21, 22).

(Robertson comments: "Paul frankly warned these new converts in this heathen environment of the many tribulations through which they must enter the Kingdom of God (the culmination at last). . . . These saints were already converted. . . . These recent converts from heathenism were ill-informed, were persecuted, had broken family and social ties, greatly needed encouragement if they were to hold out."[5])

And you who in time past were alienated and enemies in your mind by wicked works, yet now hath he reconciled in the body of his flesh through death, to present you holy and unblameable and unreproveable in his sight: if ye continue in the faith grounded and settled, and be not moved away from the hope of the gospel (Col. 1:21-23; cf. 2:4-8, 18, 19).

Moreover, brethren, I declare unto you the gospel which I preached unto you, which also ye have received, and wherein ye stand; by which also

[5]A. T. Robertson, *Word Pictures in the New Testament*, Vol. III, p. 216.

ye are saved, if ye keep in memory [*katechō*, hold fast] what I preached unto you, unless ye have believed in vain (I Cor. 15:1, 2).

(Robertson writes, "Paul holds this peril over them in their temptation to deny the resurrection."[6])

Now the Spirit speaketh expressly that in the latter times some shall depart from the faith, giving heed to seducing spirits and doctrines of devils. . . . Take heed unto thyself, and unto the doctrine; continue in them: for in doing this thou shalt both save thyself, and them that hear thee (I Tim. 4:1, 16).

For the love of money is a root of all evils: which some reaching after have strayed away from the faith and have pierced themselves through with many sorrows. But thou, O man of God, flee these things; and pursue righteousness, godliness, faith, love, endurance, meekness. Fight the good fight of faith, "get a grip" [Robertson] on eternal life (I. Tim. 6:10-12).

Evil men and seducers shall wax worse and worse, deceiving and being deceived. But continue thou in the things which thou hast learned and hast been assured of . . . the holy scriptures, which are able to make thee wise unto salvation through faith which is in Christ Jesus (II Tim. 3:13-15).

Preach the word, be instant in season, out of season; reprove, rebuke, exhort with all longsuffering and doctrine. For the time will come when they will not endure sound doctrine; but after their own lusts shall they gather to themselves teachers, having itching ears; and they shall turn away their ears from the truth, and shall be turned unto fables. But watch thou in all things, endure afflictions, do the work of an evangelist, make full proof of thy ministry (II Tim. 4:2-5).

(Those who in time to come "will not endure sound doctrine", are not the unsaved. There is no point in making such a statement concerning the lost, for they can hardly be expected to "endure sound doctrine." The peril against which Paul warns is that some of those to whom Timothy is preaching the Word "in season and out of season" will, in time to come, no longer "endure sound doctrine," but "shall turn away their ears from the truth, and shall be turned unto fables," forsaking Timothy and his faithful message for less offensive preachers more adept at tickling their ears with sermons they can "enjoy" undisturbed in heart and conscience.)

Brethren, if any of you [not *outsiders*] do err [*planaō*, go astray, wander away] from the truth, and one convert him, let him know that he who

---

[6]Robertson, *op. cit.*, Vol. IV, p. 186.

converteth the sinner from the error of his way shall save a soul from death (James 5:19, 20).

For if these things be in you and abound, they make you that ye shall neither be barren nor unfruitful [cf. John 15:1-6] in the knowledge of our Lord Jesus Christ. But he that lacketh these things is blind, and cannot see afar off, and hath forgotten that he was purged from his old sins. Wherefore the rather, brethren, give diligence to make your calling and election sure; for if ye do these things, ye shall never fall: for so an entrance shall be ministered unto you abundantly into the everlasting kingdom of our Lord and Saviour Jesus Christ (II Pet. 1:8-11).

The untaught and unsteady twist those writings as they do the other Scriptures—to their own ruin. You, therefore, dear friends, forewarned as you are, be on your guard so that you may not be carried away by the stray wanderings of the lawless, and slip from your own moorings; but grow in grace and knowledge of our Lord and Savior Jesus Christ (II Pet. 3:16-18 Verkuyl).

These be they who separate themselves, sensual, having not the Spirit. But ye, beloved, building up yourselves on your most holy faith, praying in the Holy Spirit, keep yourselves in the love of God, looking for the mercy of our Lord Jesus Christ unto eternal life (Jude 19-21).

Whoever disowns the Son, the same hath not the Father. Let that therefore remain in you which ye have heard from the beginning. If that which ye have heard from the beginning shall remain in you, ye also shall remain in the Son, and in the Father. And this is the promise that he hath promised us, even eternal life (I John 2:23-25).

Therefore we ought to give the more earnest heed to the things which we have heard, lest at any time we should drift away. For if the word spoken by angels was stedfast, and every transgression and disobedience received a just recompence, how shall we escape if we neglect so great salvation? which at the first began to be spoken by the Lord, and was confirmed unto us by them that heard him (Heb. 2:1-3).

Wherefore, holy brethren, partakers of the heavenly calling, consider the Apostle and High Priest of our profession, Christ Jesus . . . a son over his own house; whose house are we, if we hold fast the confidence and the rejoicing of the hope firm unto the end. Wherefore, as the Holy Spirit saith, Today if ye will hear his voice, harden not your hearts, as in the provocation, in the day of temptation in the wilderness. . . . Take heed, brethren, lest there be in any of you an evil heart of unbelief, in departing from the living God. But exhort one another daily, while it is called

Today; lest any of you be hardened through the deceitfulness of sin. For we are made partakers of Christ if we hold the beginning of our confidence stedfast unto the end (Heb. 3:1, 6-8, 12-14).

We shall not cite others of the many warnings against apostasy found in the Epistle to the Hebrews (which context uniformly shows to be addressed to believers) with the exception of the urgent warning found in chapter 10. The warning against "sinning wilfully after we have received the full knowledge [*epignōsis*] of the truth" (v. 26) is addressed, not to unbelievers who are halting short of faith, but to "brethren" who "have boldness to enter into the holiest by the blood of Jesus, by a new and living way" (vv. 19, 20), and who "have an high priest over the house of God" (v. 21)—men who need only to "hold fast the confession of hope without wavering" (v. 23) and to continue "the assembling of ourselves together" (v. 25) for mutual encouragement in the faith, as they "see the day [of Christ's coming, v. 37] approaching." The readers to whom the warning is addressed are ("brethren") who already "have done the will of God" (v. 36) to the present moment, and who need only to "cast not away your confidence" (v. 35) in Christ. They already are believers who now "are not of those who shrink back so as to perish, but of those who by faith preserve the soul" (v. 39 Verkuyl).

The writer exhorts them: "Let us keep on drawing near [*proserchōmetha*[7]] with a true heart in full assurance of faith. . . . Let us keep on holding fast [*katechōmen*[7]] the confession of hope without wavering . . . let us keep on considering [*katanoōmen*[7]] one another to provoke unto love and good works: not forsaking the assembling of ourselves together, as the manner of some is, but encouraging one another; and so much the more, as ye see the day approaching."

The writer follows his vigorous exhortation with an immediate urgent warning: "For if *we* [not *they*, as some seem to imagine] sin wilfully after we have received the full knowl-

---

[7] Present subjunctive, durative.

edge of the truth. . . ." In such tragic circumstance, men who actually had been sanctified by the blood of the covenant (v. 29) would be equally as guilty of apostasy (and that *graver!*) and deserving of greater punishment than those who rebelled against the law of Moses, who died without mercy. The writer urges his brethren therefore to "keep calling to remembrance" (*anamimnēskesthe*, present middle imperative, durative) the early days following their conversion, when they gladly suffered persecution and loss for Christ, setting their affections on "a better and an enduring substance in heaven" (vv. 32-34). Let them now "cast not away your confidence" (v. 35, cf. vv. 19-23). "For ye have need of patience, that, having done the will of God, ye may receive the promise. For yet a little while, and he that cometh will come, and will not tarry" (vv. 36, 37).

But he must warn them again: God has said in His Word, "Now the just shall live by faith: but if he draw back, my soul shall have no pleasure in him" (v. 38). Delitzsch comments:

The subject in both clauses is the same—the just man, the man who is justified by his faith; and the sense in which *hupostellesthai* is here used is that of not keeping faith, wavering in faith, forsaking the path of faith and the community of the faithful. The just man, the man accepted before God, lives by faith; but if he loses his faith, and faithlessly draws back from the right path, his acceptance is forfeited. That such apostasy is possible even for those who have been truly justified, *i.e.*, for Christians who have had more than a superficial experience of divine grace, is one of the main points of instruction in this epistle. To teach this lesson, the clauses of the prophetic utterance are inverted. The second, as it stands here, is a warning as from the mouth of God Himself, a warning in a high prophetic tone. But the writer, as twice before, resumes the language of comfort and encouragement after words of the saddest foreboding. He proceeds, with pastoral gentleness and wisdom, to encourage the fainthearted and establish their wavering by rousing their Christian confidence, and associating himself with them as exposed to the same dangers, and courageously defying them.

Ver. 39. *But we are not of backsliding to perdition, but of faith to the gaining of the soul* . . . The persons meant are not Christians in general, but the writer of the epistle and his readers. Our way, he says, is not that cowardly shrinking back from Christian faith and confession which the

God of prophecy has denounced as so infinitely hateful to Himself, and which leads to destruction (*apōleia*, antithesis of *zōē* and *sōteria*), but a stedfast, abiding faith and reliance . . . which bases itself on the *zēsetai* of the prophetic promise—has for its end the salvation of the soul. . . . The man who keeps his faith unto the end, he saves his soul, wins her back from the pit of destruction which threatened to devour her, and so may be said to gain and possess her for the first time as now truly his. [Cf. Jesus' words to His disciples, "In your patience, possess (*ktaomai*, gain, win) ye your souls" Luke 21:19.][8]

Other passages could be cited. But the above passages establish the fact that the warnings in the Scriptures against succumbing to the peril of apostasy are addressed, not to men who have not as yet believed and who have nothing from which to apostatize, but to men who definitely possess saving faith and are in the state of grace.

But is the peril real? Are believers actually in peril of apostatizing? Some do not think so. Many apologists for the doctrine of unconditional security, in an attempt to reconcile the warning passages with their *a priori* doctrine, explain them as being only God's means of *ensuring* that believers shall not fall away from the faith. The essence of the arguments of many is as follows: The mere fact that travelers are warned that there is a ditch alongside the road does not mean that they will fall into it. The warnings must not lead us to suppose that they will or can. God warns believers simply because, as rational beings, they are so constituted as to require motivation. He therefore appeals to their fears to keep them on the path. But the warnings do not prove that believers will fall; on the contrary, they are God's means of ensuring that they shall *not* fall.

One will not read long from advocates of the doctrine of unconditional security before encountering this "explanation" of the presence of so many urgent warnings against apostasy so obviously addressed to believers. The folly of their contention is seen in the fact that, the moment a man becomes persuaded that their doctrine of unconditional security is correct, the

[8]Franz Delitzsch, *Commentary on the Epistle to the Hebrews*, p. 201 f.

warning passages immediately lose the very purpose and value which they claim for them. Strong quotes Dr. A. C. Kendrick on Hebrews 6:4-6: "The text describes a condition subjectively possible, and therefore needing to be held up in earnest warning to the believer, while objectively and in the absolute purpose of God, it never occurs."[9] But how can there be any "earnest warning" to the believer who is sufficiently "instructed" to understand that the "warning" is directed against an impossibility? How can something be subjectively *possible* for the person who knows it to be objectively *impossible*? The only possible circumstance under which the warning passages could serve the purpose and function which they claim for them would be the total rejection of the doctrine of unconditional security and inevitable perseverance.

The renowned Reformed theologian, Dr. G. C. Berkouwer of the Free University at Amsterdam, who insists that perseverance is inevitable and "does not depend on us, but on God's grace,"[10] pleads for this bankrupt "explanation" of the warning passages. He asserts that "a central datum of the doctrine of perseverance" lies in the harmonious relation of "the gracious faithfulness of God" (which makes apostasy impossible and perseverance inevitable) and "the dynamic of the actual struggle of life" (in which it is quite necessary that we be constantly motivated by alarming threats and warnings of the dire calamity of apostasy which stalks us at every turn, so that we may continually be roused to activity, watchfulness, and prayer, and thus deliberately continue in faith).[11]

Berkouwer declares that the admonitions ". . . have as their end the preservation of the Church, which precisely in this way is established in that single direction which is and which must remain irreversible—the direction from death to life!"[12] Therefore, for the warning passages to perform their divinely

---

[9]A. H. Strong, *Systematic Theology*, p. 885.
[10]G. C. Berkouwer, *Faith and Perseverance*, p. 96.
[11]*Ibid.*, pp. 97-99.
[12]*Ibid.*, p. 121.

ordained function in securing the perseverance and preservation of the Church, it is altogether necessary, according to
Berkouwer, that the warnings be regarded with sincere alarm:

> Anyone who would take away any of this tension, this completely
> earnest admonition, this many-sided warning, from the doctrine of the
> perseverance of the saints would do the Scriptures a great injury, and
> would cast the Church into the error of carelessness and sloth.
>
> The doctrine of the perseverance of the saints can never become an
> *a priori* guarantee in the life of believers which would enable them to get
> along without admonitions and warnings. [Despite Berkouwer's protest,
> this is precisely what Calvin's doctrine of perseverance inevitably becomes
> for everyone who embraces it.] Because of the nature of the relation be-
> tween faith and perseverance, the whole gospel must abound with ad-
> monition. It has to speak thus, because perseverance is not something
> that is merely handed down to us, but it is something that comes to re-
> alization only *in the path of faith*. Therefore the most earnest and alarm-
> ing admonitions cannot in themselves be taken as evidence against the
> doctrine of perseverance.
>
> To think of admonition and perseverance as opposites, as contradic-
> tories, is possible only if we misunderstand the nature of perseverance
> and treat it in isolation from its correlation with faith. For the correct
> understanding of the correlation between faith and perseverance, it is
> precisely these admonitions that are significant, and they enable us to
> understand better the nature of perseverance.[13]

Berkouwer insists that "perseverance is not something that is
merely handed down to us, but something that comes to realization only in the path of faith." He insists that there is a real
necessity for "alarming admonitions," for they are precisely the
means which God has ordained for motivating believers and
thus securing their perseverance. But when we become sufficiently "enlightened" to understand (as Berkouwer also insists)
that perseverance is inevitable and does not depend upon us in
any manner or degree, just how are we to manage to become
alarmed by the admonitions and warnings?

It would be of interest to learn from Professor Berkouwer
how recently he himself has experienced sincere alarm at the

---

[13]*Ibid.*, p. 110 f., italics his.

reading of any of the "alarming admonitions" with which the whole gospel abounds. If he experiences sincere alarm at the reading of the "alarming admonitions," is it because he actually fears that he might turn aside from "the path of faith" and fall from grace? Or, if he does not experience sincere alarm, is it because he considers that, for himself (in contrast with all other believers), it *is* permissible for the Reformed doctrine of inevitable perseverance to constitute "an *a apriori* guarantee" which enables him to "get along without admonitions and warnings"? In the interest of understanding, let us call upon Dr. Berkouwer to make it a matter of public record whether he actually experiences sincere alarm as he contemplates the "alarming admonitions" with which the gospel abounds; and if so, to declare why; and if not, to declare why not.

Berkouwer's explanation is perhaps implied in his statement: "Faith always directs itself anew to this confidence [the inevitability of perseverance]. In this perspective it always discovers a fresh consolation, after it has allowed itself to be earnestly admonished."[14] But such a contention must be rejected for the following reasons:

First, Berkouwer's contention implies that the "consolation" passages and the "alarming admonitions" cannot be viewed with complete sincerity at one and the same time, for a person cannot be motivated by the "alarming admonitions" until he abandons his confidence in the "consolation" passages—the (supposed) promises of God that perseverance is inevitable and apostasy is impossible. Thus, a person cannot accept *all* the testimony of the Holy Scriptures at face value at one and the same time. Instead, he can only oscillate between two contradictory persuasions, both of which are supposedly equally warranted by the Scriptures.

Again, the "alarming admonitions" thus serve—not to *prevent* believers from falling into "the error of carelessness and sloth,"

---

[14]*Ibid.*, p. 122. Cf. *The Canons of the Synod of Dort*, Fifth Head of Doctrine, Article XI.

but rather only to *recover* them after they have fallen into such error. The "alarming admonitions" can begin to motivate the individual only after the error of carelessness and sloth has actually become established.

Again, Berkouwer's contention assumes that it is inevitable that the individual will eventually heed the warnings. But according to the Scriptures, this is itself a matter of contingency, as we shall observe in later chapters.

Typical of the confusion of Calvinists in their abortive attempts to reconcile the warning passages with their *a priori* doctrine of unconditional security and inevitable perseverance are Berkouwer's numerous self-contradictions. In his chapter "The Reality of Perseverance," Berkouwer asserts that there is no factor whatever in man which may in any way determine the issue of perseverance, for "in this way the consolation of perseverance would most certainly be lost, because the final outcome would be put again in the hands of persevering man."[15] But in his chapter "Perseverance and Admonition," he asserts that "the doctrine of the perseverance of the saints can never become an *a priori* guarantee in the life of believers which would enable them to get along without admonitions and warnings." But if "the consolation of perseverance" is the assurance that the final outcome is not in the hands of persevering man, does not this "consolation" constitute "an *a priori* guarantee" of perseverance for all who embrace it? If it does not constitute such a guarantee, just what *does* it constitute? And if the final outcome is in no way in the hands of persevering man, then how can the "alarming admonitions" be sincere?

In his chapter "The Reality of Perseverance," Berkouwer writes:

Nevertheless, it is clear that the Reformed doctrine intends to point out a constancy in the actual life of the believer himself. When it speaks so emphatically about perseverance as a gift, about the gracious character of God's covenant in its manifold riches, and about the power of Christ's intercession, these are indissolubly connected with a constancy in the

---

[15]*Ibid.*, p. 220.

lives of the believers themselves. . . . [The possibility of] total falling,
therefore, has had to be rejected. . . .

. . . .

[The doctrine of perseverance is a proper] subject for preaching. For this
preaching . . . is a great and moving experience for the believer, one
which constrains him to marvel about the constancy which is his in
Christ. This marvelling will always be the deepest foundation for the
thankfulness which fills the believer's life as he goes to meet the future.[16]

But just how can one continually "marvel at the constancy
which is [unconditionally and inevitably] his in Christ" and, at
the same time, reject it as "an *a priori* guarantee" of perseverance? Just how can one embrace a doctrine which denies the
possibility of total falling and, at the same time, reject it as an
a priori guarantee of perseverance?

In his chapter "The Consolation of Perseverance," Berkouwer
writes:

. . . admonition has a very important place in the life of the believer. It
occurs on almost every page of Holy Scripture. But to think that this ele-
ment of contingency expresses the entire gospel teaching regarding perseverance is to ignore completely the Scriptural teaching that faith always
rests in the steadfastness and faithfulness of God's grace. This everpresent grace is never spoken of in a simplistic fashion, as if it were something that could be taken for granted. However, the faith to which we
are incessantly called opens up to our view a marvelous continuity.[17]

But just how it is possible to view a "marvelous continuity"
which is seen as an inevitable corollary of "the steadfastness
and faithfulness of God's grace" and, at the same time, to reject
that inevitable continuity as an *a priori* guarantee of perseverance? Again, how is it possible for faith to "rest in the steadfastness and faithfulness of God's grace" and, at the same time,
to refuse to take that grace "for granted"? Surely, it must have
been a Calvinist theologian that wrote the old familiar jingle:

> The barefoot boy with boots on
> Stood sitting on the grass. . . .

[16]*Ibid.*, pp. 233, 239.
[17]*Ibid.*, p. 199.

We must reject Berkouwer's assertion that the grace of God must not be taken for granted. Quite to the contrary, the constancy of the grace of God *must* be taken for granted. True faith can have no other view of the grace of God. What must not be taken for granted is the constancy of our faith. *This* is the object and concern of the "alarming admonitions." The warning passages do not in any sense suggest that we are not to take for granted the steadfastness and faithfulness of God's grace, but rather that we are not to take for granted the constancy of our faith.

Berkouwer's difficulty stems from his erroneous assumption that the faithfulness of God ensures that we, too, must inevitably prove faithful. He asserts that, in our consideration of perseverance and continuity, we must

. . . start with the doctrine of the *faithfulness* of God's grace, which is certainly of most decisive importance for the doctrine of the perseverance of the saints. In this doctrine, there is great emphasis on the immutability of God's counsel in Jesus Christ.[18] God's grace is affirmed as the *reality* of preservation. It would not be incorrect to say that faith affirms perseverance, the constancy of God's grace, the permanency of His faithfulness and of His eternal love.

• • • • • • • • • • • • • • • • • • • •

His faithfulness does not depend on our faithfulness, nor on anything that is or will be present in us. There is rather a "nevertheless," an "in spite of."

• • • • • • • • • • • • • • • • • • • •

It is clear that one need add nothing to this faithfulness and constancy. The greatness of God's faithfulness and preservation, indeed, was a temptation to many to speak no longer of perseverance, but only of preservation.[19]

---

[18]The real root of confusion for Calvinists is their failure to recognize that the certainty of election and perseverance is with respect, not to particular individual men unconditionally, but rather with respect to the *ekklēsia*, the corporate body of all who, through living faith, are in union with Christ, the true Elect and the Living Covenant between God and all who trust in Him. See Appendix E, Section 10.

[19]*Ibid.*, pp. 219 f., 222, italics his.

But contrary to Berkouwer's assumption, the faithfulness of God does not ensure a corresponding faithfulness in us. This fact has already been observed (Chapter 8). But let us again observe that, while the faithlessness of many in Israel did not nullify the faithfulness of God in keeping His promises, neither did the faithfulness of God prevent the faithlessness of many of His covenant people (Rom. 3:3-8). The faithfulness of God with respect to Israel did not prevent "some of the branches" from being broken off through unbelief (Rom. 11:20-22), nor will it prevent a like calamity for individual Gentile believers who fail to continue to stand by faith. Paul assures us that, if we prove unfaithful, Christ will yet remain faithful. But while He cannot deny Himself, Paul assures us that He *will* deny us, if we deny Him (II Tim. 2:12, 13). His faithfulness is no unconditional guarantee against either the possibility or the consequences of our own apostasy. "Remain in me," said Jesus, "and I in you." Christ confronts all who would be His with the necessity of a living faith which has nothing in common with the barren presumptions engendered by theological sophistry.

Most aspects of Calvinism enjoy the sanctuary of the purely academic, in which realm it is perhaps possible to contrive some sort of apology for almost any hypothesis. But in its attempt to reconcile the warning passages with its *a priori* doctrine of unconditional security and inevitable perseverance, Calvinism must emerge from the sanctuary of the abstract and submit to the judgment of the conscious experience of men. It is true that we dare not define our doctrines by the measure of human experience and feelings. That is an essential axiom. But the aspect of doctrine now before us is necessarily an exception to the rule. Surely, we shall not be asked to believe that we cannot know whether we experience sincere alarm as we contemplate the "alarming admonitions" with which "the whole gospel must abound." It is impossible for one not to know whether he experiences sincere alarm. And it is equally impossible for one to be sincerely persuaded that apostasy is impossible, and also sincerely alarmed by the warnings against apostasy. Calvinism's necessary assumption is found to be false by the judgment of human experience. Completely absurd is the assumption that men are to be sincerely persuaded that apostasy is impossible and, at the same time, sincerely alarmed by the warnings. Equally absurd is any assumption that men are to oscillate between two contradictory persuasions like a pendulum and are not to view the whole testimony of the Scriptures with complete sincerity at one time, but are to be one day sincerely persuaded that the Bible warns us against apostasy, and another day sincerely persuaded that the Bible assures us that apostasy is impossible.

The fallacy of Calvinism's absurd assumption, essential to the defense of its doctrine of perseverance, is constantly demonstrated in the tragic inconsistency in the personal ministry of pastors who entertain it. They profess to believe that, while all true believers will inevitably persevere, it is only within the context of the dynamic exercise of faith that the perseverance is unfolded. They profess to believe that the warning passages are designed of God to effect this perseverance by motivating believers to continue in faith and to fear apostasy, and that the perseverance is realized only as believers take solemn heed to the warning passages. These things they profess to believe (at least, when pressed to account for the presence of the warning passages). But their preaching and teaching seem designed to *prevent* the warning passages and "alarming admonitions" from accomplishing the purpose which they profess to believe God intends them to serve. They never miss an opportunity to "explain" the warning passages in such a way as to dispel any concern which their hearers might have for them, and they continually assure them that they are unconditionally secure for all time and eternity, with no contingency whatever. They constantly do their utmost to destroy the concern of their hearers for the warnings and admonitions which they acknowledge to be God's means of motivating believers to persevere. Those who do preach the warnings with earnestness and conviction they accuse of being "confused" and "doctrinally unsound,"

and of not believing in salvation by grace. Wisdom is justified
of her children; but only eternity will reveal the full measure
of the tragedy of this popular fallacy and the inevitable inconsistency of all who embrace it.

Contrary to the assumptions of some, the warnings were not
given merely because there are no other motives by which believers may be motivated to persevere; for there are other motives, such as gratitude to God for His forgiveness and grace,
increased joy through faithfulness, concern for the spiritual
need of those who are influenced by our lives, and the promise
of more abundant reward in heaven. The warnings were given,
not to supply a lack of any motive for perseverance, but because of the existence of a real and deadly peril with which
we must reckon.

That the peril of apostasy is real, rather than imaginary, is
evident from the fact that the Bible records actual instances
of it. Numerous examples are to be found in the Bible. We shall
cite only some instances in the New Testament.

Jude warns his readers against the peril which constantly
confronts them in the insidious activities of apostate teachers
among them. In his description of apostates who "turn the grace
of God into lasciviousness and deny the only Lord God and our
Lord Jesus Christ" (v. 4) and whose wicked careers and just
condemnation "were before of old foretold" (*prographō,* to
write or describe beforehand; cf. Rom. 15:4, Eph. 3:3) by
Enoch (vv. 14, 15) and others in ancient times, Jude declares
that they are "trees whose fruit withereth, without fruit, twice
dead, plucked up by the roots" (v. 12; cf. John 15:1-6).

Some have explained the description, "twice dead," to mean
only that the false teachers are beyond redemption and their
present spiritual death is certain to culminate in "the second
death" in the world to come. But they have imagined a vain
thing. Such interpretation is mere conjecture for which there
is no warrant whatever. Jude's language is explicit. The word
apothanonta (dead) is an aorist participle, rather than an adjective, and the verbal aspect of the participle must not be over-

looked. Jude's description, literally, is "twice having died." It is concerned with the past, rather than the future.

The tragic circumstance, "twice dead," is the lot of men who, having once "passed out of death into life" through faith in Jesus Christ, have turned back to walk no more with Him, so becoming "dead in trespasses and in sins" once again. "Twice dead" can only refer to the fact that men who once were alive in Christ have again become spiritually dead by severing their union with Him "who is our life." Furthermore, Jude refers to the specific occasion and cause of their spiritual death: "They went in the way of Cain, and ran riotously in the error of Balaam for hire, and perished [apolonto, 2nd aorist indicative middle, killed themselves] in the gainsaying of Korah" (v. 11 ASV).

Like Korah and his company of old, who denied the unique authority of Moses and profanely usurped the functions of the ordained priesthood, the apostates whom Jude cites denied the unique authority of the one Mediator and the finality of His Gospel, as defined by Jesus and the Apostles. From Jude's comments, it is evident that their defection had its origin and development in their love of lascivious living and their practical repudiation of the implications of the lordship of Christ over the personal lives of all who would be His. They were therefore "without fruit" (cf. John 15:1-5, II Pet. 1:8 ff.) and, as the inevitable outcome, were plucked up by the roots (cf. John 15:2, 6) and became "wandering stars" (contra. Rev. 1:16, 20). Despite their inward spiritual defection, they still retained their outward affiliation with the believers, continuing to enjoy places of prominence and leadership. Through their spiritual defection, they had become men who had "slipped in stealthily" into positions of undeserved influence and honor. (To assume that Jude meant in v. 4 that they had originally entered the church on the strength of empty professions which were false from the beginning and that they never had been other than mere hypocrites is to contradict the historical examples which he cites—the apostates in the wilderness [v. 5] and the angels who kept not their first estate [v. 6]—and to deny his assertion that they "killed themselves" in their rebellion against the Lord after the example of Korah [v. 11] and are now "twice dead." Furthermore, to adopt such an assumption is to nullify Jude's urgent warning to believers to beware the peril of following the same tragic course as the apostates [vv. 20, 21].)

In his Second Epistle, Peter writes at length concerning apostates who, "denying [*arneomai*, disown, renounce] the Lord who bought them" (2:1), for love of "the wages of unrighteousness" (2:15), "have left the straight road and gone astray," becoming "dried-up springs" (2:15, 17 Williams). There could be no greater tragedy. "For if after they have escaped the pollutions of the world through the knowledge [*epignōsis*, full and true knowledge] of the Lord and Saviour Jesus Christ, they are again entangled therein and overcome, the latter end is worse with them than the beginning. For it had been better for them not to have known the way [*hodos*, road— "the straight road," v. 15] of righteousness than, after they have known it, to turn back [*epistrephō*] from the holy commandment delivered unto them" (II Pet. 2:20, 21).

Many have contended that the men of whom Peter wrote never were truly saved. They appeal to the metaphors in verse 22. God's children, say they, cannot be referred to as *dogs* or *sows*. But they who assume that Peter's reference to apostates as "dogs" and "sows" proves that they never were actually under grace do not likewise assume that Jeremiah's reference to the children of Israel in Judah as "a wild ass" proves that they never were "the sheep of His pasture." The shameful epithet was applied by Jeremiah (2:24) only after the people had forsaken the Lord (2:13; 17:13) and turned aside in iniquity and idolatry. Likewise, it is only after they "have forsaken the right way and are gone astray" that Peter likens apostates to dogs and sows. He could well have referred to them as "wild asses." But there were familiar proverbs about dogs and sows which so aptly illustrated their case. Let us accept the record at face value. To ignore the obvious meaning of Peter's statements by resorting to arbitrary assumptions concerning his use of metaphors is, to say the least, unwise.

Paul cites specific instances of apostasy. Urging Timothy to "continue to fight the good fight, by keeping your hold on faith and a good conscience," he declares that "some have thrust the latter aside and so have made shipwreck of their faith" (I Tim. 1:18, 19 Williams). He names Hymenaeus and Alexander as prominent among those who had shamefully apostatized.

In the same letter, Paul warns Timothy (5:9-15) against the probability that younger widows, if accepted, might wax wanton and desire to marry, breaking the vows of continence and special obligation to Christ which they must assume in order to be admitted to the company of dependent widows officially adopted for support by the church. Such defection would be no minor matter; it would constitute apostasy, incurring condemnation. The peril was real; such defection had occurred in specific instances. Some had "already turned aside to follow Satan."

Another reference to actual instances of apostasy is contained in Paul's words to Timothy, "But men who keep planning to get rich fall into temptations and snares and many foolish, hurtful desires which plunge people into destruction and ruin. For the love of money is the root of all sorts of evil, and some men, in reaching after riches, have wandered from the faith and pierced their hearts with many a pang" (I Tim. 6:9, 10 Williams).

The errors of some of the Galatians will be considered at length in a later chapter. Let us here observe that Paul refers to actual instances of apostasy among them: "All you who aim at justification by Law are dissevered from Christ; you have fallen away from grace" (Gal. 5:4 Verkuyl).

Contrary to the opinions of some, Hebrews 6:4-6 is no mere hypothesis, but a reference to actual instances of apostasy. Despite the unfortunate renderings of the Authorized Version and certain contemporary translators, no conditional particle is

present in the Greek text. The writer simply says *tous* . . .
parapesontas— "those who have fallen away" (second aorist
active participle). There is nothing in either the language or
context to indicate that the instances of apostasy cited in Hebrews 6:4-6 are only hypothetical. This fact is accurately reflected in the rendering of the American Standard Version
(1901): "For as touching those who were once enlightened
and tasted of the heavenly gift, and were made partakers of
the Holy Spirit, and tasted the good word of God, and the
powers of the age to come, and then fell away. . . ." The instances of apostasy cited by the writer are real, rather than
imaginary and hypothetical.

Some appeal to verse 9 ("But beloved, we are persuaded better things of you, and things that accompany salvation, though
we thus speak") to contend that such apostasy cannot actually
occur.[20] But they fail to reckon with the transition from the

---

[20]Berkouwer (*Faith and Perseverance*, p. 117 ff.) asserts that Heb. 6:4-6 is
not a warning against apostasy, but rather a warning against the peril of
imagining that apostasy is possible. Thus, according to Berkouwer, the passage is not a warning against the danger of apostasy, but only a grand assurance
that there is no such danger. In the course of five pages of argument from pre-
supposition, Berkouwer makes several attempts (all abortive) to reconcile his
ingenious interpretation with the obvious fact that, after all, the passage *is a
warning*. He writes: "So there is an earnest warning against this possibility
that could invade the thinking of the Church [the peril of imagining that
apostasy is actually possible]. Over against this there stands the radical 'impossible' [the impossibility of a transition from life to death, as well as of a recovery from death to life] by which, consoled and admonished, they are guided
on the only road. This passage from Hebrews 6 lets us see especially clearly
how far the Scriptures are removed from every view of the Church which
would eliminate the tension of faith and admonition" (p. 120).
    But just how does the writer to the Hebrews expect to augment "the tension
of faith and admonition" by persuading his readers that there is not the slightest possibility of apostasy? This, Berkouwer does not trouble himself to explain.
    Furthermore, if this passage were only a warning against imagining that
apostasy is possible (as Berkouwer asserts), then it would be completely contrary to the spirit and purpose of all the many "alarming admonitions" which
plainly warn that apostasy is an actual possibility and a deadly peril—admonitions with which, as Berhouwer declares, "the whole gospel must abound . . .
it has to speak thus, because perseverance is not something that is merely
handed down, but it is something that comes to realization only *in the path of*

third person ("those, they, them") in verses 4-6 to the second person ("you") in verse 9. The writer is "persuaded better things of *you*," but not of "*them*." While he is persuaded that "you" have not as yet apostatized, he declares that "they" indeed have done so. Instead of assuming that the apostasy which engulfed "them" cannot overtake "you," the writer holds "them" up before "you" as a tragic example for their solemn warning and proceeds earnestly to exhort his readers, "And we desire that every one of you do show the same diligence to the full assurance of hope unto the end; that ye be not slothful, but followers of them who through faith and patience inherit the promises" (vv. 11, 12).

The writer cites the example of Abraham (vv. 13-15) who, "after he had patiently endured, obtained the promise" (cf. 11:8-16). He exhorts his readers, after the example of Abraham, to continue to count on the faithfulness of the promise and oath of God who cannot lie, "that we who have fled for refuge may keep on having [*hina* with *echōmen*, present subjunctive, durative] strong encouragement to lay hold on the hope set before us" (v. 18). That hope is an anchor of the soul, securely fastened within the veil where Jesus our High Priest now appears in our behalf. It only remains for us to hold fast to the anchor of hope. "Let us keep on holding fast[21] the confession of hope without wavering" (10:23). "Seeing then that we have a great high priest who has passed into the heavens, Jesus the Son of God, let us keep on holding fast[21] our confession. . . . Let us keep on coming[21] with confidence to the throne of grace, that we may receive mercy and find grace to help in time of

---

faith" (p. 110 f.). If other "alarming admonitions" warn believers against apostasy as an actual peril, what moral right has the writer to the Hebrews to attempt (as Berkouwer contends) to persuade his readers that apostasy is *not* an actual peril, but is rather an absolute impossibility? Men who approach the Bible with the presuppositions of Calvinism invariably become entangled in confusion and absurd contradictions which are an offense both to common sense and (what is worse) to the testimony of the Holy Scriptures.

[21]Present subjunctive, durative.

need" (4:14, 16). Robertson comments: "In point of fact, our anchor with its two chains of God's promise and oath has laid hold of Jesus within the veil. It will hold fast. All we need to do is to be true to him as he is to us."[22]

* * *

It has been much disputed whether Judas was once a true believer, or merely an impostor from the beginning. Good arguments have been made for both views. But let us observe that, whatever the true situation of Judas, it has no bearing on the fact that other instances of actual apostasy are cited in the Scriptures. Let us beware the fallacy of "either . . . or." What is true in one instance does not govern what may or may not be true in other instances. Doubtless many in every generation have only pretended to believe, whose professions were false from the beginning. But it is equally true that others actually have departed from true faith, according to the record of the Scriptures. Whatever may have been the situation of Judas does not determine the experience or status of others.

We believe the case of Judas is an instance of true apostasy, rather than of original and prolonged imposture. The statement that Judas "fell away" (Acts 1:25; cf. Thayer on *parabainō*) from his ministry and apostleship is an assertion that, by a specific action, he disqualified himself. The necessary corollary is that he previously was qualified. The case of Judas, then, was one of apostasy, rather than original hypocrisy.

Those who contend that Judas was an impostor from the beginning appeal to John 6:64, "Jesus knew from the beginning who they were that believed not, and who should betray him." But we believe Robertson is correct in observing that "John does not say here that Jesus knew that Judas would betray him when he chose him as one of the twelve, least of all that he chose him for that purpose. What he does say is that Jesus was not taken by surprise and soon saw signs of treason in Judas. . . .

---

[22]Robertson, *op. cit.*, Vol. V, p. 379.

Judas had gifts and was given his opportunity. He did not have to betray Jesus."[23]

Jesus was always fully aware of superficiality in the "faith" of any whose professions were insincere. John records that "Jesus did not commit himself" to many who "believed in his name," because "he knew what was in man" (John 2:23 ff.). This militates against any contention that Judas was not a sincere believer when Jesus chose him, with eleven others of His disciples, to share special privileges and powers as His Apostles. The fact that Matthew, Mark, and Luke designate Judas as the betrayer, in their accounts of the choosing of the Twelve, does not afford any insight into the character of Judas at the time, but is merely their means of distinguishing him from Judas, the brother of James.

It is significant that when Jesus announced in the upper room that one of the Twelve should betray Him, the Apostles were filled with consternation and were in doubt as to the identity of the traitor. Instead of casting accusing eyes on Judas, "they began to inquire among themselves, which of them it was that should do this thing" (Luke 22:23). There had been nothing about his career as an Apostle which had distinguished Judas in any way from the other eleven. Nothing is said in Scripture to suggest that he failed to function in the exercise of the powers given to the Apostles. It is unthinkable, too, that Jesus, who so loathed the hypocrisy of the Pharisees, could ever have counted as His "own familiar friend" one whom He knew to be false (John 13:18, Psalm 41:9; cf. Psalm 55:12-14).

The events of John 6 occurred nearly a year after the choosing of the Twelve, and several months after their preaching tour. During the lapse of time, there was ample opportunity for Judas to drift from his original faith. Perhaps his faith was undermined by disappointment at the martyrdom of John, which occurred shortly before the occasion of Jesus' statement that "one of you is a devil." Martyrdom, he may have reasoned,

---

[23]*Ibid.*, p. 114.

was not the sort of thing that should happen to the friends
of the *real* Messiah. That was too unlike the triumph which the
Jews anticipated at the appearance of the Messiah. And doubtless Judas, like the crowds (and like the other Apostles), was
disappointed that Jesus refused to accede to the popular desire
to make Him king merely for immediate temporal advantage
(John 6:15).

There were the miracles, of course. But even things quite
spectacular eventually become commonplace through continual
association and familiarity. Furthermore, Judas may have concluded that the Pharisees and scribes, who apparently were not
impressed by the works of Jesus, were doubtless less gullible
than those who were. After all, there were others besides Jesus
and His apostles who performed such mighty works as casting
out demons, for example (Matt. 12:27). In any event, more
important to Judas than the question of His miracles was the
fact that Jesus no longer fit his conception of the Messiah. It
was now apparent to Judas that Jesus had no intention of being
the sort of Messiah which he believed the prophets had depicted, and he therefore concluded that his earlier impressions
of Jesus had not been correct.

His keen disappointment destroyed the last vestiges of faith
which had remained, and his latent selfishness swiftly moved in
to fill the vacuum in his soul. He now decided that his best
course was to continue outwardly with the movement for the
sake of some possible personal advantage—a purpose which was
later to manifest itself in his perfidy as treasurer of the group
(John 12:4-6) and, ultimately, in his betrayal of the Son of
man for a few silver coins. Even then, there was forming in
his mind the evil thought that he might turn the situation to
advantage by betraying Jesus into the hands of powerful enemies who already were planning to destroy Him (John 6:71;
cf. Phillips' excellent rendering of *emellen paradidonai auton,*
"was planning to betray him"). The thought was to be encouraged, rather than resisted; and the love of money eventually was to drown him in destruction and perdition. Although

outwardly he was to continue to follow Jesus, Judas' heart went with the crowds who, following His discourse in the synagogue at Capernaum, turned back to walk no more with Him. His inward defection, unknown to the others of the Twelve, was fully apparent to Jesus. For He who never committed Himself to men of superficial faith "knew all men, and needed not that any should testify of man, for he knew what was in man" (John 2:24, 25).

That such defection was possible for the others, as well as for Judas, is clearly affirmed in John 6:66-71. Jesus asked His Twelve the searching question, "Will ye also go away?" The language of the text anticipates a negative answer. But that does not mean that Jesus' question was merely rhetorical or that the peril of defection was, for them, only hypothetical. The peril was real, and Jesus was probing the inmost recesses of their hearts.

The answer of Peter was a splendid affirmation of faith and fidelity. But it contained an unmistakable note of self-confidence which constituted a distinct peril. The use of the pronoun *hēmeis* (v. 69) is emphatic, indicating the strength of the contrast which Peter presumed to exist between the Twelve and the disciples who withdrew to walk no more with Jesus. The answer of Jesus was a pointed rebuke to such self-assurance that, though others turn back, never will we! "Jesus answered them, Have not I chosen you twelve? Yet one of you is a devil." What is He saying to Peter and the others? Just this: "Peter, do not be too sure that you can never turn back from following me. Have I not chosen you twelve, of all my disciples, to be my inner circle—my Apostles and my constant companions? Yet, already, one of you is now a devil!" It had happened among the Twelve! There was need, not for such bouyant self-confidence, but for holy fear.

Friend in Christ, there can be no place for smug self-assurance in our hearts if we heed the admonition of Peter (who had learned much since the days of John 6), "pass the time of your sojourning here in fear" (I Pet. 1:17). "Let him who feels

sure of standing firm beware of falling" (I Cor. 10:12 Verkuyl).
"Of how much greater punishment, suppose ye, shall he be
thought worthy who hath trodden under foot the Son of God,
and hath counted the blood of the covenant, wherewith he was
sanctified, an unholy [commonplace] thing, and hath done despite unto the Spirit of grace? . . . We shall not escape if we
turn away from Him from heaven" (Heb. 10:29; 12:25). Robertson's comment on Heb. 10:29 is apropos as one contemplates the appalling career of Judas: "It is an unspeakable tragedy that should warn every follower of Christ not to play with
treachery to Christ."[24]

"If we deny him. . . ."

---

[24]*Ibid.*, p. 414.

"Sin Shall Not Have Dominion"

Likewise reckon ye also yourselves to be dead indeed unto sin, but alive unto God through Jesus Christ our Lord. Let not sin therefore reign in your mortal body, that ye should obey it in the lusts thereof. Neither yield ye your members as instruments of unrighteousness unto sin: but yield yourselves unto God as those that are alive from the dead, and your members as instruments of righteousness unto God. For sin shall not have dominion over you: for ye are not under the law, but under grace.

What then? shall we sin, because we are not under the law, but under grace? God forbid. Know ye not that to whom ye yield yourselves servants to obey, his servants ye are to whom ye obey, whether of sin unto death, or of obedience unto righteousness? . . . For the wages of sin is death, but the gift of God is eternal life in Jesus Christ our Lord.

ROMANS 6:11-16, 23

CHAPTER XIII

SIN SHALL NOT HAVE DOMINION

THERE ARE but two possible reasons why any man on earth is unsaved. Either he has not heard the Gospel, or he is unwilling to accept the condition of repentance and discipleship whereby the Gospel of Christ may become for him, personally, "the power of God unto salvation."

Jesus commissioned His disciples to preach "repentance and remission of sins in his name among all nations" (Luke 24:47). There can be no remission without repentance. Paul testified "both to the Jews and also to the Greeks repentance toward God and faith toward our Lord Jesus Christ" (Acts 20:21). One cannot believe in Christ as his Saviour from sin apart from repentance toward God. The God whose "commandment is life everlasting" is the God who "now commands all men everywhere to repent" (John 12:50, Acts 17:30). Men cannot share His life everlasting apart from repentance toward Him.

"We will not have this man to reign over us!" Such is the attitude of all men who deliberately reject the Gospel. Men refuse Christ for one reason alone: they want to be "free"—free of the lordship of Christ, free of divine restraint, and of all holy obligation. They are, indeed. But they are also free of the remission of sins, free of saving grace, and free of eternal life and all prospect of heaven. Every man is "free"—either of the dominion of Christ and the prospect of heaven, or of the dominion of sin and the prospect of hell.

Every man is likewise a servant—either of the Lord Jesus Christ and His kingdom of righteousness, or of the devil and the tyranny of sin. There is no middle ground. "He who is not with me," said Jesus, "is against me" (Matt. 12:30). Men who would be free of the tyranny of sin must accept the lordship of Christ over their personal lives. He who said "Come unto me and I will give you rest" said also "Take my yoke upon you" (Matt. 11:28, 29). No man can find rest for his soul in Christ who does not take His yoke upon him. "No man can serve two masters," said Jesus. "Ye cannot serve God and mammon" (Matt. 6:24). There are but two masters. Every man must serve one; no man can serve both. Every man faces the question, Who is to be my master? His answer determines, for him, all the issues of time and eternity.

If Christ is to be Saviour and Lord, a definite decision must be made. A tragic failure of many pastors and churches is the failure to confront men with the necessity of making a definite decision for Christ. Preaching which fails to confront hearers with the Person and claims of Christ in such a manner that decision becomes mandatory is altogether too vague and nebulous to accomplish the purpose of Him who is pleased "by the foolishness of preaching to save them that believe" (I Cor. 1:21).

There is a sense, of course, in which no man is without a personal decision with respect to Christ. "He who is not with me is against me." There is no "middle road." The decision, for every man, is *no* until he makes it *yes*. If Christ is to be Saviour and Lord, the choice must be made—definitely and deliberately. And it must be made with a sense of finality. One cannot receive Christ as his personal Saviour and Lord without a sincere intention to trust and follow Him always, through life into eternity. Any "faith in Christ" is completely insincere apart from such intention.

It would be a mistake, however, to suppose that the choice of Christ as Saviour and Lord can or must be made but once. Marriage is supposedly "until death do us part." No one has a right to enter into marriage with any other intention. But unless the vows exchanged at the altar are continually reaffirmed and implemented in deed and life, the inner spiritual essence of marriage will perish and the outward form most likely will be terminated by something other than death.

The commitment of oneself to Christ in accepting Him as Saviour and Lord is the necessary starting point. But the initial decision must be reaffirmed and implemented in the life which follows. We must continue to choose between the lordship of Christ and the dominion of sin. It never becomes true that we may somehow serve both God and mammon. "Know ye not," asks James, "that the friendship of the world is enmity with God? Whosoever therefore will be a friend of the world is the enemy of God" (4:4). We cannot negotiate a special arrangement whereby we may serve two masters. God is a jealous God. Christ cannot be the Lord of men who do not give Him their true allegiance. "Why call ye me, Lord, Lord, and do not the things which I say?" (Luke 6:46). The "Christian" who fancies that he can carry water on both shoulders and get along well enough by "doing his bit" for God while hobnobbing with the devil is cherishing a fatal delusion.

"Love not the world," writes John, "neither the things that are in the world. If any man love the world, the love of the Father is not in him. For all that is in the world, the lust of the flesh, and the lust of the eyes, and the pride of life, is not of the Father, but is of the world. And the world passeth away, and the lust thereof [and all who live for these things]; but he who keeps on doing[1] the will of God abides for ever" (I John 2:15-17).

Jesus came to "save His people from their sins." Many seem to wish somehow to be "His people," but they do not quite desire to be saved from their sins. They wish only to be saved from the *consequences* of their sins. Any "salvation" which does not save one from his sins, as well as from their consequences, is a delusion. One cannot be a part of "His people" while giving his allegiance to the world, the flesh, and the devil.

---

[1]*Poiōn*, present participle. Cf. Williams, "whoever perseveres in doing God's will lives on forever."

Perhaps more than any other city in Paul's day, Corinth was notorious for its sensuality and lasciviousness. As in other places and times, religion and lust had been made handmaids one of another. "What impressed [Paul] at Corinth may perhaps be gathered from the fact that there he wrote the last section of the first chapter of the Epistle to the Romans, 'the moral history of a heathenism delivered over to the lust of its own heart.' "[2] Understandably, the Gentile converts in the church at Corinth had much to overcome in their conflict with old habits and patterns firmly entrenched through long acceptance and cultivation. They were saved; but they were yet carnal. Their carnality was expressed, not only in the "envying, strife, and divisions" (I Cor. 3:3) among them, but also in their apparent indifference to the presence of incest in their midst (chapter 5) and in the common tendency among them toward immorality (6:13-20).

Paul was patient; but he could not condone their carnality, and it would have been a mistake for them so to have construed his patience. His statement, "ye are yet carnal," implies that they were not to remain so. The sharpness of some of his rebukes and warnings indicates the intensity of his concern for them. They are on dangerous ground if they imagine that the feast of "Christ our passover" can be kept with "the leaven of malice and wickedness." On the contrary, it must be kept "with the unleavened bread of sincerity and truth" (5:7, 8). They must therefore "purge out the old leaven," which is not merely a matter of excommunicating a certain flagrant offender, but more especially of judging themselves, lest they be judged of the Lord, chastened, and (if not corrected) ultimately condemned with the impenitent world (11:31, 32). They must realize that they cannot continue as sons and daughters of the Father if they are unwilling to "cleanse [themselves] from all filthiness of the flesh and spirit, perfecting holiness in the fear of God" (II Cor. 6:14-7:1). Citing the example of many of the

---

[2]J. Massie, *The New Century Bible: Corinthians* (ed. W. F. Adeney), p. 7.

children of Israel in the wilderness, Paul implores the Corinthians to profit by their tragic example, to discard foolish presumption and vain self-confidence, and to "flee from idolatry" and all the evil associations which it represents (I Cor. 10:1 ff.).

They must beware receiving his warning lightly. The consequences of their present tendencies, if unchecked, must be fatal. For "ye cannot drink the cup of the Lord, and the cup of devils: ye cannot be partakers of the Lord's table, and of the table of devils" (10:21). The "cup of the Lord" of which Paul speaks is not merely the vessel used in the observance of the Lord's Supper. He considers the ordinance at length in 11:17-34 and mentions it incidentally in 10:16; but he is concerned in v. 21 with a spiritual partaking, rather than a physical act at the communion table. (Cf. vv. 17, 4.) Then, as now, many who delighted to "drink" of the cup of devils *did* drink from the cup of the Lord at the table of Holy Communion. Although they might do so physically, it was impossible to do so spiritually. The peril in view in Paul's warning therefore is the peril of presuming to continue to partake of Christ spiritually while consciously and deliberately embracing sin. This was the error of many of Israel (10:1-10). It was a real and constant peril for both Paul (9:27) and the Corinthians (10:6-21). For Paul and the Corinthians, as well as for the men who heard His voice in Galilee, the Lord's dictum stands: "No man can serve two masters."

The warning of James is ever timely: "Sin, when it is fully matured, brings forth death" (1:15). Let us observe that, contrary to many evangelistic sermons, James' warning is not directed to unbelievers. It is not possible for sin to "bring forth death" in them, for they already are "dead in trespasses and in sins." James directs his solemn warning, not to outsiders who make no profession of faith in Christ, but to "my beloved brethren" (v. 16). They must reckon with the peril of incurring spiritual death through surrender to habitual deliberate sin. In his instructions to Timothy concerning the care of widows in the church, Paul declares that those who abandon themselves to voluptuous living incur spiritual death: "She who lives in pleasure is dead [spiritually] while she lives [physically]" (I Tim. 5:6).

That surrender to the dominion of sin is fatal, spiritually, is clearly implied in II Corinthians 12:21 wherein Paul expresses his fear that, should he return to Corinth, he should be obliged to mourn over many who, despite his warnings by letter and in person, "have sinned already, and have not repented of the uncleanness and fornication and lasciviousness which they have committed."

Some understand Paul to imply that the impenitent of whom he writes have never repented of their original sins and so have never been converted. This is not so. Were this the case, he should not have been obliged to distinguish them from the others in the church by identifying them as *tōn proēmartēkotōn*. For who among them had not previously practiced habitual sinning during the days of their paganism? Had Paul meant persons who never as yet had repented and experienced conversion, there would have been no occasion for him to identify them as men who have sinned heretofore, but rather merely as those who have not yet repented. Again, in 13:2, he distinguishes between those who "heretofore have sinned, and all others," a distinction which would be impossible were Paul referring to the habitual sinning which characterized them before the time of their conversion. Meyer comments: "But as the evils adduced in ver. 20 only set in *after* the conversion, we are not warranted . . . to assume for the sins named in ver. 21 the time *before* conversion, as, indeed, 1 Cor. v. 1 also points to the time *after* conversion. . . . [Paul's] *pro* [prefix of *proēmartēkotōn*] looks back into the past of the Corinthians that had elapsed since their conversion. . . ."[3]

[Paul] had no doubt learned from Titus that 'many' of the immoral persons were none the better for his warnings, and over these he fears that

---

[3]H. A. W. Meyer, *Critical and Exegetical Hand-Book to the Epistles to the Corinthians*, p. 695, italics his.

he will have to *mourn*. This cannot mean a mourning of mere pity and sorrow, as if these men were carried away by the infirmities of nature. The original term properly denotes mourning for the dead, and here signifies grief for those who will suffer the chastisement which he declares (xiii. 2) that he will inflict. As they belonged to the same class with the notable offender of I Cor. v., it may be inferred that he contemplates passing the same sentence of excommunication upon them that he did upon him, and so should have to sorrow over them as severed and, for a while at least, *dead* members of the visible Church.[4]

That some in the church at Corinth (in addition to the man guilty of incest) definitely had incurred spiritual death is evident, not only from Paul's sorrowful words in II Cor. 12:21, but also from his expression of gratification at the news through Titus of how they had profited by his stern rebuke and had been led to repent—unto salvation:

For though I made you sorry with a letter, I do not reget it, though I did [for a while] regret it. For I see that that letter grieved you, though but for a while. Now I rejoice, not because you were made sorrowful, but because you were made sorrowful toward God, so that in no way should you suffer injury by us. For the sorrow toward God works repentance unto salvation [and is] without regret; but the sorrow of the world works death. For behold this very thing—your being made sorrowful toward God—what earnest care it wrought in you, yea, what clearing of yourselves, what indignation, what fear, what longing, what zeal, what avenging! In every way you have proved yourselves to be pure in this matter (II Cor. 7:8-11).

Neither Paul nor the Corinthians had cause any longer to regret the sorrow occasioned by his stern letter of reproof; for it had accomplished his purpose and they had been led to repent, with the happy consequence of restoration in grace.

Paul's reference to their having been moved by his rebuke to such sorrow toward God that they were led to repentance

---

[4] Joseph Waite, *The Second Epistle to the Corinthians* (*The Bible Commentary*, ed. F. C. Cook), Vol. III, p. 474. We would reject any suggestion that excommunication imposed spiritual death. It was pronounced, not to impose spiritual death, but in recognition of the fact that spiritual death already had occurred, the evidence of which had become unmistakable.

unto salvation cannot be construed as a reference to their initial conversion. For that had occurred (for most of them, at least) during Paul's personal ministry among them, and obviously prior to the occasion of his letter of rebuke. The repentance to which he refers occurred as their response to a letter written after they had fallen into the perilous attitude of complacency toward sin which is so apparent in I Corinthians.[5] That complacency, apparently widespread among them, had made them apathetic toward a case of incest among them. For many of them, it ultimately had issued in spiritual death. Happily, however, in response to Paul's stern reproof, they had returned to repentance and grace (although, as Paul feared, possibly not all of them, II Cor. 12:21; 13:5).

Paul points out (7:12) that he had written his letter of reproof, not merely out of regard for the man who had been guilty of incest, nor for the man who had been wronged in that shameful instance, but in order that the whole church might be made aware of their care for Paul himself, especially with respect to his Apostolic authority, which some had challenged. (The text of v. 12 is disputed; ASV follows the reading favored by most scholars.) Regard for Paul and his authority as an Apostle would (and did) lead them to heed his rebuke and warning. But he had written, not as one who exercised "dominion over your faith," but as one who sought to be a "helper of

---

[5] We cannot know how many letters Paul wrote to the Corinthians. It is evident that there was at least one prior to what we call "I Corinthians" (Cf. I Cor. 5:9). He doubtless wrote numerous letters to them (cf. II Cor. 10:10). It seems evident that the letter to which he refers in II Cor. 7:8 is not the one we call "I Corinthians." I Corinthians ". . . as a whole . . . scarcely corresponds to the great agitation of mind described by the apostle as the accompaniment of the writing. And it is of the letter as a whole that Paul speaks (ii. 3, 4, vii. 8ff.): does it seem natural to believe that I Corinthians ('that letter,' vii. 8) 'vexed them,' or that of I Corinthians Paul had for a while 'repented' or felt inclined to repent? It seems more natural to believe in an intermediate letter, one of greater stringency, probably of greater brevity and concentration, directed exclusively to the point at issue; and such a belief has, in recent times, steadily grown." —J. Massie, *The New Century Bible: Corinthians* (ed. W. F. Adeney), p. 46.

your joy," that by faith they might continue to "stand" (1:24; cf. Rom. 11:20). Paul's dealings with the Corinthians illustrate the solemn obligations enjoined in the admonition of Hebrews 13:17, "Obey them that have the rule over you, and submit yourselves: for they watch for your souls as they that must give account; that they may do it with joy, and not with grief: for that is unprofitable for you." And certainly the experience of the Corinthians confirms the truth of our Lord's dictum, "No man can serve two masters." No man can submit to both the dominion of Christ and the dominion of sin; and surrender to the dominion of sin is fatal, spiritually.

In Romans 6:14, Paul writes, "For sin shall not have dominion over you: for you are not under the law, but under grace." Some consider Paul's statement to imply that it is impossible for sin to become the master of one who is under grace. They understand Paul to mean that, just as Christ, having died and risen again, has forever been freed from any possibility of becoming subject again to the dominion of death (v. 9), so the Christian who has entered by faith into the death of Christ for sin has been freed forever from the possibility of becoming subject again to the dominion of sin.

Their interpretation ignores two things. First, it ignores the nature of saving faith which, as we have considered earlier, is not the act of a single moment whereby all the benefits of Christ's life, death, and resurrection suddenly become the irrevocable possession of the individual, per se, despite any and all eventualities. It is, to the contrary, a present condition whereby the believer shares the eternal life of Him "who is our life" and who "is able to continue saving to the uttermost those who are ever drawing near to God through Him, seeing that He is ever living to intercede for them" (Heb. 7:25 Montgomery).

Again, their interpretation ignores the immediate context. Far from asserting the impossibility of our submitting to the dominion of sin, Paul insists that we shall remain free of sin's dominion only as we implement the deliverance which has been won for us by Christ: "Likewise reckon ye also yourselves to be dead indeed unto sin. . . . Let not sin therefore reign in your mortal body. . . . Neither yield ye your members as instruments of unrighteousness unto sin" (vv. 11-13). "Know ye not," he asks, "that to whom ye yield yourselves servants to obey, his servants ye are to whom ye obey, whether of sin unto death, or of obedience unto righteousness?" (v. 16).

There are two masters, and the believers at Rome must continue to choose between them. It is true that they previously had chosen to obey the Gospel and, in so choosing, they became no longer "the servants of sin," but were made free from sin and "became the servants of righteousness" (vv. 17, 18). But the choice was not irrevocable; the initial decision must continually be reaffirmed and implemented. "For, as ye have yielded your members servants to uncleanness and to iniquity unto iniquity, even so now yield your members servants to righteousness unto holiness" (v. 19). Paul reminds them that the end of those things which they had pursued when they were "the servants of sin, free from righteousness," is death (vv. 20, 21), whereas, "having been made free from sin and having become servants of God," the end of their present servitude is everlasting life (v. 22). Let them therefore continue as servants of righteousness and beware yielding themselves as servants of iniquity. For it is still true for the believers at Rome that "the wages of sin is death [cf. Jas. 1:12-16, Gal. 6:7-9], but the gift of God is eternal life through Jesus Christ our Lord" (v. 23)—a gift they can continue to share only as they continue to submit to His dominion, as opposed to the dominion of sin. (Rom. 6:23 is another verse which is a popular text for evangelistic sermons, and rightly so. But let us observe that the warning is addressed, not to outsiders who make no profession of faith in Christ, but to the Christians themselves.)

Let no one imagine that Paul is contending for salvation by works, rather than grace, in contradiction to many other passages which declare that salvation is by grace through faith. Not at all. Paul is only contending for the necessity of implementing the principle laid down by Jesus Himself: "Verily, verily, I say unto you, He that believeth on me, the works that I do shall he do also. . . . Greater love hath no man than this, that a man lay down his life for his friends. Ye are my friends—if ye do whatsoever I command you" (John 14:12; 15:13, 14). Like master, like disciple. We are again confronted with the point on which James is so insistent, a truth so aptly summarized by Melanchthon's dictum, "It is faith, alone, which saves; but the faith that saves is not alone." Not all "faith" is saving faith. "For as the body without the spirit is dead, so faith without works is dead also" (Jas. 2:26). Such "faith" cannot save.

Paul makes the same point in Galatians 5:6, "For in Jesus Christ neither circumcision availeth anything nor uncircumcision, but faith working by love." Lightfoot comments: "These words *di' agapēs energoumenē* bridge over the gulf which seems to separate the language of St. Paul and St. James. Both assert a principle of practical energy, as opposed to a barren, inactive theory."[6] Jesus is the Saviour, not of all who profess faith in Him, but "of all them that obey him" (Heb. 5:9). Only obedient faith is saving faith. Consider John 3:36: "He that believeth [*pisteuō*] on the Son hath everlasting life, but he that does not obey [*apeitheō*] the Son shall not see life, but the wrath of God abideth on him." The use of two different words in the Greek text (a fact not indicated in the Authorized Version) lends emphasis to obedience as an essential aspect of saving faith. There is no saving faith apart from obedience.

John insists, "He that saith, I know him, and keepeth not his commandments is a liar and the truth is not in him. But whoso keepeth his word, in him verily is the love of God perfected: hereby know we that we are in him. He that saith he abideth in him ought himself also so to walk even as he walked" (I John 2:4-6). "Ought?" Indeed! For unless he sincerely endeavors to "walk even as He walked," his profession of faith is vain pretense whereby he deceives—perhaps most of all—himself! (Consider the deadly possibility cited in I John 2:9-11, Jas.

---

[6]J. B. Lightfoot, *The Epistle of St. Paul to the Galatians*, p. 205.

1:22, 26.) It is vain for one to speak of his faith in Christ as Saviour who is not definitely committed to the lordship of Christ and positively opposing the dominion of sin in his personal life. (What revival would come to churches everywhere if all "Christians" should become aware of this solemn fact!)

Whether sin shall have dominion over us must remain, throughout our earthly pilgrimage, a matter of prayerful concern and continual decision. Liddon comments on Romans 6:14, "Sin will not become lord over you (*kurieusei*, not merely *basileusei*) unless you will it."[7] The necessity of continuing to choose whether we shall be servants "of sin unto death, or of obedience unto righteousness" and life is vividly set before us by Paul in Romans 8:12-14: "Brethren, we are debtors, not to the flesh, to live after the flesh. For if ye live after the flesh, ye shall die: but if ye through the Spirit do mortify the deeds of the body, ye shall live. For as many as are led by the Spirit of God, they are sons of God." The consequence of choosing the wrong master and living after the flesh is spiritual death. Again, let us observe that the warning is directed, not to outsiders, but to believers. Godet comments:

The life of the Spirit is not realized in the believer without his concurrence merely from the fact that the Spirit has once been communicated to him. There is needed on man's part a persevering decision, an active docility in giving himself over to the guidance of the Spirit. For the guidance of the Spirit tends constantly to the sacrifice of the flesh; and if the believer refuses to follow it on this path, he renounces the life of the Spirit and its glorious privileges.[8]

Even as Paul warned the Galatians (6:7-9), we, too, must choose whether we shall continue to sow to the Spirit and reap life everlasting, or grow weary and faint in our task of sowing to the Spirit and, sowing to the flesh, reap destruction. If we are wise, we shall heed Paul's exhortation, "Let us not be weary in well doing [sowing to the Spirit], for in due season we shall

---

[7]H. P. Liddon, *Explanatory Analysis of St. Paul's Epistle to the Romans*, p. 113.

[8]F. L. Godet, *Commentary on the Epistle to the Romans*, p. 307.

reap [life everlasting—salvation final and irrevocable] **if we faint not**" (v. 9).

The writer to the Hebrews bids his readers "exhort one another, while it is called Today, lest any of you be hardened through the deceitfulness of sin" (3:13). David feared the peril of tolerating sin. Consider his prayer in Psalm 19: "Who can understand his errors? Cleanse thou me from secret faults. Keep back thy servant also from presumptuous sins; let them not have dominion over me: then shall I be upright, and I shall be innocent from the great transgression" (vv. 12, 13). Delitzsch comments:

. . . [David] prays for forgiveness in respect of the many sins of infirmity—though for the most part unperceived by him—to which even the pardoned one succumbs. . . . No one can discern his faults, on account of the heart of man being unfathomable and on account of the disguise, oftentimes so plausible, and the subtlety of sin. Hence, as an inference, follows the prayer: pronounce me free also [of] all those sins which even he who is most earnestly striving after sanctification does not discern, although he may desire to know them, by reason of the ever limited nature of his knowledge both of himself and of sin. . . . The prayer for justification is followed in ver. 13 by the prayer for sanctification, and indeed for preservation against deliberate sins. . . . Presumptuous sins, when they are repeated, become dominant sins which irresistibly enslave the man . . . hence the last member of the climax (which advances from the *peccatum involuntarium* to the *prœreticum,* and from this to the *regnans*): let them not have dominion over me. . . . Then, when Thou bestowest this twofold favour upon me, the favour of pardon and the grace of preservation, shall I be blameless . . . from great transgression.[9]

According to Delitzsch, the Hebrew word rendered *great transgression* means "to spread out, go beyond the bounds, break through, trespass," and is "a collective name for deliberate and reigning, dominant sin, which breaks through man's relation of favour with God, and consequently casts him out of favour,—in one word, for apostasy."[10]

---

[9]Franz Delitzsch, *Biblical Commentary on the Psalms,* Vol. I, p. 288 f.
[10]*Ibid.,* p. 289.

As the climax of prolonged striving against the reproof of the Spirit, it is possible that one might consciously and deliberately discard the yoke of Christ through a signal act of rebellion, to end the conflict. But it is much more likely that final obstinance should be arrived at imperceptibly and that the Spirit should quietly abandon His striving without the man's being aware of His departure. Samson "knew not that the Lord was departed from him" (Judges 16:20). John cites the tragic circumstance of the man who "says he is in the light," but "walks in darkness and knows not where he is going, because darkness has blinded his eyes" (I John 2:9-11). On his way to hell, he still imagines himself to be on the way to heaven. He still professes faith, and all seems well to him. He is quite unaware of his apostasy.

Spiritual hardening through the deceitfulness of sin (Heb. 3:12, 13) is hardly likely to come about as an immediate cataclysm. There is little likelihood that a believer suddenly should recoil from true devotion and trust and, shaking his fist in the face of Christ, exclaim, "Depart from me! I no longer wish you to be my Saviour and Lord!" The real peril is that the believer may gradually become increasingly tolerant of sin until he begins to excuse himself for his sins, no longer confessing and seeking forgiveness and cleansing, and ignoring the patient rebukes of the Holy Spirit. If he continues to quench Him and to refuse His faithful reproof, his prolonged obstinance ultimately becomes "despite unto the Spirit of grace" (Heb. 10:29). The words "hath trodden under foot the Son of God" seem descriptive of a catastrophic act of deliberate repudiation. But context indicates that it is the aggregate effect of an extended pattern of willful sinning. The present active participle *hamartanontōn* (v. 26) indicates persistent sinning rather than a single act. The warning in Hebrews 10:26 ff. is not against an isolated act of rebellion, but against habitual deliberate sinning which ultimately constitutes a repudiation of the Saviour, shameful indifference toward the holy blood of the covenant, and a spurning of the Holy Spirit's gracious ministry of guidance and reproof.

Context indicates that "forsaking the assembling of ourselves together," while not necessarily an indication of actual apostasy as yet, at least is a symptom of perilous drifting and an invitation to spiritual disaster. The Christian who prefers to absent himself from the worship services of his church obviously has little interest in the kingdom of Christ and feels no need for spiritual encouragement. He is in process of surrendering "the good fight of faith." Final surrender occurs imperceptibly. The person still imagines himself to be a Christian; but he only deceives himself—a subtle peril against which the Bible warns frequently and urgently. Millions of "Christians," satisfied with their "Christian experience" (all in the past) and complacent in their indifference toward Christ and His Church, are in desperate need of examining themselves to see whether they are in the faith (II Cor. 13:5). The love of the world is the path of compromise. It ends in disaster.

Kierkegaard, the great theologian, told the "Parable of the Wild Duck" which flew in the springtime northward across Europe. On his flight he happened to come down in a barnyard in Denmark where there were some tame ducks. The wild duck ate and enjoyed some of their corn and remained for a while. At first he decided to stay only one hour, then for one day. Then he remained a week, and then a month; and because he liked the good food and the safety of the barnyard he stayed all summer.

One autumn day when his wild mates were winging their way southward again, they passed over the barnyard where he was. He heard their cries and was so stirred by the old thrill of joy and delight that he flapped his wings and rose to join his mates in their flight. But he had become so soft and so heavy that he could not rise above the top of the barn. He sank back again to the barnyard and consoled himself with the thought, "Oh well, my life is safe here, and the food is good."

Every spring and every autumn when the wild ducks flew over his barnyard, he heard their cries. His eyes would gleam for a moment, and he would begin to lift his wings to join his mates. But the day came

when the wild ducks flew over him and uttered their cries and he paid
not the slightest attention. The compromise was complete.[11]

Friend in Christ, we shall be foolish indeed if we assume that
the warnings in God's Holy Word against the peril of apostasy
do not apply to us and that we need not concern ourselves with
the possibility of ultimate submission to the dominion of sin.
To the contrary, "holy brethren, partakers of the heavenly calling," let us beware the peril of becoming tolerant of the sins
which nailed Jesus to His cross, lest we "be hardened through
the deceitfulness of sin," and lest, at last, "there be in any of
[us] an evil heart of unbelief, in departing from the living God"
(Heb. 3:1, 13, 12). Let us steel our hearts against the siren
song of Vanity Fair, lest the voice of our Saviour and the call
of His Spirit be lost to our hearing.

> If I gained the world, but lost the Saviour,
>   Were my life worth living for a day?
> Could my yearning heart find rest and comfort
>   In the things that soon must pass away?
>
> If I gained the world, but lost the Saviour,
>   Would my gain be worth the lifelong strife?
> Are all earthly pleasures worth comparing
>   For a moment with a Christ-filled life?
>
> Had I wealth and love in fullest measure,
>   And a name revered both far and near,
> Yet no hope beyond, no harbor waiting,
>   Where my storm-tossed vessel I could steer;
>
> If I gained the world, but lost the Saviour,
>   Who endured the cross and died for me,
> Could then all the world afford a refuge
>   Whither, in my anguish, I might flee?
>
> O what emptiness!—without the Saviour
>   'Mid the sins and sorrows here below!
> And eternity, how dark without Him!—
>   Only night and tears and endless woe!

----
[11]*The Intermediate Leader,* Volume 40, Number 2 (Second Quarter, 1957),
p. 41. Published by the Sunday School Board of the Southern Baptist Convention, Nashville 3, Tennessee. Used by permission.

What, though I might live without the Saviour,
  When I come to die, how would it be?
O to face the valley's gloom without Him!
  And without Him all eternity!

ANNA ÖLANDER

"More Than Conquerors"

Who shall separate us from the love of Christ? shall tribulation, or distress, or persecution, or famine, or nakedness, or peril, or sword? . . . Nay, in all these things we are more than conquerors through him that loved us. For I am persuaded that neither death, nor life, nor angels, nor principalities, nor powers, nor things present, nor things to come, nor height, nor depth, nor any other created thing shall be able to separate us from the love of God which is in Christ Jesus our Lord.

ROMANS 8:35, 37-39

Chapter XIV

MORE THAN CONQUERORS

"Am I a soldier of the cross, a follower of the Lamb?" asks Isaac Watts in his inspiring hymn. No one is a follower of the Lamb who is not a soldier of the cross. "My son, be strong in the grace which is in Christ Jesus," wrote the veteran warrior Paul to young Timothy. "Endure hardship as a good soldier of Jesus Christ. . . . Fight the good fight of faith, get a grip[1] on eternal life."

Paul wrote, not as an "armchair general" (there are none among the soldiers of Jesus Christ), but as one who had fought the good fight on the field of bloody battle and now awaited the victor's crown. The conflict had been long and arduous, the battles fierce. But from the outset, victory had been certain— in Christ. Earlier, in his letter to the Romans, Paul had surveyed the host of all possible adversaries—physical and spiritual, present and future. In the face of them all, he had exclaimed triumphantly, "In all these things, we are more than conquerors through him who loved us!"

What comfort and encouragement in the day of battle! Consider the force of Paul's argument (Rom. 8:31 ff.): God is for us; who then can prevail against us? God justifies; who can condemn? Christ died, rose, and intercedes for us; who can separate us from His love? "I am persuaded," writes Paul, "that neither death nor life, nor angels nor principalities nor powers, nor things present nor things to come, nor height nor depth nor

---

[1]A. T. Robertson, *Word Pictures in the New Testament*, Vol. IV, p. 594.

any other created thing shall be able to separate us from the love of God which is in Christ our Lord" (vv. 38, 39). No power in all the universe can separate from Christ one who is trusting in Him.

But we must be careful to distinguish between all the foes which Paul enumerates (every possible foe) and the believer himself. There is no possibility that some power or circumstance may snatch from Christ's hand even the weakest one who trusts in Him. There is perfect safety and security in the Saviour and in the Father for the weakest sheep who follows the Good Shepherd and listens to His voice (John 10:27-29). The sole peril is that we may fail to listen to His voice and to follow Him. We may fail to abide in Him (John 15:4-6) and thus fail to continue to share His life and victory. Commenting on Romans 8:31-39, Liddon writes:

This passage does not afford countenance to that theory of the Final Perseverance of the Saints which makes their salvation independent of responsibility and free-will. That forfeiture of Grace which God the Father and our Lord never will, and which no external power or circumstance ever can effect, may be brought about by the free-will of the Christian himself.[2]

Similar is the comment of Godet:

It is a fact of the moral life which is in question, and in this life liberty has always its part to play . . . from the first moment of faith. What Paul means is that nothing will tear us from the arms of Christ against our will, and so long as we shall not refuse to abide in them ourselves.[3]

We have before alluded to Hengstenberg's remark on John 10:28, 29:

It is a cold consolation to say, "If and so long as they remain my sheep they are secure and shall never perish." The whole strength of our soul's

---

[2]H. P. Liddon, *Explanatory Analysis of St. Paul's Epistle to the Romans*, p. 146.

[3]F. L. Godet, *Commentary on the Epistle to the Romans*, p. 333.

desire is for a guarantee against ourselves! That there is such a guarantee
is [here] assured. . . .'

As has been pointed out, it is evident that Hengstenberg overlooked the condition laid down by the Saviour in verse 27—the
necessity of listening to His voice and following Him. Hengstenberg's demand for "a guarantee against ourselves" cannot be
granted, by reason of the nature of man as God created him:
a moral agent with the privilege and power (and responsibility)
of spiritual initiative and decision—not merely once, but continually throughout his earthly sojourn. So far from offering
them "a guarantee against themselves," Jesus admonished His
disciples, "In your patience [hupomonē, steadfastness, constancy, endurance] possess [ktaomai, gain, acquire] ye your
souls" (Luke 21:19). He counsels all who would be His, "Remain in me, and I in you" (John 15:4).

Westcott has well said: "If man falls at any stage in his spiritual life, it is not from want of divine grace, nor from the
overwhelming power of adversaries, but from his neglect to
use that which he may or may not use. We cannot be protected
against ourselves in spite of ourselves."[5]

Unfortunately, the familiar rendering in Romans 8:37, "we
are more than conquerors," has tended to obscure the force
of Paul's statement. A more precise rendering of the present
active indicative verb hupernikōmen is "we more than conquer," or "we win total victory," or "we triumphantly overcome." The familiar rendering, "we are more than conquerors
through him who loved us," conveys a strong suggestion that
we are somehow merely passive, rather than active, in the conquest. It suggests that, the moment we receive Christ as Saviour, we are suddenly made conquerors for all time to come,
without further ado and regardless of any and all eventualities.
It strongly suggests that the conflict is immediately resolved in
glorious victory for all time to come, and the conqueror's gar-

---

'E. W. Hengstenberg, *Commentary on the Gospel of St. John*, Vol. I, p. 532.
[5]B. F. Westcott, *The Gospel According to St. John*, p. 158.

land is placed upon our brows as we recline in ease and splendor. Not so. Our conflict but begins the moment we accept Jesus Christ as Saviour and Lord. It is unfortunate that what Paul sounded as a battle cry has been regarded by many as a lullaby.

Williams' excellent rendering conveys the full force of Paul's words: "In all these things we keep on gloriously conquering through Him who loved us." We are to be active, rather than passive, in the conflict. No one ever became a conqueror without conquering. Jesus summons all who would be His to be soldiers; whether we prove to be *conquerors* depends on whether we remain "strong in the grace which is in Christ Jesus" and "endure hardship as good soldiers of Jesus Christ." We cannot be excused from "fighting the good fight of faith." With Timothy, we, too, are under the necessity of "getting a grip on eternal life."

Some may object that this makes man virtually his own savior. The objection is unwarranted. The necessity of the believer's "fighting the good fight of faith" and conquering through Christ is to be understood in exactly the same sense as the many admonitions in the Scriptures in which human responsibility in individual salvation is in view. Man must appropriate what God has provided and graciously offers to men through Christ. The conflict in which we are called to engage, "the good fight of faith," is real. The issues are life and death. Maclaren has well said that our freedom in Christ brings with it

. . . the necessity for continual warfare against all that would limit and restrain it—namely, the passions and desires and inclinations of our baser or nobler, but godless, self. These are, as it were, deposed by the entrance of the new life. But it is a dangerous thing to keep dethroned and discrowned tyrants alive, and the best thing is to behead them, as well as to cast them from their throne. 'If ye, through the Spirit, do put to death the deeds (and inclinations and wills) of the flesh, ye shall live'; and if you do not, they will live and will kill you. So the freedom of the new life is a militant freedom, and we have to fight to maintain it. As Burke said about the political realm, 'the price of liberty is eternal vigilance,' so we say about the new life of the Christian man—he is free only on condition that he keeps well under the hatches the old tyrants, who are ever plotting and struggling to have dominion once again.[6]

The eighth chapter of Romans, as someone has said, "begins with no condemnation and ends with no separation." It is well to observe, however, that it is punctuated with sharp warnings that "if ye live after the flesh ye shall die, but if ye through the Spirit do mortify the deeds of the body, ye shall live" (v. 13); that only such as are led by the Spirit of God are truly sons of God (v. 14); that only if we suffer with Christ shall we be glorified together with Him (v. 17); and that, despite our infirmities but aided by the Spirit, we must continue to wait in patience and hope (vv. 24-27) for the ultimate realization of salvation and the full manifestation of our divine sonship (vv. 16-23), "the glory which shall be revealed to us . . . *if* so be that we suffer with Him" (cf. II Tim. 2:12).

We have strong encouragement in the hour of trial. We have the assurance that "all things go on working together for the good of those who keep on loving God" (v. 28 Williams). We have the assurance that an eternal purpose of God is at work to issue in the ultimate glorification (full conformity to the image of His Son) of all who keep on loving Him (vv. 29, 30). We have the encouragement of Paul's argument (vv. 31-39) that, since God is for us and Christ intercedes for us, no external power or circumstance can separate us from the love of God in Christ. But certainly these precious assurances are intended, not to mitigate the sharp warnings of the earlier part of the chapter, but to encourage us to "keep on gloriously conquering through Him who loved us" (v. 37 Williams).

Paul writes: ". . . stand fast in one spirit, with one mind striving together for the faith of the gospel. . . . For unto you it is given in the behalf of Christ, not only to believe on him, but also to suffer for his sake, having the same conflict which ye saw in me and now hear to be in me" (Phil. 1:27, 29, 30). Peter writes of "the trial of your faith" (I Pet. 1:7) and admonishes

---

[6]Alexander Maclaren, *Expositions of Holy Scripture: St. John,* Vol. I, p. 157f.

us to "think it not strange concerning the fiery trial which is to try you, as though some strange thing happened unto you: but rejoice inasmuch as ye are partakers of Christ's sufferings, that, when his glory shall be revealed, ye may be glad also with exceeding joy" (4:12, 13). Paul urges Timothy to "put them in remembrance" that only if we suffer (*hupomenō*, endure, persevere) with Christ shall we reign with Him, and that if we deny Him, He also will deny us (II Tim. 2:12). Our unfaithfulness cannot impair His faithfulness nor cause Him to deny Himself in any way (v. 13); but our unfaithfulness and denial of Him assuredly will cause Him to deny us (v. 12). "The good fight of faith" is a conflict real and grave, and the issues are fraught with everlasting glory and joy, or shame and despair.

A popular doctrine which seems to have much to commend it has served to obscure the desperate gravity of the conflict and the fateful consequences of the outcome. It is the assertion that the believer has two natures, one of which is carnal and can do nothing but sin, and the other of which is spiritual and cannot possibly sin. It is assumed that, when a Christian sins, it is only a manifestation of his old carnal nature; but his new spiritual nature is not involved. (This erroneous doctrine provides a convenient means of solving many problems of interpretation, e.g., reconciling I John 1:8 and 3:9. But the "solutions" it affords are incorrect because they rest on a false premise.)

The doctrine of "the two natures of the believer" is an erroneous assumption. It is true that the believer has a carnal nature, and certainly it causes him to sin—to his sorrow. (Neither the Bible nor experience substantiates the claims of the advocates of the doctrine of eradication and sinless perfection. Their false doctrine is a subtle snare of Satan leading the unwary away from a sense of present need for the saving grace of Christ and His intercession before God. Denying the fact of their sin, they become devoid of the truth and His Word (I John 1:8-10) and, in their smug self-righteousness, they are left without the Saviour.) But, contrary to the assumptions of some, the believer does not possess two natures. While he does have a carnal nature, he does *not* possess a new spiritual nature, per se. Rather, he is only a "partaker of the divine nature" (II Pet. 1:4) who "partakes of His holiness" (Heb. 12:10) through submission and faith in Jesus Christ. Kuyper rightly observes:

What Peter calls "to become partaker of the divine nature" is called in another place, to become *the children of God*. But altho Christ is the *Son* of God and we are called the *children* of God, this does not make the Sonship of Christ and our sonship to stand on the same plane and to be of the same nature. We are but the *adopted* children, altho we have another descent, while He is the *actual* and eternal Son. While He is essentially the eternal Son, partaker of the divine nature which in the unity of His Person He unites with the human nature, we are merely *restored* to the likeness of the divine nature which we had lost by sin. Hence as *"to be adopted as a child"* and *"to be the Son forever"* are contrasts, so are also the following: *"to have the divine nature in Himself"* and *"to be only partakers of the divine nature."*

. . . .

. . . accepting [God's] great and precious promises, believers become partakers of the divine nature, altho in themselves wholly devoid of that nature. Partaker does not denote what one possesses in himself, as his own, but a partial communication of what does not belong to him, but to another.

Despite the assumptions of many, the Christian does not have two natures. To the contrary, he is a single spiritual entity who can act only as an integer. Whatever the Christian does at any moment, he does—not as "Dr. Jekyl" or as "Mr. Hyde," but as *the whole man*. The whole of his person is involved in whatever he does "after the Spirit," and in whatever he does "after the flesh." As a spiritual integer, he is continually confronted with the necessity of choosing whether to walk after the flesh, or after the Spirit; whether to sow to the flesh, the ultimate outcome of which is to reap destruction, or to sow to the Spirit, the consequence of which is to reap life everlasting. Whichever he does he can do only as *the whole man*.

---

[7]Abraham Kuyper, *The Work of the Holy Spirit*, p. 333 f., italics his.

No man can walk two directions at once. No man can go hopping along on one foot "after the Spirit" toward life and at the same time hop along on the other foot "after the flesh" toward destruction. He can walk but one direction. If he walks after the Spirit, however imperfectly, he is a Christian. His steps may be halting. He may stub his toe now and then, and occasionally he may even turn his ankle and limp rather badly. But still, as he walks after the Spirit, he walks but one direction. God is patient and understanding. He is not looking for perfection in men. But He is profoundly concerned about their *direction*. To those whose direction is toward Him through obedient faith in Jesus Christ, He imparts the perfection of His sinless Son and shares with them His own divine nature. But this He can do only for men whose direction is toward Him. And men can walk but one direction at a time. Whether a man walks "after the Spirit," or "after the flesh," he walks with both feet as the whole man.

The popular concept of "the strife of the two natures of the believer" may seem to be substantiated by Paul's account of the conflict which he experienced within himself, as recorded in Romans 7:7-25. But the passage, which is historical and autobiographical, depicts the conflict between conscience and conduct, between aspirations and inclinations, which Paul experienced while still under the Law. (The "therefore" of 8:1 reverts to 7:6, and 7:7-25 is parenthetic.) The dismal conclusion which Paul reached in the conflict within himself under Law is stated (following a parenthetic exclamation in vv. 24, 25a) in verse 25b: "So then with the mind I myself serve the law of God; but with the flesh the law of sin." But now that he has found deliverance through Jesus Christ our Lord and by faith has come to be "in Christ Jesus" (8:1), no longer can he resign himself to such a miserable conclusion. Far from accepting such a conclusion, Paul insists that we who are in Christ Jesus must "walk, not after the flesh, but after the Spirit" (v. 4). For the man who is "in Christ Jesus," such a course is mandatory. But it is not inevitable, even though he is "not in the flesh but in the Spirit" through His indwelling presence (v. 9). The Christian must continue to choose whether to be "carnally minded," which tends toward death, or to be "spiritually minded," which tends toward life and peace (v. 6). Paul sharply admonishes his brethren who are in the Spirit to remember that "we are debtors, not to the flesh, to live after the flesh" (v. 12). We must recognize that two courses are open to us, and we can follow but one. We must weigh carefully the consequences of following either course. If we live after the flesh, we shall die; if we live after the Spirit, we shall live (v. 13). Only men who consent to be led of the Spirit can be sons of God (v. 14), and only such as consent to suffer with Christ will ultimately be glorified together with Him (v. 17).

Another passage which may seem to lend support to the erroneous concept of "the strife of the two natures of the believer" is Galatians 5:17, "For the flesh lusteth against the Spirit, and the Spirit against the flesh: and these are contrary the one to the other: so that ye cannot do the things ye would." But let us observe that "the works of the flesh" (vv. 19-21) are not deeds somehow done by "the flesh" as an entity separate and distinct from the person himself; they are deeds done by the *whole person* in response to the inclinations of the only nature which is his own—"the flesh." Paul warns sharply, *"They* [the *whole persons*] who do such things shall not inherit the kingdom of God" (v. 21).

"The strife of the two natures of the believer" is a mistaken concept and quite misleading. It suggests that the believer himself is only a bystander observing the struggle—an interested spectator, but not actually a participant. But such is not the case. The spiritual conflict within the believer is, in reality, nothing less than his own personal striving against the Spirit. It is the struggle to determine whether the whole of his person shall surrender to the inclinations of his own carnal nature, or to the demands of the divine nature of which he partakes by faith. It is the conflict to determine whether he shall continue under the dominion of Christ, or return to the dominion of sin.

It is so easy for us to excuse ourselves for our defeats and to pass the blame. In Eden, Adam protested, "The woman—!" and Eve, "The serpent—!" A young man, overtaken in a flagrant sin, shrugged his shoulders and excused his wickedness with the defense, "The devil got me down." Perhaps so. But it is well to remember that the devil cannot compel us to act contrary to our own will and consent. He has no power beyond that of influence, and we have the promise that he must flee when we resist him, submitting ourselves to God (Jas. 4:7).

In our wrestling with "the rulers, authorities, and cosmic powers of this dark world . . . the spirit-forces of evil challenging us in the heavenly contest" (Eph. 6:12 Williams), the field of battle is within ourselves. It is there that the conflict is won or lost—a conflict in which every believer must continue to engage throughout his earthly pilgrimage if he is to reign with Christ (II Tim. 2:12). In His messages to the churches (Rev. 2 and 3), our risen Lord offers to all His followers, in their day of conflict, blessed incentives and encouragements to "keep on gloriously conquering through Him who loved us":

To him that overcometh will I give to eat of the tree of life, which is in the midst of the paradise of God. . . . Be thou faithful unto death, and I will give thee the crown of life. . . He that overcometh shall not be hurt of the second death. . . . To him that overcometh will I give to eat of the hidden manna, and will give him a white stone,[8] and in the stone a new name written, which no man knoweth saving he that receiveth it. . . . That which ye have already hold fast till I come. He that overcometh and keepeth my works unto the end, to him will I give power over the nations: and he shall rule them with a rod of iron; as the vessels of a potter shall they be broken to shivers, even as I received of my Father (cf. Psalm 2:7-9). And I will give him the morning star. . . . Thou hast a few names even in Sardis which have not defiled their garments; and

---

[8]"Used in courts of justice, black pebbles for condemning, white pebbles for acquitting." —A. T. Robertson, *Word Pictures in the New Testament*, Vol. VI, p. 307.

they shall walk with me in white: for they are worthy. He that overcometh, the same shall be clothed in white raiment; and I will not blot
out his name out of the book of life, but I will confess his name before
my Father, and before his angels. . . . Him that overcometh will I make
a pillar in the temple of my God, and he shall go no more out: and I
will write upon him the name of my God, and the name of the city of
my God, which is new Jerusalem, which cometh down out of heaven
from my God: and I will write upon him my new name. . . . To him
that overcometh will I grant to sit with me in my throne, even as I also
overcame, and am set down with my Father in his throne.

What blessed incentives to overcome are these precious
promises of our Saviour. But the enemy is strong and the conflict
is fierce. How can we overcome? The secret of victory is given
in Revelation 12:11, "And they overcame him [Satan, the ac-
cuser of the brethren, v. 10] by the blood of the Lamb,[9] and
by the word of their testimony;[10] and they loved not their lives
unto the death" (cf. 2:10; John 12:25).

In Christ there is victory for every man who will grasp it.
We may "keep on gloriously conquering" every conceivable foe
"through him who loved us." "Who is he that overcometh the
world, but he that believeth that Jesus is the Son of God?"
(I John 5:5). John did not refer to a mere intellectual assent
to the fact of the deity of Jesus. At the time John wrote 4:15,
5:1, and 5:5, it *meant* something to believe and confess Jesus as
the Christ and the Son of God. Such testimony could cost a
man his freedom. It could mean banishment to the lonely isle
of Patmos (Rev. 1:9). Such testimony could mean crucifixion,
or burning at the stake. It was no small matter openly to confess
Jesus as Son of God and Lord and Saviour. But "faith" without
open confession was the same delusion then as now. Then,

---

[9]"The blood of Christ is here presented by *dia* as the ground for the victory,
and not the means, as by *en* in 1:5, 5:9. Both ideas are true, but *dia* with
the accusative gives only the reason. Christ conquered Satan, and so makes our
victory possible (Luke 11:21 f.; Heb. 2:18)."—Robertson, *Word Pictures in
the New Testament*, Vol. VI, p. 394.

[10]"The same use of *dia*, 'because of their testimony to Jesus,' as in John's
own case in 1:9."—*Ibid.*

as now, the prospects were poor indeed for all "secret believers" in Him who said, "Whosoever shall confess me before men, him will I also confess before my Father which is in heaven" (Matt. 10:32 f.). And a profession of faith with the lips, but not with the life, has ever been a vain thing (cf. Luke 6:46, John 14:12, 21-23; 15:10-14, Titus 1:16, I John 2:4).

In orthodox evangelical circles today, the popular conception of the nature of saving faith is tragically inadequate. "By grace, through faith, plus nothing" has become the watchword. This is well and good, except for the fact that saving faith can never be "plus nothing." For saving faith cannot exist apart from repentance. And repentance is concerned, not only with the past, but even more with the present and the future. It involves not only sorrow for the sins of the past, but the submission of the soul and life to the lordship of Christ for the present and the future. There is a sense in which we must believe in Christ, not only "with all our heart," but with all our life as well. We must believe with head, heart, and hand. To be hearers of the Word, but not doers, is to deceive ourselves (Jas. 1:22). Faith without works is as dead and worthless as the body without the spirit (Jas. 2:14-26). "Faith" in Christ which leaves the "believer" free of any real allegiance and devotion to Him is sheer presumption. A "plus-nothing" faith avails nothing. Only obedient faith is saving faith—living, conquering faith that "overcomes the world."

The spirit of submission and obedience, as an essential aspect of saving faith, is vividly in view in Hebrews 5:7-9 (Williams): "For [Jesus] during His human life offered up prayers and entreaties, crying aloud with tears to Him who was always able to save Him out of death, and because of His [godly fear] His prayer was heard. Although He was a Son, He learned from what He suffered how to obey, and because He was perfectly qualified for it He became the author of endless salvation for all who obey Him."[11] Williams' comment in his footnote on 5:9

---

[11]As a matter of preference, I have departed from Williams' rendering of *eulabeia* in v. 7, substituting *godly fear* for *beautiful spirit of worship*.

is excellent: "The whole process of deliverance from sin to maturity in heaven, so conditioned on obedience; not in conflict with Paul's teaching, saved by faith." Not, indeed! It serves only to qualify the *kind* of faith which saves. Translators have done well who have rendered John 3:36 somewhat as follows, "He who believes in the Son has eternal life; but he who does not obey [*apeitheō*, rather than merely *apisteō*] the Son shall not see life." To believe in Christ as Saviour requires that one obey Him as Lord. Only obedient faith is saving faith, and the faith by which "we keep on gloriously conquering through Him who loved us."

Solemn indeed are two essential truths which our Lord declared in His discourse on the Vine and the Branches (John 15). First, we can bear fruit only as we remain in Him: "Remain in me, and I in you. As the branch cannot bear fruit of itself, except it remain in the vine, no more can ye, except ye remain in me" (v. 4). Profoundly awesome is the second truth: we can remain in Christ only as we bear fruit: "I am the vine, ye are the branches: he that remains in me, and I in him, the same brings forth much fruit. . . . Every branch in me that beareth not fruit [my Father] taketh away. . . . Remain in me, and I in you" (vv. 5, 2, 4a).

"Teach them to observe all things whatsoever I have commanded you," said Jesus. Keeping His commandments is not optional for men who would enter into life. It is an essential aspect of saving faith. (Cf. Luke 6:46-49, John 3:36 RSV; 14:21, 23; 15:8-10, 13, 14, Jas. 1:22, II Pet. 1:8-11, I John 2:3-5; 3:24a, Jude 12.) There is no saving faith apart from obedience. The obedience of even the most godly Christian will be imperfect; but though imperfect, it must nevertheless be real. Let us repeat: only obedient faith is saving faith, and the faith by which "we keep on gloriously conquering through Him who loved us."

The power for spiritual conquest is not of ourselves. Commenting on Romans 8:37, Godet writes:

And in what strength [are we to conquer]? The apostle, instead of saying: through the love of the Lord, expresses himself thus: *through the Lord that loved us.* It is His living person that acts in us. For it is He, Himself, in His love who sustains us. This love is not a simple thought of our mind; it is a force emanating from Him.[12]

"Without me," said Jesus, "ye can do nothing" (John 15:5). But "I can do all things," wrote Paul, "through Christ who strengthens [empowers] me" (Phil. 4:13). "Christ liveth in me," he wrote, "and the life which I now live in the flesh I live by faith in the Son of God[13] who loved me and gave himself for me" (Gal. 2:20). The power for conquest is freely available to all who trust in the Saviour.

. . .this dying Lover of our souls communicates to us all, if we will, the strength whereby we may coerce all outward things into being helps to the fuller participation of His perfect love. Our sorrows and all the other distracting externals do seek to drag us away from Him. Is all that happens in counteraction to that pull of the world, that we tighten our grasp upon Him, and will not let Him go; as some poor wretch might the horns of the altar that did not respond to his grasp? Nay! what we lay hold of is no dead thing, but a living hand, and it grasps us more tightly than we can ever grasp it. So because He holds us, and not because we hold Him, we shall not be dragged away by anything outside of our own weak and wavering souls; and all these embattled foes may come against us, they may shear off everything else, they cannot sever Christ from us unless we ourselves throw Him away. 'In this thou shalt conquer.' 'They overcame by the blood of the Lamb, and by the word of His testimony.'[14]

> He that overcometh in the fight
> Shall be clothed in raiment white and pure;
> In the ever-blessed book of life
> Shall his name eternally endure.

---

[12]Godet, *op. cit.,* p. 333.

[13]Not "by the faith of the Son of God," as incorrectly rendered in AV. "*Which is in the Son of God (tēi tou huiou tou theou).* The objective genitive, not the faith of the Son of God." —Robertson, *Word Pictures in the New Testament,* Vol. IV, p. 290.

[14]Alexander Maclaren, *Expositions of Holy Scripture: Romans,* p. 208.

When my Father on His dazzling throne
Sits, with myriad angels all around,
I'll confess His name, to men unknown;
Heaven and earth shall listen to the sound.

Who, with such a glorious end in view,
Would not in the heavenly conflict join?
Strange that willing soldiers are so few,
Strange so many faint, who once were Thine.

Oh, it is a service blest indeed!
Though the strife be long, the end is sure;
And our Leader gives to all who need,
Grace that they may to the end endure.

'Neath Thy standard be my place, O Lord:
Grant me strength and grace, that I ere long
May obtain that rich and full reward.
Then, as conquering I sheath my sword,
Thou, my Captain, shall be all my song.

                    FRANCES RIDLEY HAVERGAL

"The Race Set Before Us"

And we desire that every one of you do show the same diligence to the full assurance of hope unto the end: that ye be not slothful, but followers of them who through faith and patience inherit the promises.

* * *

Cast not away therefore your confidence, which hath great recompence of reward. For ye have need of patience, that, after ye have done the will of God, ye might receive the promise. For yet a little while, and he that shall come will come, and will not tarry. Now the just shall live by faith: but if he draw back, my soul shall have no pleasure in him.

* * *

For by faith the elders obtained a good report. . . . These all died in faith, not having received the promises, but having seen them afar off, and were persuaded of them, and embraced them and confessed that they were strangers and pilgrims on the earth. For they that say such things declare plainly that they seek a country. . . . And these all, having obtained a good report by faith, received not the promise: God having provided some better thing for us, that they without us should not be made perfect.

Wherefore seeing we also are compassed about with so great a cloud of witnesses, let us lay aside every weight, and sin which doth so easily beset us, and let us run with patience the race that is set before us, looking unto Jesus the author and finisher of faith; who for the joy that was set before him endured the cross, despising the shame, and is set down at the right hand of the throne of God.

* * *

Let us keep on going forth therefore unto him outside the camp, bearing his reproach. For here we have no enduring city, but we seek one to come.

From the Epistle to the Hebrews

CHAPTER XV

THE RACE SET BEFORE US

WHO WROTE THE Epistle to the Hebrews? When? Where? What was the original title? To whom was it sent? How did it become the common property of the Church? Many questions surround the "Epistle to the Hebrews"—questions which must remain unanswered until the time when we shall no longer know in part.

Nevertheless, reverent scholars through the centuries have agreed that the epistle bears its own seal of divine inspiration and authenticity. "And if we hold that the judgment of the Spirit makes itself felt through the consciousness of the Christian Society, no Book of the Bible is more completely recognized by universal consent as giving a divine view of the facts of the Gospel, full of lessons for all time, than the Epistle to the Hebrews."[1] No epistle speaks with greater earnestness to the hearts of reverent readers.

The Epistle to the Hebrews was written, not to all Hebrew Christians in general, as some have assumed, but to a specific company of believers with whom the writer had fellowshipped in the past and whom he expected soon to visit (13:19, 23). They needed encouragement in the faith. Many of their expectations remained unfulfilled. Why had Jesus not returned in power and judgment to usher in the Messianic Kingdom? Were the brave promises of the prophets to remain unfulfilled? Were the meek never to inherit the earth? Was there no bright prospect for Israel? And what of Jesus Himself? Was He ac-

---

[1] B. F. Westcott, *The Epistle to the Hebrews*, p. lxxi.

tually the promised Messiah? Or had the whole thing been a grand deception? Was it possible that Jesus had somehow been mistaken about Himself? Did He really rise from the dead? If so, was He never to be vindicated in the eyes of His critics and before the world? And were they, as His followers, to suffer reproach forever? Perhaps it might be wiser to return to Moses. He had stood the test of centuries, and the religion of the fathers offered tangible aids to worship and the dignity of long established custom. Why continue the embarrassment? Why not return to the fold?

What need they had for encouragement in the faith! Of all the epistles of the New Testament, none is more given to exhortation and admonition. Half or more of the letter is devoted to exhortation,[2] and the writer implies in his conclusion that "the word of exhortation" has been the burden of his letter and his principal purpose in writing (13:22). Consider the following analysis of the Epistle to the Hebrews:

teaching

Didactic (1:1-14):	Jesus superior to prophets and angels.
Hortatory (2:1-4): *exhortation*	Warning against drifting away from the Gospel and neglecting so great salvation announced first by the Lord Himself, and confirmed by men who heard Him.
Didactic (2:5-3:6):	Jesus to have universal dominion and, having suffered for man's redemption, to be the Head over His own house—the faithful.
Hortatory (3:6-4:16):	Warning against being hardened through the deceitfulness of sin, lapsing into unbelief, and departing from God and from Jesus, our High Priest.

---

[2]Of 303 verses, 160 are hortatory.

Didactic (5:1-10): Jesus a high priest forever after the order of Melchisedec and the source of eternal salvation to all who obey Him.

Hortatory (5:11-6:20): Warning against falling away and failing to press on in faith and patience to final attainment of all that God has promised in salvation.

Didactic (7:1-10:18): Jesus a high priest forever after the order of Melchisedec—the reality, of which the Aaronic priesthood and ministrations were only the shadow. His sacrifice, alone, actually efficacious; but His one offering eternally so.

Hortatory (10:19-12:29): Warning against failing to hold fast the confession of hope and to run with patience the race before us as did the faithful of old in their day, and against turning away from the Father of spirits, in rebellion against His corrective discipline.

Didactic (13:1-6): Practical aspects of Christian discipleship.

Hortatory (13:7-17): Warning against failing to continue in faith in Jesus, alone, as the all-sufficient Altar and the sole Way to an enduring city yet to appear.

Conclusion (13:18-25): Matters of immediate personal interest, the benediction, and a final appeal to heed "the word of exhortation" which has been the author's burden in writing.

The writer alternates between exalting Jesus and exhorting his readers. In no other book of the New Testament does exhortation play so large a part. In this respect, the Epistle to the Hebrews has much in common with the Book of Deuteronomy in the Old Testament.

It is obvious that the Epistle to the Hebrews was written to men whose background was Judaism. But their exact spiritual status has been a matter of dispute. Some have contended that, to a great extent, the writer viewed them as men who still halted between two opinions and had not as yet actually abandoned Judaism for Christ. Such a contention, of course, is unavoidable for men whose theology places them under the necessity of interpreting the numerous warnings against the peril of apostasy as being addressed, not to actual believers, but to men whose professions of faith in Christ have been either inadequate or insincere. Accordingly, they must also insist that those involved in instances of apostasy cited by the writer were not actually believers. The Scofield Reference Bible, the editors of which believed that apostasy is impossible for men who have experienced saving grace, asserts that "Hebrews 6:4-8 presents the case of Jewish professed believers who halt short of faith in Christ after advancing to the very threshold of salvation" and declares that "it is not said that they had faith."[3] Kuyper argues similarly in commenting on the same passage: "It is true the apostle declares that the men guilty of this sin 'were once enlightened,' and 'have tasted of the heavenly gift,' and 'were made partakers of the Holy Ghost,' and 'have tasted the good Word of God and the powers of the age to come;' but they are never said to have had a *broken and a contrite heart*."[4]

We must concede to Scofield and Kuyper that indeed "it is not said that they had faith" or that they "have had a broken and a contrite heart." We must further concede that it is not

---

[3]The *Scofield Reference Bible*, p. 1295, copyright 1909, 1917, by Oxford University Press, New York. Used by permission.

[4]Abraham Kuyper, *The Work of the Holy Spirit*, p. 610, italics his.

here said of them that they ever asked, "What must I do to be saved?" or that they ever prayed, "God be merciful to me a sinner." Nor is it said of them that they had called upon the name of the Lord, or that they had believed in their hearts, or that they had confessed with their mouths, or that they had become new creations in Christ, or that they had passed out of death into life. We must concede that many, many things "are not said of them" in the passage before us. But then, one cannot say *everything* in such brief compass. What the writer *did* say of them can be said only of men who have experienced the saving grace of God in Christ. Surely, Scofield and Kuyper have leaned upon a slender reed in their argument.

Contrary to the assumptions of many, the Epistle to the Hebrews was not written to men who, in the writer's opinion, had halted short of true faith in Christ as Saviour and Lord. Consider the following evidences of the fact that the writer assumes his readers to be true believers:

1. In his warning (2:1-4) against the peril of slipping away from "the things which we have heard"—things involving "so great salvation"—the writer assumes that his readers have fully accepted, and still firmly retain, the saving Gospel. In his use of the first person *we* he includes himself as being equally subject with his readers to the peril of drifting away.

2. He addresses his readers as "holy brethren, partakers of the heavenly calling," for whom Jesus is "the Apostle and High Priest of our confession" (3:1).

3. He includes his readers with himself ("we") as among those who already are Christ's "own house" and need only to hold fast their confidence and hope firm to the end (3:6).

4. The peril confronting his readers is not the possibility of failing to arrive at a proper relationship with God through Christ, but of departing from their present relationship through surrender to deceitful sin and unbelief—a condition which, as he assumes, has not as yet developed (3:6-19).

5. In the face of the peril of subsequently coming short of the promised rest and of falling after Israel's example of unbelief (3:16-4:13), the writer and his readers need only to "keep on holding fast" (present subjunctive, durative) their present confession of faith and to "keep on coming" (present subjunctive) to the throne of grace in confident faith (4:14-16).

6. The writer is persuaded "better things" of his readers—"things holding on to salvation," rather than things involving apostasy (6:9-12). His readers need not to enter into faith, but only to "show the same diligence to the full assurance of hope unto the end" and to continue as "followers of them who through faith and patience inherit the promises."

7. The writer includes his readers among those who "have fled for refuge" and whose hope in Jesus, their forerunner now within the veil, is for them "an anchor of the soul" (6:18-20).

8. He exhorts his readers to "keep on drawing near" (present subjunctive, durative) and to "keep on holding fast [present subjunctive] the confession of our hope without wavering . . . not forsaking the assembling of ourselves together" as they "see the day approaching" (10:19-25).

9. He reminds his readers (10:32-34) that they have been enlightened (with "the full knowledge of the truth"—v. 26) and that they already have endured great persecution for their faith and testimony. It remains only for them to "cast not away their confidence" and, in patience, to continue to live by faith, avoiding the error of those who withdraw unto perdition, and continuing with "them that believe to the saving of the soul" (vv. 35-39).

10. He assumes that his readers already have entered upon "the race that is set before us" and need only to continue along the way, guarding against the peril of despising God's corrective chastening and turning away from Him (12:1-29).

11. He writes (13:1-6) of practical aspects of conduct of concern to Christians and admonishes his readers to keep on

submitting to the under-shepherds who are responsible for guiding them in doctrine, faith, and practice (vv. 7, 17, 24).

12. He reminds them that "we have an altar" (Christ) and exhorts them to "keep on going forth [present subjunctive] unto Him" in anticipation of an enduring city yet to come (vv. 10-14).

13. He appeals for their prayer help (v. 18) and exhorts them as "brethren" to give heed to "the word of exhortation" which constitutes the principal burden of his letter to them (v. 22).

14. He anticipates seeing them shortly with "our brother Timothy" (v. 23).

15. His benediction (vv. 20, 21) is applicable only to true believers, among whom the writer obviously includes his readers (vv. 24, 25).

Those who contend that the writer to the Hebrews views his readers as men who have halted short of saving faith in Christ, rather than as true believers, do so out of regard for the necessities of their theology. The evidence of the epistle is against them.

Others agree that the Epistle to the Hebrews obviously is addressed to true believers, but contend that the writer's purpose is not to sound a warning against apostasy, but to share with his readers the secret of spiritual progress. His call to them, as they contend, is not "Don't turn back!"—but "Let us go on!"[5] Again, such opinion is dictated by the necessities of their theology, rather than by the contents of the epistle.

The phrase "let us go on" appears but once (6:1). "Let us go on," he writes, "unto perfection." The writer may have reference to his intention to proceed to the more advanced development of "the doctrine of Christ" to which he proposes

---

[5] Cf. W. H. Griffith Thomas, *Let Us Go On*, Zondervan Publishing House, Grand Rapids, Michigan.

to lead them in the course of his letter. Or, it may be a call to his readers to advance from the spiritual infancy in which he found them (5:11-13) toward the maturity (v. 14) which is possible for all who will grasp it. Actually, both things are within the writer's purpose. Certainly it is his intention to proceed toward the fuller development of his Christology, which is the grand theme of the didactic portions of his letter. But the presentation of his Christology is not an end in itself; it is offered for the profit of his readers. The didactic portions of his letter are but the base from which he launches his frequent exhortations, the principal burden of which is not "let us go on," but "let us hold fast."

Certainly he is concerned that his readers "go on unto perfection." But his first concern is that they "hold fast the confession of hope without wavering." If they do, they *will* go on toward perfection. The Christian life, a living relationship proceeding upon a living faith in a living Saviour, is never static. "[Jesus] said unto them, Take heed what ye hear: for with what measure ye mete, it shall be measured unto you: and unto you that hear shall more be given. For he that hath, to him shall be given: and he that hath not, from him shall be taken even that which he hath" (Mark 4:24, 25). Robertson's comment is worth pondering: "The man who does not acquire soon loses what he thinks that he has. This is one of the paradoxes of Jesus that repay thought and practice."[6] Growth in grace, or spiritual decline, may be hardly perceptible in many instances; nevertheless, it remains true that a Christian either grows or degenerates. The Christian life is never static. The congregation to whom the Epistle to the Hebrews was written had not merely failed to grow in their Christian lives; they had *degenerated* to the point of becoming spiritual infants again (5:11, 12).

They had become with the years less quick in understanding, and not more quick according to a natural and healthy development. . . . The

---

[6]A. T. Robertson, *Word Pictures in the New Testament*, Vol. I, p. 288.

Hebrews had through their own neglect become young children again.
. . . As yet however this dulness had not extended to action, though
such an issue was not far off (c. vi. 12; comp. 2 Pet. ii. 20).[7]

Their peril of finally apostatizing increased in proportion as
they declined spiritually. The writer's concern for them is reflected in his frequent and urgent exhortations.

In contrast with the exhortation "let us go on unto perfection," which occurs but once, the exhortation "let us hold fast
our confession" occurs twice (4:14; 10:23) and the epistle
abounds with cognate exhortations: "if we hold fast the confidence and rejoicing of the hope firm unto the end" (3:6);
"if we hold the beginning of our confidence stedfast unto the
end" (3:14); "lest there be in any of you an evil heart of unbelief in departing from the living God" (3:12); "lest any of
you be hardened through the deceitfulness of sin" (3:13); "lest
at any time we should slip away" (2:1); "if we neglect so great
salvation" (2:3); "harden not your hearts" (3:8, 15); "lest any
man fall after the same example of unbelief" (4:11); "show the
same diligence to the full assurance of hope unto the end"
(6:11); "let us keep on drawing near with a true heart in full
assurance of faith" (10:22); "cast not away therefore your
confidence" (10:35); "for ye have need of patience, that . . .
ye might receive the promise" (10:36); "the just shall live by
faith: but if he draw back, my soul shall have no pleasure in
him" (10:38); "lest ye be wearied and faint" (12:3); "despise
not the chastening of the Lord nor faint when thou art rebuked of him" (12:5); "be in subjection unto the Father of
spirits, and live" (12:9); "lest that which is lame be turned
out of the way" (12:13); "lest any man fail of the grace of
God" (12:15); "lest there be any fornicator, or profane person, as Esau, who sold his birthright" (12:16); "if we turn
away from Him who speaks from heaven" (12:25); "be not
carried away with divers and strange doctrines" (13:9); "let
us keep going forth unto Him outside the camp, bearing His

---

[7]Westcott, op. cit., p. 132 f.

reproach" (13:13). Any emphasis in the Epistle to the Hebrews on going on toward spiritual maturity is secondary. The burden of the writer's "word of exhortation" is that his readers "hold fast the confession of their hope" in Jesus Christ as the only Saviour and "the Source of eternal salvation unto all who obey Him."

Countless sermons have been preached on the familiar exhortation (12:1, 2) to "run with patience the race set before us." It has often been considered only a call to faithful endeavor toward spiritual maturity and attainment, having nothing to do with the question of salvation. But it is an integral part of the most extended exhortation in the epistle (10:19-12:29), the burden of which is "let us hold fast the confession of our hope without wavering" (10:23), for "the just shall live by faith: but if he draw back, my soul shall have no pleasure in him" (10:38); "we shall not escape if we turn away from Him who speaks from heaven" (12:25). The "race" to be run is the lifelong trial of our faith through constant temptation to turn back and abandon our pilgrimage. This is the reason for the writer's citation of the galaxy of the faithful in days of old (chapter 11). These all "obtained a good report through faith" (11:39, 2)—faith which believed God for things as yet "not seen," but "hoped for" (v. 1). Although in the days of their pilgrimage they "received not the promise" (v. 39), with patience and enduring faith they finished their race, despite trials and testings. In the light of context, the exhortation to "run with patience [hupomonē, stedfastness, endurance] the race set before us" can only be an exhortation to continue in the faith, despite manifold temptations to turn aside and fall by the way. (Cf. II Tim. 2:12, hupomenō.)

Prominent among the men of enduring faith cited in chapter 11 is Abraham who, at God's call, "went out, not knowing whither he went." In chapter 6 he is presented as an example of patience and faith. Urging his readers to "show the same diligence to the full assurance of hope unto the end" and to be "followers of them who through faith and patience inherit the promises" (6:11, 12), the writer declares that it was only "after he had patiently endured"—long after the promise was first announced to him—that Abraham "obtained the promise" (v. 15). From the time of the first announcement of the promise until the time when he "died in faith," Abraham's earthly pilgrimage was a test of "patient endurance" and of being "persuaded of the promises," though only "seeing them afar off" (11:13).

Patient, enduring faith, like that of Abraham, is presented (6:11 ff.) as the sole alternative of the apostasy cited in vv. 4-8. Such apostasy, an everpresent peril for the writer and his readers, was a peril also for Abraham. If he and "Isaac and Jacob, the heirs with him of the same promise" (11:9), had grown weary of "looking for a city which hath foundations, whose builder and maker is God" (v. 10) and of counting themselves "strangers and pilgrims on earth" (v. 13) seeking "a better country, that is, an heavenly" (vv. 14, 16), they could have returned to "that country from whence they came out" (v. 15). Growing weary of setting their affection on things above, they could have returned to both the literal and the spiritual Ur of the Chaldees, dismissing the anticipation of "an heavenly country" and a "city which hath foundations" as of no practical consequence for the present. Demas "loved this present world" and therefore withdrew. It was a tragic mistake; for "if any man love the world, the love of the Father is not in him" (I John 2:15), and "the friendship of the world is enmity with God" (Jas. 4:4). Therefore, "love not the world, neither the things that are in the world" (I John 2:15). For "the world passeth away, and the lust thereof"—and all who live for this world. For only "whoever perseveres in doing God's will lives on forever" (v. 17 Williams).

The possibility of returning to "that country from whence [we] came out" is a peril which ever confronts us while we are yet "pilgrims and strangers on the earth." We do well constantly to remember that, even as Abraham, "we have here no enduring city, but we seek one to come" (Heb. 13:13). There is but one way to the Father's house and the "city which hath foundations, whose builder and maker is God." Jesus said, "I am the way [*hodos*, road] . . . no man cometh unto the Father but by me." "Let us therefore keep on going forth unto Him outside the camp, bearing His reproach."

In Hebrews 10:38 is stated a divine maxim four times affirmed in the Holy Scriptures: "The just shall live by faith." This is the cardinal axiom governing man's relation to God and His saving grace throughout his earthly experience. It was so for Adam in Eden. Faith in the word of his Creator concerning a death he neither had experienced nor observed was the one condition whereby he *avoided* that death and continued to share the eternal life of God. After the Fall, faith remained the condition whereby Adam could experience restoration and continue to share in the saving grace and eternal life of God. Faith in the word of God concerning a coming Redeemer and the ordinance of animal sacrifice as the approved approach to a merciful God for guilty sinners was the condition whereby fallen men could know forgiveness and saving grace. It was "by faith," not by chance, that Abel offered "a more excellent sacrifice." For the ante-deluvian saints, for the patriarchs, and for all the saints in Israel, it was true that "the just shall live by faith." In the present era, it is still the principle governing man's participation in the eternal life of God in Christ. "The just shall live by faith: but if he draw back, my soul shall have no pleasure in him." How essential, then, that we "run with patient endurance the race set before us!" This is the burden of the writer to the Hebrews—a burden shared by all the New Testament writers, and by our Saviour Himself.

James writes, "Blessed is the person who endures trial, for when he stands the test, he will receive the crown of life which God has promised to those who love Him" (Jas. 1:12 Williams). Similar are the words of our Lord, "Each one of you must prove to be faithful, even if you have to die, and I will give you the crown of life. Whoever conquers will not be hurt at all by the second death" (Rev. 2:10, 11 Williams). The patient endurance which James enjoins in 1:12 is the antithesis and the sole alternative of submission to sin which, "when it is finished, brings forth death," as he declares in his warning to his brethren (1:13-16).

Peter urges us (II Pet. 1:5-11) to be diligent to add to our faith virtue, knowledge, temperance, patience, brotherly kindness, and charity, assuring us that "if these things be in you and abound, they make you that ye shall neither be barren nor unfruitful in the knowledge of our Lord Jesus Christ." To be "barren and unfruitful in the knowledge of Christ" is an invitation to spiritual disaster. Jesus warned that "every branch in me that beareth not fruit [my Father] taketh away" (John 15:2). Such barrenness is the inevitable corollary of failing to abide in Him (vv. 4, 5), which issues in death (v. 6). Peter further urges us (v. 10) to "give diligence to make your calling and election sure: for if ye do these things, ye shall never fall." He assures us (v. 11) that "so an entrance shall be ministered unto you abundantly into the everlasting kingdom of our Lord and Saviour Jesus Christ." He further admonishes us (3:17) to "beware lest ye also, being led away with the error of the wicked, fall from your own stedfastness." The "stedfastness" of which he writes is more than a matter of consecration and zeal in service, as some have assumed. For the "error" against which he warns is the fatal error of those who "wrest the scriptures, unto their own destruction" (v. 16).

The burden of Jude is that his readers continue to fight the good fight of faith. His extended consideration of actual instances of apostasy, both historical and contemporary, lends strong emphasis to his exhortation, "But you, dearly beloved, must continue to build yourselves up on the groundwork of your most holy faith and to pray in the Holy Spirit; you must keep yourselves in the love of God and continue to wait for the mercy of our Lord Jesus Christ, to bring you to eternal life" (vv. 20, 21 Williams).

John bids us shun the course followed by the "many antichrists" (I John 2:18) who denied the Son (and therefore

the Father also—vv. 22, 23) and "went out from us" (v. 19),
and who now seek to seduce others to do likewise, through
their false doctrine which denies that Jesus is truly Christ
(vv. 26, 27). John's consideration of the "many antichrists"
follows immediately his warning to his children in the faith to
"stop loving the world, or the things that are in the world. If
anyone persists in loving the world, there is no love for the
Father in his heart, because everything that is in the world,
the things that our lower nature and eyes are longing for, and
the proud pretensions of life, do not come from the Father,
but from the world; and the world is passing away, and with
it the evil longings it incites; but whoever perseveres in doing
God's will lives on forever" (vv. 15-17 Williams). Context thus
suggests that it was the love of the world that led the "many
antichrists" to deny the Son and thus to "go out from us."
John is anxious lest his readers fall into the same tragedy, and
therefore warns: "No one who disowns the Son can have the
Father. Whoever owns the Son has the Father too. Let what
you have heard from the beginning continue to live in your
hearts; if you do, you will always remain in union with the
Son and the Father. And the very thing that He Himself has
promised us is eternal life. I write you this with reference to
those who are trying to lead you astray. The anointing of the
Spirit which you received still remains in your hearts, and so
you have no need that anyone should teach you. But just as
that anointing of His teaches you about everything, and as it
is true and no falsehood, and as it has taught you to do so,
you must continue to live in union with Him. And now, dear
children, I repeat, you must continue to live in union with
Him, so that if He is unveiled, we may have unshaken confidence and not shrink away from Him in shame when He
comes" (vv. 23-28 Williams).

The concern of Paul that his converts run with patient endurance the race set before them is seen in Acts 14:21, 22,
"they returned again to Lystra, and to Iconium and Antioch,
confirming the souls of the disciples and exhorting them to

continue [*emmenō,* remain] in the faith, and that we must through much tribulation enter into the kingdom of God." Such concern for his converts is reflected in his letters. To the Galatians he writes, "Be not deceived; God is not mocked: for whatsoever a man soweth, that shall he also reap. For he that soweth to his flesh shall of the flesh reap destruction; but he that soweth to the Spirit shall of the Spirit reap life everlasting. And let us not be weary in well doing: for in due season we shall reap, if we faint not" (6:7-9).

Writing to the Romans, whom he hoped to visit in order to strengthen them in the faith (1:11), Paul warns that "we are debtors, not to the flesh, to live after the flesh. For if ye live after the flesh, ye shall die: but if ye through the Spirit do mortify the deeds of the body, ye shall live. For as many as are led by the Spirit of God, they are sons of God" (8:12-14). Again, he reminds the Gentiles in the church at Rome that they only "stand by faith" (11:20, cf. II Cor. 1:24) and that they must "be not arrogant, but fear;" for since God did not spare the "natural branches" of Israel, but broke them off because of their unbelief, neither will He spare *them* if they abandon the faith by which they stand. "Behold therefore the goodness and severity of God: on them that fell, severity; but toward thee, goodness, if thou continue in His goodness: otherwise thou also shalt be cut off" (v. 22).

Writing to the Colossians, Paul declares that God, who has reconciled us to Himself in the body of Christ's flesh through His death, will "present you holy and unblameable and unreproveable in his sight—if ye continue in the faith grounded and settled and be not moved away from the hope of the gospel which ye have heard" (1:22, 23). Similarly, he writes to the Corinthians of "the gospel which I preached unto you, which also ye have received, and wherein ye stand; by which also ye are being saved [present indicative passive] if ye hold fast the word which I preached to you, unless ye have believed in vain" (I Cor. 15:1, 2).

Paul admonishes Timothy that, though "some will turn away from the faith because they continuously give their attention to deceiving spirits and the things that demons teach through the pretensions of false teachers," he must "make it your habit to pay close attention to yourself and your teaching. Persevere in these things, for if you do you will save both yourself and those who listen to you" (I Tim. 4:1, 16 Williams). Again, he admonishes Timothy, "But bad men and impostors will go on from bad to worse, misleading others and misled themselves. But you, on your part, must continue to abide by what you have learned and been led to rely upon . . . the sacred Scriptures which can give you wisdom that leads to salvation through the faith that leans on Christ Jesus" (II Tim. 3:13-15 Williams). Other similar exhortations from the pen of Paul may be cited. But these suffice to indicate something of the concern he felt for the continued spiritual safety of his fellow believers.

Concerning himself, Paul writes to the Philippians (3:7-14) of his intense desire to "gain Christ, and be found in him." Not, of course, that he has not as yet "gained Christ" or is not yet to be "found in him." But he purposes to continue in the Way. "To have been brought to Christ is a beginning, and not an end," as Westcott[8] comments on Hebrews 4:1. Therefore, Paul not only has "*counted* loss for Christ" all other grounds for confidence and hope; he firmly declares that "I *do count* them but rubbish, that I may gain Christ and be found in him," continuing in that righteousness which is "through faith in Christ." His race is not yet won. It is his purpose, then, to run with patience the race before him, continuing to "press toward the goal for the prize of the upward calling of God in Christ Jesus."

Paul reckoned with the fearful possibility of failing in the race. Not everyone who runs wins. "Know ye not that they which run in a race run all, but one receives the prize? So run, that ye may obtain" (I Cor. 9:24). Paul therefore con-

---

[8]Westcott, *op. cit.*, p. 92.

tinually disciplined himself lest, though having preached to others, he himself should become a castaway. As we have considered in Chapter 4, Paul's meaning in his use of the word *adokimos* is clearly indicated by his use of the word in II Cor. 13:5, where he exhorts the Corinthians to determine whether they actually are in the faith, asserting that Jesus Christ does not dwell in any who are *adokimoi*. The meaning of the word, as he uses it in I Cor. 9:27, is further defined by context. After frankly acknowledging his deep concern lest he should become *adokimos*, he immediately cites instances of apostasy among the Israelites:

Paul draws an analogy (10:1 ff.) between the experience of the children of Israel in the wilderness and our experience in the present era. He points out that they, too, were baptized. Their miraculous passage through the sea was a symbol of their union—not merely with Moses, but with the One of whom Moses was the ordained representative. Their "baptism" was a confession of their faith in Him who had called them from Egypt to journey to the Promised Land. Furthermore, on their journey "they did all eat the same spiritual meat and did all drink the same spiritual drink" as we. The manna and the water from the rock were symbols of the same Rock as are the bread and wine in our era, and the physical sustenance which they received was symbolic of spiritual sustenance from the same saving Person whom we know as Jesus Christ. Paul does not contend that they were especially aware of the symbolic aspects of the manna and the water. But the manna and the water were nevertheless symbolic of Christ and the grace and life eternally vouchsafed in Him from before the foundation of the world and divinely dispensed in all ages to all who believed God and obeyed His Word as revealed in their day. And so "they drank the same spiritual drink [as we]: for they drank of that spiritual Rock that followed them: and that Rock was Christ. But with many of them God was not well pleased: for they were overthrown in the wilderness" (vv. 4, 5). The tragedy in Israel's case is that most of them did not continue in obedient faith. Paul's warning is that such could happen to us in our day.

Jesus Himself frequently warned His disciples of the necessity of continuing in faith if they are to continue in saving grace. To certain Jews who believed on Him, He said, "If ye continue in my word, then are ye my disciples indeed; and ye shall know the truth, and the truth shall make you free" (John 8:31, 32). Some have asserted that Jesus did not mean that continuance in truth and grace is conditional; He offered only a criterion by which true disciples may be identified. But they have overlooked the significance of Jesus' statement on the same occasion (v. 51), "Verily, verily, I say unto you, If a man keep my word, he shall never see death." Criterion, or condition? Obviously the latter.

Our Lord's solemn words in John 15:1-14 clearly depict the urgent necessity of perseverance. The lesson of six of our Saviour's parables[9] is the necessity of perseverance in the faith, and such necessity is plainly implied in numerous other parables. In Luke 12:35-46, Jesus associates the grave importance of perseverance with the promise of His return—an association found many times in the Scriptures. "By your endurance," said Jesus to His disciples, "you will win your souls" (Luke 21:19 Williams; cf. Matt. 24:13, Heb. 10:35-37, Jas. 5:7-11).

The many urgent warnings of the New Testament writers and of our Saviour reflect their holy concern that we run with endurance the race set before us. We shall be foolish indeed if we fail to share that concern. The issues are of everlasting consequence.

*   *   *

The supreme example of one who ran with patient endurance the race set before him is Jesus who, in the days of His flesh, "endured such contradiction of sinners against himself," resisting even "unto blood" (Heb. 12:3, 4). The writer to the

---

[9]The Sower (Luke 8:4-15), The Goodman (Luke 12:35-40), The Steward (Luke 12:42-48), The Tower Builder (Luke 14:28-30), The Savorless Salt (Luke 14:34, 35), and The Ten Virgins (Matt. 25:1-13).

Hebrews bids us run our race "looking unto Him Who is the leader and finisher of Faith, even Jesus, Who, for the joy that was set before Him, endured the cross, despising shame, and hath sat down on the right hand of the throne of God" (v. 2).[10] Westcott writes:

Christ in His humanity—*Jesus*—is "the leader and consummator of faith." To Him our eyes are to be turned while we look away from every rival attraction. From Him we learn Faith. The "faith" of which the Apostle speaks is faith in its absolute type, of which he has traced the action under the Old Covenant. The particular interpretations, by which it is referred to the faith of each individual Christian as finding its beginning and final development in Christ, or to the substance of the Christian creed, are foreign to the whole scope of the passage, which is to show that in Jesus Christ Himself we have the perfect example—perfect in realisation and in effect—of that faith which we are to imitate, trusting in Him. He too looked through the present and the visible to the future and the unseen. In His human Nature He exhibited Faith in its highest form, from first to last, and placing Himself as it were at the head of the great army of heroes of Faith, He carried faith . . . to its most complete perfection and to its loftiest triumph. This ascription of "faith" to the Lord is of the highest importance for the realisation of His perfect humanity. Comp. c. v. 8; ii. 13; iii. 2; John v. 19; xi. 41.[11]

In His birth as Jesus, Son of Mary, the eternal Word humbled Himself to be made what He had not been before, and what He must forever remain—Son of God,[12] and Son of Man. We might suppose that Jesus had some divine insight into the nature of His Person almost from infancy, and that there was no occasion or necessity for Him to exercise faith with respect to the fact of His unique relation to the Father. But we must

---

[10]Westcott, *op. cit.*, p. 392.

[11]*Ibid.*, p. 395.

[12]Cf. Heb. 1:5, "Thou art my Son, this day have I begotten thee. And again, I will be to him a Father, and he shall be to me a Son." Some understand the fulfillment of Ps. 2:7 to be the resurrection of Jesus, because of Paul's words in Acts 13:33 and Rom. 1:4. But while the Resurrection is full *confirmation* of His divine Sonship, it is not the *occasion* of it. The Incarnation marks the occasion of the implementation of the eternal purpose of God declared in Ps. 2:7 and II Sam. 7:14a.

remember that it was under the circumstance of the *Kenosis* (Phil. 2:5-8) that Jesus lived His life on earth. The Scriptures reveal that Jesus' understanding developed only gradually, in full accord with His circumstance. The fact of His peculiar relation to God doubtless entered His consciousness only gradually, as He matured, and was a precious truth which, more and more, He grasped by faith.

We may be sure that Mary and Joseph told Him of the holy circumstance of His birth. But their testimony could be accepted only by faith. Did they not also tell His sisters and His brothers, James, Joses, Simon, and Judas? Yet their testimony seems to have made little impression on Jesus' brothers and sisters. It is altogether likely, too, that there was scandal attached to the "premature" birth of Jesus by the tongue-waggers of Nazareth. The true circumstance of His birth remained a holy truth which Jesus could accept only by faith.

It seems evident that at the age of twelve, at the time of His visit to Jerusalem, Jesus was conscious of a special relation to the Father, doubtless without any full understanding of the implications as yet. But as far as we know from the Scriptures, the first overt affirmation of His divine Sonship came to Him on the occasion of His baptism, when the Holy Spirit descended on Him and the Father broke the silence of the heavens to declare, "Thou art my beloved Son; in thee I am well pleased."

Even so, the fact of His divine Sonship yet remained for Jesus a truth to be grasped and held fast by faith. It was precisely at this point that Satan launched his temptation of Jesus in the wilderness. "If thou be the Son of God, command these stones. . . ." Satan's challenge was an effort to induce Jesus to seek, through miraculous demonstration, tangible confirmation of a fact He was expected to accept by faith, on the testimony of the Father—both through the manifestation at His baptism, and inwardly in His heart by the Spirit. Satan's attack indicates that, at the outset of His ministry, Jesus had to accept the fact of His divine Sonship by faith. In the days that followed, His response to "the things heard of my Father" was faithful, and the certainty of His relation to the Father became fully established in His mind and heart, a certainty which included a consciousness that "before Abraham was, I am," and a veiled awareness of "the glory that I had with thee before the world began." But at the outset, it was not so. To impose John 17 on Jesus at Luke 4 is to deny that Satan's temptation was valid at this point and to reject the clear indication of the Scriptures that it was by faith that Jesus accepted the fact of His divine Sonship. The Gospel narratives portray the implicit faith in the Father which characterized Jesus throughout His earthly experience, all the way to the cross. The life of Jesus, from beginning to end, is the supreme example of a life of faith in God.

The perfect humanity of Jesus, the realm in which faith functioned, was essential to the fulfillment of His redemptive mission. It was as the Son of *man* that Jesus was obedient unto death, even the death of the cross. The Gospels record Jesus as speaking of Himself only as "the Son of man" in His references to His death. Even in the Gospel of John, with its emphasis on Christ as the eternal Word and the Son of God, only the term *Son of man* is used by Jesus in reference to His death. In the Epistles, with respect to His death, the emphasis is on His role of Son of man. It was as the second Adam that He wrought redemption for mankind (I Cor. 15:21, 22, 45, Rom. 5:12-19). It was as the one perfect, sinless man that Jesus took our sins and was "made sin for us, that we might be made the righteousness of God in him." His cry on the cross, "My God, My God, why hast thou forsaken me?" was the cry of the Son of *man*. It is not the role of God to be tempted to sin, to practice obedience, to be made sin, or to die. For these experiences, in His accomplishment of the redemption through which God might realize His purpose of bringing many sons unto glory through Him, the Word was made flesh—very man (cf. Heb. 2:9-18, Phil. 2:5-8).

Rationalists who deny the Incarnation see Jesus only in terms of humanity. They are mistaken. But we who know Him to be the Word Incarnate tend to overlook the *significance* of His humanity and all that was involved in His *Kenosis*. We have failed to appreciate both the reality and the necessity of such things as His increasing in wisdom and in favor with God, His accepting by faith the fact of His divine Sonship, His learning obedience by the things which He suffered, His putting His trust in God for His own deliverance out of death, His being heard in prayer because of His holy fear, God's loving Him supremely because of His submission to the Father's will—even to the point of the death of the cross, and His being annointed with the oil of gladness above His fellows—not because of divine relationship, but because He loved righteousness and hated iniquity. We have failed to appreciate all that is implied in such statements of Jesus as, "Because I lay down my life, therefore doth my Father love me" (John 10:17). His sufferings and His accomplishments in His redemptive career were all purely voluntary, and God loved Him for them all.

As the Son of man, Jesus' life did not automatically unfold in the fulfillment of God's will without the necessity of His own deliberate decision and earnest striving. There was nothing artificial or merely hypothetical about His temptations and testings. They were fiercely real. It is true that His redemptive career had been foretold and, having been written, "the Scriptures must be fulfilled." But the prophecies were given, not to determine what He *must* do, but to declare what He *would* do. Jesus' fulfillment of the Scriptures was entirely voluntary. The fact that He could have turned aside from the path of His redemptive mission was declared by our Saviour in His words to Peter in Gethsemane, "Put up thy sword. . . . Thinkest thou that I cannot now pray to my Father and he will immediately send me more than twelve legions of angels? But how then shall the scriptures be fulfilled, that thus it must be?" (Matt. 26:52-54). All that was written in the Law of Moses and in the Prophets and in the Psalms concerning Jesus was entirely voluntary on His part. Jesus declared that the Father would have concurred immediately in His withdrawal from the path to the cross, sending legions of angels to deliver Him, had He so chosen. He asserted that the fulfillment of the Scriptures with respect to His redemptive career as Messiah was to be determined by His personal decision alone. All therefore that Jesus endured and achieved in His redemptive career was purely voluntary on His part, rather than the inevitable unfolding of some inexorable divine decree. From Nazareth to Calvary, Jesus was under no constraint or coercion other than His own desire to fulfill the will of His Father, whose will was His meat and His delight.

Jesus' fierce rebuke of well-meaning Peter for his suggestion that He avoid the sufferings and death which awaited Him at Jerusalem (Matt. 16:23) reflects the persistence and power of the temptation which confronted Him all the way from Jordan to Gethsemane and the cross. Could Jesus actually have turned aside from His redemptive mission? Certainly the issue was not in doubt insofar as God was concerned. He had declared the outcome through His prophets of old, an outcome which He had foreseen from eternity. But it does not follow that God's foreknowledge, of itself, determined the outcome of Jesus' mission. Nor did God's eternal decree to give the Son, of itself, determine the outcome; for the decree of the Father was not a unilateral decree which left the Son no alternatives—a decree which imposed absolute necessity upon Jesus, depriving Him of all possibility of concurring with the Father's will on a purely voluntary basis. The Father chose to give the Son—even unto death; but unto death, only on condition that the Son should freely choose to die. (Cf. John 10:17, 18: "For this reason does my Father love me, because I lay down my life, that I may take it again. No one [neither the Father nor man] takes it from me, but I lay it down of myself. I have authority to lay it down, and I have authority to take it up again. This charge I received from my Father." The final decision was Christ's, as He affirmed in Matt. 26:53.) Victory in His redemptive mission was therefore actually, rather than merely hypothetically, contingent on

Jesus' voluntary and uncoerced submission to the will of the Father.

Let us repeat: the outcome was never in doubt in the mind of God. In the eternal counsels of God (in which the uncreated Word concurred "in the beginning") the victory of Jesus in His redemptive career was foreseen as certain. But it was certain, only on the basis of the foreseen voluntary and uncoerced submission of the Son of Man to the will of the Father. And in the circumstance of the *Kenosis,* it was only by faith that Jesus, "the pioneer and perfecter of faith" (Heb. 12:2), embraced the fact of His unique relation to the Father and pursued His role as Messiah. Victory in His redemptive mission therefore was truly contingent on His own decision and perseverance, and it is abundantly evident from the Scriptures that Jesus so regarded it. He found Himself beset on every hand by fearful possibilities of failure—possibilities which He did not dismiss as unreal or somehow incapable of actually materializing because of some eternal decree. The decision whether to summon twelve legions of angels was not made before creation in some inexorable decree of God; it was made by Jesus in Gethsemane, and the Father would have concurred in His decision either way, according to the statement of our Saviour. His fulfillment of the Scriptures pertaining to the redemptive career of the Messiah Jesus regarded as entirely contingent on His own uncoerced submission—finally unto death itself, a death which was for Jesus the Son of Man the supreme act of faith in His God and Father.

This does not mean that God is only an interested spectator in His universe and is not positively at work in the accomplishment of an eternal purpose. But it does mean that individuals are free to choose how they shall relate themselves to God's eternal purpose of "bringing many sons unto glory." This was true for Jesus in His redemptive career, and it is equally true for all men. It was the will of the Father that Jesus die for the sins of mankind. But the will of the Father did not in any way ignore or coerce the will of the Son. It is the will of God that all men be saved and none perish (I Tim. 2:4, II Pet. 3:9). But the will of God does not ignore or coerce the will of men, and many perish.

In Eden, God foresaw and declared the victory of the Seed of the woman, the Son of man—a victory which was the consequence of the voluntary submission of Jesus to the Father's will. God foresaw also the salvation of the elect of all ages—a salvation which, individually, was not inevitable except on the basis of the voluntary submission of individual men to the will of God. What God foresaw in Eden, He had beheld from eternity. But that fact does not destroy the voluntary character of the response to His will, either of Jesus, or of those who are elect in Him. Jesus fulfilled His redemptive role because He delighted in the Father's will. And Jesus declared that only men who will to do God's will can know the truth of His teaching (John 7:17) and the way of grace and life eternal through Him. God wills to have all men to be saved; but if they so choose, individual men can thwart God's will and purpose for them (Luke 7:30, cf. Verkuyl, Williams, RSV, *et al.*).

It is impossible to surmise what might have followed, had Jesus turned aside from the cross. Would that have constituted sin? Evidently not, since the Father could not have concurred in His decision to avoid the cross (as Jesus declared He would do) had such a decision constituted sin. Let us remember that, since Jesus was without sin, His submission to death was not obligatory, but substitutionary and purely voluntary. As far as the Father was concerned, He gave the Son to die; but only as the Son Himself *chose* to die. The decision of the Son was as free and deliberate as that of the Father. It was impossible that the cup should pass from Him—not *absolutely*, but only if He chose to save others rather than Himself. The answer to our Saviour's agonizing prayer in Gethsemane came, not from the Father in heaven, but from the heart of Jesus Himself. Jesus laid down His life of His own will (John 10:18). In His death, He was not simply passive and submissive; for He was not only sacrifice, He was equally priest. He was not merely slain; He voluntarily *"offered* Himself without spot to God" (Heb. 9:14). "As Moses lifted up the serpent," said Jesus, "even so must the Son of man be lifted up." Let us not assume that Jesus meant that He *had* to die—simply because He was *Jesus,* or because God somehow had decreed it. Jesus *had* to die only if He were to save others. Saving others, Himself He could not save. Therefore He *must* be lifted up—not because of inexorable divine necessities which He could not avoid, but only in order "that whosoever believeth in Him should not perish, but have eternal life." Jesus died only because He *chose* to die. The decision was completely His own. Because He chose as He did, the Father loves Him supremely (John 10:17) and has highly exalted Him and given Him a Name above every name (Phil. 2:8-11).

We need not speculate about what might have happened, had Jesus chosen to avoid the cross. He did not so chose. But let us recognize that it was a possibility—a real possibility with which Jesus fully reckoned. Let us recognize that God's decree of death for the Son of Man was not unilateral; it depended on the voluntary compliance of the Son who, in submission to the Father's will, chose not to summon legions of angels to save Him from the hands of wicked sinners for whom He chose to die. In wonder and in praise, let us thank our Saviour that He chose as He did, at such frightful cost to Himself.

Jesus' victory in His redemptive career was not conferred; it was *won*—at the cost of tears, blood, and death. His eternal victory over sin, death, and hell was a victory we could never have won. He won it, only to share it. In infinite grace, He shares His victory with us: but only as we trust Him in obedient faith and, after His example, run with stedfast endurance the race set before us. Our victory in our race is but a secondary victory; but it is essential: it is the prerequisite for sharing Christ's eternal victory.

He who was determined to run His race—even to the death of the cross—said to His disciples: "If any man will come after me, let him deny himself and take up his cross and follow me.

For whosoever will save his life shall lose it: and whosoever will lose his life for my sake shall find it. For what is a man profited if he shall gain the whole world and lose his own soul? or what shall a man give in exchange for his soul? For the Son of man shall come in the glory of his Father with his angels, and then he shall reward every man according to his works. . . . To him that overcometh will I grant to sit with me in my throne, even as I also overcame and am set down with my Father in His throne. . . . Be thou faithful unto death, and I will give thee the crown of life. He that hath an ear, let him hear what the Spirit saith unto the churches: He that overcometh shall not be hurt of the second death."

If we would be Christ's and forever share His eternal victory over sin, death, and hell, "let us lay aside every encumbrance, and sin which doth so easily beset us, and let us run with endurance the race set before us, looking unto Jesus, the leader and perfecter of faith" in its supreme manifestation. For all who trust Him in obedient faith, He who ran His race to everlasting victory is now the object of faith, the fount of grace, and the source of strength. Victory is certain—as we continue "looking unto Jesus."

"The Deceitfulness of Sin"

Wherefore, holy brethren, partakers of the heavenly calling, consider the Apostle and High Priest of our confession, Christ Jesus . . . Whose house are we, if we hold fast the confidence and the rejoicing of the hope firm unto the end.

Wherefore . . . take heed, brethren, lest there be in any of you an evil heart of unbelief, in departing from the living God. But exhort one another daily, while it is called Today, lest any of you be hardened through the deceitfulness of sin. For we are made companions of Christ, if we hold the beginning of our confidence stedfast unto the end.

HEBREWS 3:1, 6, 12-14

CHAPTER XVI

THE DECEITFULNESS OF SIN

IT HAS BEEN SAID that a large segment of the church today has great zeal for the new birth, but little concern for the newborn. Not so the Apostles in the first generation of the church. Prominent in the epistles of the New Testament is the note of intense concern, not only for the growth and maturity, but for the spiritual safety—the very survival—of the saints in all the various churches.

"I feel a divine jealousy for you," writes Paul to the believers at Corinth, "as I betrothed you to Christ to present you as a pure bride to her one husband. But I am apprehensive that, somehow or other, as the serpent by his cunning deceived Eve, your thoughts may be turned aside from single-hearted devotion to Christ" (II Cor. 11:2, 3 Williams). Such would be as great a spiritual disaster for the Corinthians as that suffered by Eve in Eden.

Wherever Paul labored, he seemed invariably to be followed by "sham apostles, dishonest workmen, masquerading as apostles of Christ" (v. 13 Williams) and preaching "another gospel" which they represented as a necessary advance upon Paul's incomplete teaching. The unflagging efforts of the Judaizers were a continual vexation for the first-generation church. Their arguments were difficult to combat.

Many of the earliest churches were composed largely of Jews. And in virtually all of the churches which were predominantly Gentile, there were strong nuclei of Jewish believers. Understandably, many of the customs and habits which had been so

255

deeply ingrained in the Jews from childhood continued to cling to them after their conversion. This, in itself, was not wrong. The Scriptures indicate that Paul himself continued all his lifetime occasionally to manifest various habits and customs which had been part of his earlier life as a Pharisee. Furthermore, the church never had undertaken any deliberate crusade against Judaism. Indeed, the church in council at Jerusalem (Acts 15) had explicitly requested Gentile converts to avoid conduct which would unnecessarily offend the adherents of Judaism in Antioch and in Syria and Cilicia (and, implicitly, anywhere else). Paul, by request of James and the elders at Jerusalem, entered upon a ceremonial vow involving a sacrifice, in an attempt to demonstrate to Jewish believers (and doubtless to unbelievers as well) that he was not, as they had assumed, deliberately hostile toward the teachings of Moses and the customs of the fathers (Acts 21:18-26). This was in keeping with Paul's principle of avoiding unnecessary offense and endeavoring to be "all things to all men" (I Cor. 9:19-22) in his effort to win some to Christ. It is evident from the New Testament that, for Jewish Christians, any lingering aspects of Judaism which were mere matters of custom and habit were, of themselves, neither necessarily right nor wrong. However, any attempt to impose any aspects of Judaistic ceremonialism on Gentile Christians was positively wrong; for it implied that such were essential to salvation.

The "certain men from Judea" and the Pharisees (Acts 15:1, 5) were doubtless sincere in insisting that Gentile converts must be circumcised and be brought under the law of Moses, if they were to be saved. But after Spirit-led deliberation, the council of the church at Jerusalem declared that the yoke of the law, with circumcision and various other ceremonial aspects, is not to be thrust upon the necks of Gentile believers. While not wrong in themselves, such things are not a part of the Gospel of Christ and the new economy of Grace. They are not means to justification. As Peter declared, God had clearly demonstrated in the house of Cornelius that justification is apart from any observance of ceremonial ordinances. Peter and his fellow Jewish believers, who throughout their lifetime had endeavored conscientiously to observe the law, were to be saved through the grace of the Lord Jesus Christ alone (v. 11), even as the Gentiles whose hearts God had purified solely on the ground of faith (v. 9). The pronouncement was clear, definite, and final. Henceforth no one, with good conscience, could advocate the necessity of circumcision or other ceremonial aspects of Judaism for justification before God. To do so would be contrary to a clear directive of the Holy Spirit (v. 28).

Following the historic council at Jerusalem, men who continued to advocate the necessity of circumcision and other aspects of Judaism were obviously "false brethren" preaching "another gospel." Their efforts to win converts to a rigid ceremonialism were vigorously opposed by Paul and all faithful ministers of the Gospel of Christ. It was no minor issue. The "full gospel" of the Judaizers, with their insistence on ceremonial circumcision and calendar observances (which Paul decried as "weak and beggarly elements"), constituted a deadly peril. It was fatal to all who embraced it; for it completely nullified the simple "faith which leans on Christ Jesus" (II Tim. 3:16 Williams) which is the sole condition whereby men know the joy of God's gracious salvation.

The churches of Galatia seemed especially vulnerable to the teachings of "false brethren" who "perverted the gospel of Christ" through the preaching of "another gospel." The Galatians' heathen background of pagan ritualism involving flagrant physical mortification provided a disposition which made them easily "bewitched" by the clever Judaizers who preached the "gospel" of the cross, the knife, and the calendar.

Paul was dismayed to learn that, under the persuasive spell of the Judaizers, some of the Galatians already had turned from simple faith in Christ and had submitted to ceremonial circumcision in an effort to ensure their justification. He feared that others were on the verge of so doing. "Behold," he warns them, "I Paul say unto you that if ye receive circumcision [in

an effort to ensure justification], Christ will profit you nothing.
. . . Ye are severed from Christ, ye who would be justified by
the law; ye are fallen away from grace. For we through the
Spirit by faith wait for the hope of righteousness. For in Christ
Jesus neither circumcision availeth anything, nor uncircumci-
sion; but faith working through love" (5:2, 4-6 ASV).

Paul expresses his confidence (v. 10) that, ultimately, they
will not rest content with an erroneous view of this vital question which must determine the issue of their very salvation. Although when they were "running beautifully" (v. 7 Williams)
some allowed a false apostle to "cut into their way" to turn them
from obeying the truth of the Gospel, Paul is yet confident that,
if duly warned, they will resume a proper view of the matter
and return to obedience to the truth of the simple Gospel of
salvation by grace, through faith. He does his utmost, therefore,
to convince them that it is *faith* alone, in *Christ* alone, which
justifies men before God and vouchsafes His gracious salvation.
A divided faith which rests partly on Christ and partly on circumcision, calendar observances, or other "weak and beggarly
elements," is completely ineffective and unacceptable before
God.

Circumcision and other ceremonial aspects of Judaism had
had their proper place in the former economy, having been
commanded of God for observance by His children in the
"paedagogue" era. Under certain circumstances, their continued
observance was not harmful. But when they were deliberately
embraced in a conscious effort to ensure justification, they con-
tradicted faith in Jesus Christ, severing the individual from
Him. The transfer of faith from Christ *alone* to Christ *plus
other things* is fatal. Thus, things which of themselves are not
wrong may yet constitute a deadly snare. Beware "the deceitfulness of sin."

(The basic error of Seventh Day Adventism is the equation
of obedience, an essential aspect of faith, with legalistic observances which pertained to the old economy. Such preoccupation
with "shadows" [Col. 2:16 ff.] is not for our day, since the

"body" [Christ] has come. The Adventist cult is committed to the propagation of an error vigorously condemned in the New Testament because of the peril that men may transfer their faith from Christ, alone, to mere fleshly observances. The fatal snare into which many of the Galatians fell in Paul's day is precisely the snare into which Mrs. White's "gospel" of the cross, the day, and the diet leads many today.)

In his later letter to the Colossians, Paul inveighs against a false teaching similar to that which troubled the Galatians. The surface manifestations differed somewhat, but the basic issue was the same. Paul warns the Colossians to beware "lest any man should beguile [*paralogizomai*, Thayer: to cheat by false reckoning, to deceive by false reasoning; hence to deceive, delude] you with enticing words" (2:4), leading them away from "the stedfastness of your faith in Christ" (v. 5) in which Paul rejoiced. As they have once received Christ, so must they continue to "walk in Him, rooted and built up in Him and established in the faith" (vv. 6, 7). They must "take care that nobody captures [*sulagōgeō*, Thayer: to capture and carry off as booty; hence, to lead away from the truth and subject to one's sway] you by the idle fancies of his so-called philosophy, following human traditions and the world's crude notions instead of Christ" (v. 8 Williams). It is in Christ that all the fulness of the Godhead dwells embodied, and it is only in Him that they are spiritually complete (vv. 9, 10). They must "allow no one, therefore, to be your judge in regard to eating and drinking or the observance of a festival or a new moon or a Sabbath. These are shadows of things to follow, but the body is Christ. Let no one defraud you of salvation's victory prize, no one who indulges in assumed humility and the cult of angel-worship; who brags of visions and though empty, is inflated by his worldly mind, instead of keeping hold on that Head from which the whole body, gathering vigor and held together by ligaments and sinews, grows with God's increase" (vv. 16-19 Verkuyl).

Throughout his epistle are found expressions of Paul's ". . . intense anxiety for the Churches of Colossae and the neighbourhood, lest they should be led astray by a spurious wisdom to desert the true knowledge."[1] The ultimate expression of that spurious wisdom lay in an assumed humility in which men worshipped angels.

The motive of this angelolatry it is not difficult to imagine. There was a show of humility, for there was a confession of weakness in this subservience to inferior mediatorial agencies. It was held feasible to grasp at the lower links of the chain which bound earth to heaven, when heaven itself seemed far beyond the reach of man. The successive grades of intermediate beings were as successive steps, by which man might mount the ladder leading up to the throne of God. This carefully woven web of sophistry the Apostle tears to shreds. The doctrine of the false teachers was based on confident assumptions respecting angelic beings of whom they could know nothing. It was moreover a denial of Christ's twofold personality and His mediatorial office. It follows from the true conception of Christ's Person that He, and He alone, can bridge over the chasm between earth and heaven; for He is at once the lowest and the highest. He raises up man to God, for He brings down God to man. Thus the chain is reduced to a single link, this link being the Word made flesh. As the *pleroma* resides in Him, so is it communicated to us through Him. To substitute allegiance to any other spiritual mediator is to sever the connexion of the limbs with the Head, which is the centre of life and the mainspring of all energy throughout the body.[2]

There is but one bridge between God and man. Especially vivid is the translation of I Timothy 2:5 by the Roman Catholic scholar, the late Monsignor R. A. Knox of England: "There is only one God, and only one mediator between God and men, Jesus Christ, who is a man, like them, and gave himself a ransom for them all."[3] What a tragedy that Roman Catholic dogma and practice are so far removed from the cardinal truth so beautifully stated in Monsignor Knox's translation. Dr. Donald Grey Barnhouse relates an interesting experience:

---

[1] J. B. Lightfoot, *Saint Paul's Epistles to the Colossians and to Philemon*, p. 99.

[2] *Ibid.*, p. 103 f.

[3] From the New Testament in the translation of Monsignor Ronald Knox, Copyright 1944, Sheed and Ward, Inc., New York. Used by permission.

Some years ago I was living in one of the Alpine valleys of Southern France, preaching to one of the little Huguenot congregations while I was pursuing my studies at the University of Grenoble. Every Thursday morning I walked four miles up the valley to a little centre where I instructed a score of children in the things of God. In that village there lived a Roman priest who on Thursday used to come down the valley to a village near the one where I lived. Frequently our paths crossed, and at times we found ourselves going the same direction. One day as we went along together he said to me, "Why do you Protestants object so strongly to our praying to the saints?" I asked him to explain what advantage there was to be gained from praying to the saints. He replied, "Well, suppose, for example, that I wanted an interview with the President of the Republic, Monsieur Poincaré. I could go to Paris and arrange for an interview with any one of the members of the cabinet. I could go to the Minister of Agriculture, or to the Minister for the Colonies, or to the Office of the Interior, the Navy, National Defense, or any other of the ministries. They would facilitate my obtaining an interview with the President. In the same way I may obtain the intercession of the Virgin and the saints on behalf of my desires as I pray." He looked rather triumphant as he completed his illustration. Then I said to him, "Monsieur le Curé, let me ask you a question. Suppose that my name is Poincaré, and that my father is the President of the French Republic. Suppose that I live in the Palace of the Elysée with him, sit at his table three times a day, and am frequently the object of his tender solicitations, and know the touch of his loving hand. Do you think for a moment that if I have a problem to present to him I am going to go across Paris to one of the ministries, pass all the guards and secretaries that surround a cabinet member, and finally reaching his office, say, 'Monsieur le Ministre, would you be so kind as to arrange an interview for me to talk with *my daddy?*' Do you not rather think that I will look him in the eye at one of the moments when he puts his arm across my shoulder in a gesture of affection, and then tell him that I have a request to make?"

The Curé was taken aback. He looked at me and his mouth opened and closed and opened again as though he were seeking for words that would not come. Then I took my little French Testament from my pocket and turned to two or three passages of Scripture and had him read them aloud. To "as many as received Him (Christ), to them gave He the authority to become the sons of God, even to them that believe on His Name" (John i. 12). "Therefore being justified by faith, we have peace with God through our Lord Jesus Christ: by Whom also we have *access* by faith into this grace wherein we stand, and rejoice in hope of the glory of God" (Rom. v. 1, 2). "Seeing then that we have a great high priest, that is passed into the Heavens, Jesus the Son of God, let us hold fast our profession. For we have not an high priest which cannot be touched with the feeling of our infirmities; but was in all points tempted like as we are, apart from sin. Let us therefore come boldly unto the throne of grace, that we may obtain mercy and find grace to help in time of need" (Heb. iv. 14-16).

He had me write down the references that he might look them up in what he called a Catholic Bible, and frequently thereafter he stopped me with questions, coming as a learner to discover some of the wonders that are ours in Christ.[4]

To depart from utter dependence upon Jesus Christ alone as the sole Mediator between God and men is to become severed from the Saviour, "not continuing in connection with the Head" (Col. 2:19 Williams). To such tragedy can men be led by the deceitfulness of sin, which is never more deceitful than when it masquerades as wisdom. "Wisdom" was a threat to the Ephesians, as we discern from Paul's First Epistle to Timothy (Williams):

As I begged you to do when I was on my way to Macedonia, I still beg you to stay on in Ephesus to warn certain teachers to stop devoting themselves to myths and never-ending pedigrees, for such things lead to controversies rather than stimulate our trusteeship to God through faith. But the aim of your instruction is to be love that flows out of a pure heart, a good conscience, and a sincere faith. Some people have stepped aside from these things and turned to fruitless talking. They want to be teachers of the law, although they do not understand the words they use or the things about which they make such confident assertions.

. . . .

. . . continue to fight the good fight, by keeping your hold on faith and a good conscience; for some have thrust the latter aside and so have made shipwreck of their faith.

. . . .

Now the Spirit distinctly declares that in later times some will turn away from the faith, because they continuously give their attention to

[4]Donald Grey Barnhouse, *Life by the Son*, pp. 43-46. Used by permission of The Evangelical Foundation, Inc., Philadelphia, publishers of *Eternity* magazine.

deceiving spirits and the things that demons teach through the pretensions of false teachers, men with seared consciences, who forbid people to marry and teach them to abstain from certain sorts of food which God created for the grateful enjoyment of those who have faith and a clear knowledge of the truth. For everything in God's creation is good, and nothing to be refused, provided it is accepted with thanksgiving, for in this way it is consecrated by the word of God and prayer.

If you continue to put these things before the brothers, you will be a good minister of Christ Jesus, ever feeding your own soul on the truths of the faith and of the fine teaching which you have followed.

• • • • • • • • • • • • • • • • • • •

Make it your habit to pay close attention to yourself and your teaching. Persevere in these things, for if you do you will save both yourself and those who listen to you.

• • • • • • • • • • • • • • • • • • •

Timothy, guard what has been intrusted to you; continue to turn away from the worldly, futile phrases and contradictions of what is falsely called "knowledge," by professing which some individuals have failed in the faith.

Human nature has not changed since the day of Paul. Stratagems then employed by Satan with such success are equally successful today. The perils which confronted men then continue to confront men today. Witness Seventh Day Adventism with its rank legalism obscuring grace and turning the hearts of men from simple faith in Christ, alone. Witness the self-realization cults with their pseudo-Biblical formulae for attaining present bliss and heaven itself by means of back-patting self-propulsion. Witness Roman Catholicism with its myriads of mediators diverting men from the One Mediator between God and men, who said, "Come unto *Me*," and through whom we may "come boldly unto the throne of grace." Men will trust in many things—days and diets and fine assortments of "weak and beggarly elements"; self-improvement and noble endeavor; saints and angels and Mary of Nazareth—anything and anyone, save Jesus Christ the Holy Son of God and Man and the only Mediator between God and men!

One may be wrong about many things, doctrinally, and yet be saved. But one dare not be wrong about the object of his faith and the ground of his hope for God's salvation. Christ Himself must be the sole object of one's faith and the exclusive ground of all his hope for heaven and eternity. To be wrong at this point is to miss the Way. Men who rest their faith on foundations other than Christ, or in addition to Christ, are destined for everlasting disappointment and despair. Jesus said, "Strait is the gate and narrow the way which leads to life, and few there be that find it. . . .I am the door. . . . I am the way . . . no man comes unto the Father but through me."

> There is a green hill far away,
>   Without a city wall,
> Where the dear Lord was crucified,
>   Who died to save us all.
>
> He died that we might be forgiven,
>   He died to make us good,
> That we might go at last to heaven,
>   Saved by His precious blood.
>
> There was no other good enough
>   To pay the price of sin;
> He only could unlock the gate
>   Of heaven and let us in.
>
> Oh, dearly, dearly, has He loved,
>   And we must love Him, too;
> And trust in His redeeming blood,
>   And try His works to do.
>
> CECIL F. ALEXANDER

It is essential that we "try His works to do;" for any "believing" which does not lead to *doing* is completely insincere. But our faith must never rest in all our *doing*. All our trust and hope must be "in His redeeming blood"—in Christ alone, and not in other things to even the smallest degree, no matter how good and right they may be, of themselves. One dare not trust Christ—and baptism; or Christ—and church membership; or Christ—and noble Christian living; or Christ—and faithful

Christian service. All these things—baptism, church member-ship, upright living, faithful service—are good and important and pleasing in the sight of God. They are obligations of every Christian, according to the Holy Scriptures. The man who has no concern for such things has no saving faith in Christ and no warrant for assuming that he is a child of God on his way to the Father's House. But these important obligations are only the *expression* of faith. They must never become the *objects* of our faith. All our faith must rest in Christ alone.

"If thou wilt make me an altar of stone," said God to the children of Israel, "thou shalt not build it of hewn stone: for if thou lift up thy tool upon it, thou hast polluted it" (Ex. 20:25). God's provision of the perfect Sacrifice upon His eternal altar needs not to be supplemented by human effort. In another object lesson, God smote Uzzah with death (II Sam. 6:6, 7) because he disobeyed the divine injunction against touching the ark of the covenant (Num. 4:15-20) whereon was the mercy seat of God. The perfect grace of a holy God needs not to be supported or sustained by the efforts of sinful men. To presume to supplement grace through human endeavor (the error of some of the Galatians) is to become severed from Christ and the saving grace of God which is ours through Him alone.

"Though I might have confidence in the flesh," wrote Paul to the Philippians, "what things were gain to me, those I counted loss for Christ. And indeed I do continue to count[5] . . . them but rubbish, that I may gain Christ and be found in him, not having mine own righteousness, which is of the law, but that which is through faith in Christ, the righteousness which is of God by faith" (3:4, 7-9).

> My hope is built on nothing less
> Than Jesus' blood and righteousness;
> I dare not trust the sweetest frame,
> But wholly lean on Jesus' Name.

EDWARD MOTE

---

[5]Paul's use of five particles with the present middle indicative is emphatic.

One of the false "sweet frames" on which multitudes of sincere people rest their hope for eternity is the erroneous doctrine of unconditional security. Many who deplore the fact that some trust in church membership, baptism, decent living, and other false frames yet rest all their hope for salvation on a false frame just as deadly. Many, quite unconsciously, have transferred their faith from Christ Himself to the fact of a past conversion experience and the assumed validity of the popular doctrine of "once in grace, always in grace." Their confidence now rests, not actually in Christ Himself, but in their conversion experience sometime in the past. They know the time and the place they were saved; but they do not know Christ. They have no sense of present need for Him—no sense of present dependence on Christ for saving grace, no living faith in a living Saviour. They are abiding, not in Christ the Living Vine, but in a popular doctrine. "I trusted Christ years ago," say they. But they have long since ceased trusting in Him and now are trusting in their past conversion experience and in the erroneous assumption that "once in grace, always in grace."

"Cromwell on his death-bed questioned his chaplain as to the doctrine of final perseverance, and, on being assured that it was a certain truth, said: 'Then I am happy, for I am sure that I was once in a state of grace.' "[6] What unspeakable tragedy that men should live and die with their confidence and hope fixed, not on Christ Himself, but on the fact of their past conversion and the assumed validity of a popular, but erroneous, doctrine.

Aware of the exceeding "deceitfulness of sin" and knowing its diabolical power to cheat us, let us refuse all sweet frames of hope, save Jesus Christ Himself. Trusting only in Him, let us "hold the beginning of our confidence stedfast unto the end" (Heb. 3:14) that we may be "partakers of Christ"—His fellows and companions, by His grace, in God's endless perfect day.

---

[6] A. H. Strong, *Systematic Theology*, p. 886.

When He shall come with trumpet sound,
Oh, may I then in Him be found;
Dressed in His righteousness alone,
Faultless to stand before the throne.

On Christ, the solid Rock, I stand;
All other ground is sinking sand.

EDWARD MOTE

"Kept by the Power of God"

Blessed be the God and Father of our Lord Jesus Christ, who according to his abundant mercy hath begotten us again unto a living hope by the resurrection of Jesus Christ from the dead, to an inheritance incorruptible and undefiled, that fadeth not away, reserved in heaven for you, who are kept by the power of God through faith unto salvation ready to be revealed in the last time. Wherein ye greatly rejoice, though now for a season, if need be, ye are in heaviness through manifold temptations: that the trial of your faith, being much more precious than of gold that perisheth, though it be tried with fire, might be found unto praise and honor and glory at the appearing of Jesus Christ: whom having not seen, ye love; in whom, though now ye see him not, yet believing, ye rejoice with joy unspeakable and full of glory: receiving the end of your faith, the salvation of your souls.

I Peter 1:3-9

And they that know thy name will put their trust in thee: for thou, Lord, hast not forsaken them that seek thee.

Psalm 9:10

Chapter XVII

KEPT BY THE POWER OF GOD

"I'D LIKE TO BE a Christian. But what's the use? I know I couldn't last." How often do we hear such statements! Many, acutely aware of the weakness of the flesh, honestly fear that perseverance in the Christian life is beyond their poor powers. And indeed it is. But there is a sublime truth which many fail to recognize: Christ does not ask us to "go it alone" as His followers. He has promised to be with His own all the days, even to the end of the age. Surrounding and sustaining all who follow Him in obedient faith is His infinite grace and all the power of Almighty God!

The purposes of God in the salvation of men encompass the unending ages of eternity to come. To the Colossians (1:21, 22), Paul writes that they who in time past were alienated from God by hostility and wicked works now have become "reconciled in the body of Christ's flesh through death" in order that He may "present you holy and unblemished and unreproveable before Him" in His everlasting holy presence.

Paul had perfect confidence in the keeping grace of God. Knowing that he was near the end of his pilgrimage and warfare, he wrote to Timothy, "The Lord will deliver me from every evil work and will preserve [save] me unto his heavenly kingdom" (II Tim. 4:18).

Jude addresses his letter ". . . 'to the called, who have been kept for Christ;' namely, in order to belong to Him in time and in eternity."[1] In his closing doxology, he writes, "Now unto

---

[1] J. E. Huther, *Critical and Exegetical Handbook to the General Epistles of James, Peter, John, and Jude*, p. 669.

him who is able to keep you from falling, and to present you faultless before the presence of his glory with exceeding joy . . . the only wise God our Saviour. . . ." (v. 24 f.).

Peter writes of "an inheritance incorruptible and undefiled that fadeth not away, reserved in heaven for you" (I Pet. 1:4). What a precious heritage! Nor is this the whole of the wondrous truth. Peter declares in the same sentence that we are "kept by the power of God unto salvation ready to be revealed in the last time" (v. 5). What a glorious word! An everlasting heritage, to be revealed in the last time, is now reserved in heaven for us who, by the mighty power of God, are kept for that heritage.

But did you notice that, in our quotation of I Peter 1:5, two words were omitted? Only two words; but quite essential. And yet, many seem to omit them—if not in quoting, at least in comprehension. The words? "Through faith!" Peter declares that we are "kept by the power of God *through faith!*" The words do not seem to register in the minds of many. Recently a radio preacher, speaking on the keeping grace of God, referred twice to I Peter 1:5. In neither instance did he quote more than the words, "kept by the power of God. . . ." Although he said many good things in his message, there was no recognition whatever of the fact that it is *through faith* that we are "kept by the power of God." We can ill afford to ignore the essential condition governing the keeping grace of God. Bishop Moule writes:

"Able to keep." I know well how liable is this blissful truth, like every other, to distortions and misuse. It is possible so to state it, or rather so to ignore other truth beside it, as almost to deny our immortal personality, or our present responsibility.[2]

Paul did not lose sight of "our present responsibility" in his consideration of the preserving grace of God at work in our behalf to bring us to the everlasting enjoyment of the Father's presence. Writing to the Colossians of God's purpose to present holy and unblemished and unreproveable in His presence those

---

[2]H. C. G. Moule, *Thoughts on Christian Sanctity*, p. 68.

whom He has reconciled to Himself through the death of His Son, Paul is faithful to warn the Colossians that God's purpose can finally be realized in them only "if ye continue in the faith grounded and settled [stedfast], and be not moved away from the hope of the gospel" (1:23). Bishop Moule comments:

But that prospect is only yours *if,* an emphatic "if" *(eige), you are abiding by your (tēi) faith,* holding fast to that great secret, simplest reliance on the all-sufficient Saviour, and on no substitute for Him; *founded* as on the Rock, *and steady* in the resolve to rest there for ever; *and not yielding to movements* (*metakinoumenoi,* a present participle, indicating a chronic liability to disturbance) *away from the hope* (the blessed hope of the Lord's Return for the final salvation of His waiting and faithful ones), the hope *of the Gospel which you heard* when you were first evangelized.[3]

Paul's confidence that "the Lord will deliver me from every evil work and will preserve me unto his heavenly kingdom" was the confidence of one who could say, "I have fought the good fight, I have finished my course, I have kept the faith" (II Tim. 4:7) and who, in his letter, faithfully exhorts the pastor of the church at Ephesus "to continue thou in the things which thou hast learned . . . the holy scriptures which are able to make thee wise unto salvation through faith in Christ Jesus" (3:14, 15).

While the short Epistle of Jude begins and ends on a sublime note of the keeping power of God, in between are numerous sharp warnings of the peril and tragedy of apostasy. In his brief summary of the Epistle of Jude, A. T. Pierson writes:

It is a *warning against apostasy. Faith* makes *faithful* saints who, contending for the faith and persevering, are preserved by Grace and presented in Glory. The contrast is marked between those who *kept not* their first estate and *are kept* for judgment, and those who *keep themselves* and *are kept* from falling. Apostasy is presented in representative examples: Antinomians, who turn gracious liberty into lascivious license; unbelieving Israel in the Exodus; disobedient angels; lustful Sodomites; self-righteous Cain; greedy Balaam; presumptious Korah; and blasphemous mockers. All of us are either reserved for the Day of Condemnation,

---

[3]Moule, *Colossian Studies,* p. 97 f., italics his.

or preserved for the Day of Presentation. If we keep ourselves in the Love of God, fighting for the faith, building up ourselves upon the faith, praying in the Holy Ghost and looking for the coming of the Lord, God will keep us (guard as with a garrison).[4]

(Although he succeeded admirably in presenting the gist of the Epistle of Jude in his brief résumé, the godly Dr. Pierson, when contemplating other Scriptures, was not always so fully cognizant of the important truth which Jude emphasizes. For example, in *The Heart of the Gospel*, he writes: "You ask me whether I believe in the perseverance of the saints. I tell you, no. I have no confidence in the saints and their perseverance; but I believe in the perseverance of Jesus Christ. The reason why the saints persevere in grace is because Jesus Christ perseveres in the saints."[5] Much to the contrary, however, Jesus affirmed that the condition whereby *He* perseveres in the *saints* is that *they* persevere in *Him*. "Remain in me, and I in you. . . . If a man remain not in me, he is cast forth. . . ." [John 15:4, 6].)

Jude, who assures us of the keeping grace of God, warns us that there is a corresponding responsibility resting on us. Having cited actual instances of apostasy, both historical and contemporary, Jude turns from a consideration of apostates who "separate themselves, sensual [earthly-minded], having not the Spirit" (v. 19), to address an urgent warning to his readers: "But ye, beloved [in contrast with the apostates], building up yourselves on your most holy faith, praying in the Holy Ghost, keep yourselves in the love of God, looking expectantly for the mercy of our Lord Jesus Christ unto eternal life" (v. 20 f.). Concerning Jude's exhortation, "keep yourselves," Robertson comments on *tērēsate*: "First aorist active imperative (of urgency) of *tēreō*. In verse 1 they are said to be kept, but note the warning in verse 5 from the angels who did not keep their dominion."[6]

---

[4]A. T. Pierson, *Keys to the Word*, p. 158 f. italics his.

[5]Pierson, *The Heart of the Gospel*, p. 130.

[6]A. T. Robertson, *Word Pictures in the New Testament*, Vol. VI, p. 194.

The keeping grace of God is a precious fact. But the Scriptures reveal that there is a prerequisite "keeping" which is the responsibility of man. Both are in view in principle in our Lord's exhortation, "Remain in me, and I in you." Many places in the Scriptures, God's keeping and man's keeping are closely associated. In addition to the above example from Jude, consider the following:

1. Jesus declared to the church at Philadelphia (Rev. 3): ". . . thou hast kept my word and hast not denied my name. . . . Because thou hast kept the word of my patience, I also will keep thee from the hour of temptation which shall come upon all the world" (vv. 8, 10).

2. Assuming that the reading of the Vatican Manuscript is correct, I John 5:18 contains a precious reference to the keeping grace of Christ: "We know that no one who is born of God makes a practice of sinning, but the Son who was born of God continues to keep him" (Williams; cf. RSV). But close by is the admonition, "Little children, keep yourselves from idols" (v. 21); and John already had warned his dear children in the faith to beware the peril of apostasy arising through the enticements of the "many antichrists" who were attempting to "seduce" them and to lead them away from the Gospel which they had heard from the beginning (2:18-26).

3. Paul writes to the Thessalonians of his confidence that God, in His faithfulness, will preserve their spirits, souls, and bodies "blameless unto the coming of our Lord Jesus Christ" (I Thess. 5:23, 24) and prays (3:11-13) that God may "establish your hearts unblameable in holiness before God, even our Father, at the coming of our Lord Jesus Christ with all his saints." But he does not assume that there is no corresponding responsibility resting upon the Thessalonians themselves. Quite to the contrary, he expresses his deep concern that they "stand fast in the Lord" and in the faith (3:1-10).

4. Paul, who had suffered much as an Apostle and preacher of the Gospel, was not ashamed; for he was fully confident that

He whom he had believed, and for whom he gladly had suffered, "is able to keep that which I have committed unto him against that day" (II Tim. 1:12). But his expression of sublime confidence in the keeping grace of God is immediately followed by an urgent admonition to Timothy: "Hold fast the pattern of sound words, which thou hast heard of me, in faith and love in Christ Jesus. That good thing which was committed unto thee keep by the Holy Ghost who dwells in us" (vv. 13, 14). The guarding of the Gospel committed to him was for Timothy more than merely his obligation as a minister; it was essential to his own salvation. Continuing in the true Gospel, though evil men and seducers grow worse and worse—deceiving others and themselves more and more, Timothy would continue "wise unto salvation through faith in Christ Jesus" (3:13-15). By continuing in the true doctrine in a day when many depart from the faith (I Tim 4:1), Timothy would save both himself and all who hear and heed him (v. 16).

5. In his prayer of intercession just before His passion, Jesus prayed, "Holy Father, keep through thine own name those whom thou hast given me, that they may be one, as we are. . . . I pray not that thou shouldest take them out of the world, but that thou shouldest keep them from the evil [one]" (John 17:11, 15). Some assert that it is impossible that any who once believe on Jesus should subsequently be lost, since God must answer the prayer of His Son. But Jesus prayed for those who sent Him to the cross, "Father, forgive them, for they know not what they do." Are we to assume that, because Jesus so prayed, all the members of the Sanhedrin, Pilate, Herod, Judas, the soldiers, and all the mocking multitude were forgiven, simply because Jesus prayed for them? Are we to assume that the whole lot were immediately destined for salvation, simply because Jesus prayed for them? Jesus prayed aloud at the grave of Lazarus for the benefit of "the people which stand by, that they may believe that thou hast sent me" (John 11:42). Are we to assume that all who heard His prayer and for whom he

prayed were necessarily persuaded that He was indeed sent of God? Obviously not. It is evident from John's account that, while many of the Jews who witnessed the raising of Lazarus believed in Jesus, others did not.

Certainly there is nothing ineffectual about the keeping grace of the Father; it is infinite. But neither was there anything lacking in the keeping power of Jesus, who said, "While I was with them in the world, I kept them in thy name: those that thou gavest me I have kept, and none of them is lost, but the son of perdition" (John 17:12). Those whom the Father gave Him[7] Jesus kept—except one. Neither the Father nor the Son can keep those who do not wish to accept the conditions under which they may be kept. It is not, as some foolishly assert, a question of whether men are "stronger than God." Nor is it a question of what God *could* do. It is only a question of what God *does* do, as revealed in the Holy Scriptures. The Scriptures declare that men are free to depart from God, and believers are solemnly warned against so doing (Heb. 3:12). Jesus said of those whom He kept, "they have kept thy word" (John 17:6). This is of more than incidental significance, as we may discern from the promise (and warning) of Jesus, "If a man keep my word, he shall never see death" (John 8:51). "Keeping His word" is more than a momentary reception; it must be habitual, after the example of Jesus Himself, who said, "I know [the Father] and keep His word" (v. 55). Jesus said: "He that hath my commandments and keepth them, he it is that loveth me: and he that loveth me shall be loved of my Father, and I will love him, and will manifest myself to him. . . . If a man love me, he will keep my words: and my Father will love him, and we will come unto him and make our abode with him. . . . As the Father hath loved me, so have I loved you: remain [*menō*] in my love. If ye keep my commandments, ye shall remain in my love, even as I have kept my Father's commandments and

---

[7]For a discussion of the question, Whom Does the Father Give to Jesus? see Appendix B.

remain in His love" (John 14:21, 23; 15:9, 10). Those who *keep* are kept.

6. The writer to the Hebrews bids us "be content with such things as ye have: for he himself hath said, I will never leave thee nor forsake thee" (13:5). If anything can foster contentment in any circumstance, it is the promise that the Lord will not forsake His own. But shortly before his reminder of the Lord's promise not to forsake His own, the writer had warned his readers, "See that ye refuse not him that speaketh. For if they escaped not who refused him that spake on earth, much more shall not we escape if we turn away from him that speaketh from heaven" (12:25). Throughout his letter, he had warned his readers many times against the dreadful peril of forsaking the Lord, a peril which constantly confronted them.

The Old Testament passage from which the writer to the Hebrews quotes the Lord's promise not to forsake His own (Deut. 31:6, 8) contains the Lord's solemn warning that when the children of Israel forsake Him and break His covenant, His anger will be kindled against them and He will forsake them (vv. 16 ff. Cf. I Chron. 28:9, II Chron. 15:2, Ps. 9:10, Ezra 8:22). The peril is never that the Lord may forsake His people; but rather that His people may forsake Him. "If we deny him," warns Paul, "he also will deny us" (II Tim. 2:12). "Remain in me, and I in you."

> Alone, O Christ, on earth,
>   Thy saving Name is given:
> To turn aside from thee is hell;
>   To trust in thee is heaven.
>   *(Selected)*

7. Those whom Peter exhorts to "commit the keeping of their souls to God in well doing, as unto a faithful Creator" (I Pet. 4:19) he yet admonishes to "be sober, be vigilant, because your adversary the devil, as a roaring lion, walketh about seeking whom he may devour: whom resist stedfast in the faith" (5:8, 9). He already had admonished them, as pilgrims and strangers on earth, to "abstain from fleshly lusts which war

against the soul" (2:11). God's faithful keeping of our souls does not obviate our responsibility to "keep ourselves in the love of God, looking for the mercy of our Lord Jesus Christ unto eternal life" (Jude 21). Our keeping ourselves in His love, in faithful anticipation of the mercy of our Saviour unto eternal life, is prerequisite to His safekeeping of our souls. We can trust Christ to save us, and we can trust Him to keep us; but we *must* trust Him.

8. Let us consider again I Peter 1:5. Peter declares that it is "through faith" that we are "kept by the power of God unto salvation ready to be revealed in the last time." Immediately following his reference to the necessity of faith as the condition whereby we are kept by the power of God unto final salvation, Peter encourages us to stand firm in our present trials and testings (vv. 6-9) and declares that it is on the basis of our *now believing* that we are *now receiving* the end of our faith, the salvation of our souls (vv. 8, 9). We can trust Christ to save us, and we can trust Him to keep us all the way; but we *must* trust Him—all the way. The necessity of keeping ourselves in the saving grace of Christ is quite as much a doctrine of the Holy Scriptures as the power and faithfulness of Christ to save and keep all who trust in Him.

Paul commended the Thessalonians for the stedfastness of their faith, as expressed in "your patience and faith in all your persecutions and tribulations that ye endure: which is a manifest token of the righteous judgment of God, that ye may be counted worthy of the kingdom of God, for which ye also suffer" (II Thess. 1:4, 5). It seems a staggering thing that there could be any sense whatever in which we—sinners that we are—could ever be accounted "worthy of the kingdom of God." And yet our Lord declares of the few in Sardis who had not defiled their garments that "they shall walk with me in white: for they are worthy. He that overcometh, the same shall be clothed in white raiment; and I will not blot out his name out of the book of life, but I will confess his name before my Father, and before his angels" (Rev. 3:4, 5).

It is true that we can be accounted worthy of the kingdom of God and worthy to walk with Christ before the Father and His angels only by the grace of our loving Saviour who is Himself our "righteousness, sanctification, and redemption" (I Cor. 1:30), even as He is our very life (Col. 3:4). But the righteousness and the saving life of the risen Christ (Rom. 5:10) cannot avail for unfaithful men. The righteousness which God requires of men who are to be part of His everlasting kingdom is the "righteousness of God which is through faith in Jesus Christ unto all and upon all them who believe" (Rom. 3:22)—not merely for a moment, but habitually and persistently, through trials and testings. Paul was faithful to exhort his converts to "continue in the faith [because] we must through much tribulation enter into the kingdom of God" (Acts 14:22)—the actual realization of "the everlasting kingdom of our Lord and Saviour Jesus Christ" (II Pet. 1:11), the final salvation which now must be anticipated by living faith in our living Saviour.

The Christian life is a life of spiritual warfare, and all who would be forever Christ's must necessarily "fight the good fight of faith" and continually "lay hold on eternal life" in the conflict against "the wiles of the devil [and] the world-rulers of the darkness of this age" and against "fleshly lusts which war against the soul." James writes, "Blessed is the man who endures temptation: for when he is tried [lit., having become approved] he will receive the crown of life which the Lord has promised to them that love him" (1:12). Some insist that the promise of which James writes is not life itself, but only a *crown* of life. The life, say they, is a gift; but the crown (only a symbol of that life, say they) is a reward. But *tēs zōēs* in Jas. 1:12 (as in our Lord's promise in Rev. 2:10) is the genitive of apposition, and therefore the crown in view is life itself. Robertson comments, "It is the genitive of apposition, life itself being the crown."[8] Mayor declares, "Gen. of definition . . . 'the crown which consists of life eternal.' "[9]

---

[8]Robertson, *op. cit.*, p. 17.

[9]J. B. Mayor, *The Epistle of St. James*, p. 49.

It is true that eternal life is the free gift of God to undeserving sinners. But just as the acceptance of the gift is costly (as we considered in Chapter 2), so is the retention of that gift, once received. There is therefore a sense in which eternal life, though God's gracious gift to undeserving men, is yet a reward to those who faithfully endure as Christ's overcomers and who "become approved" as James declares. The promises of Jesus to overcomers confirm the fact that the promised crown is not merely a symbol, but eternal life itself: "Be thou faithful unto death, and I will give thee the crown of life. . . . He that overcometh shall not be hurt of the second death. . . . I will not blot out his name out of the book of life, but I will confess his name before my Father, and before his angels. . . . To him that overcometh will I give to eat of the tree of life, which is in the midst of the paradise of God" (Rev. 2:10, 11; 3:5; 2:7). The conflict is real, and the issue is life everlasting.

Conquer we must, if we are to reign eternally with Christ. He has promised, "To him that overcometh will I grant to sit with me in my throne, even as I also overcame and am set down with my Father in his throne" (Rev. 3:21). "If we patiently endure," writes Paul, "we will reign with Him too. If we disown Him, He will disown us too" (II Tim. 2:12 Williams). Only if we suffer with Christ shall we be glorified together with Him (Rom. 8:17). "He that overcometh shall inherit all things; and I will be his God, and he shall be my son. But the fearful [*"Tois deilois*, old word . . . for the cowardly who recanted under persecution."[10]] and unbelieving [*"Apistois*, faithless, untrustworthy, in contrast with Christ *'ho pistos'* (1:5)."[10]] . . . shall have their part in the lake which burneth with fire and brimstone: which is the second death" (Rev. 21:7, 8). Conquer we must, if we are to inherit the things prepared for them that love Him.

Let us not think it strange concerning "the fiery trial" which tries us, as though some strange thing happened to us. Rather

---

[10]Robertson, *op. cit.*, p. 469.

let us rejoice in "the trial of our faith." Let us "rejoice, inasmuch as we are partakers of Christ's sufferings; that, when his glory shall be revealed, we may be glad with exceeding joy" (I Pet. 4:13). With Paul, let us consider that "the sufferings of this present time are not worthy to be compared with the glory which shall be revealed to us . . . if so be that we suffer with Him, that we may also be glorified together" (Rom. 8:18, 17). Let us rejoice in the trials of our faith; they are an evidence of sonship and a pledge of good things to come. Let us remember that it is "through much tribulation" (Acts 14:22) that we must enter into the kingdom of God— the ultimate entrance into "the everlasting kingdom of our Lord and Saviour Jesus Christ" (II Pet. 1:11) in its tangible divine manifestation, when faith becomes sight.

With Paul, we may be fully confident that, as we trust in Him, "the Lord shall deliver [us] from every evil work and preserve [us] unto his heavenly kingdom" (II Tim. 4:18). If we trust and follow Him, He will be with us all the way, and the day of His triumph will find us among them of whom it is written, "And they overcame him [Satan] by the blood of the Lamb, and by the word of their testimony, and they loved not their lives unto death" (Rev. 12:11). Our present concern need be only that "with purpose of heart, we cleave unto the Lord" (Acts 11:23).

Sometime ago, a young father shared the burdens of his heart with me as we talked together in the quiet of my study. He had known recent bereavement, and was passing through deep waters of ill health, loss of income, and mounting expense. Never shall I forget his words. After a moment's quiet, he looked up and calmly said, "But those nail-pierced Hands are mine. They're holding me fast."

Above the doorway of his Pastor's College in London, Spurgeon affixed the words, "Holding, I am held." A precious truth! But neither the first clause, nor the latter, can stand alone. They are complementary. Together, they comprehend the meaning of our Saviour's words, "Remain in me, and I in you."

So the sum of this whole matter is—abide in Christ. Let us root and ground our lives and characters in Him, and then God's inmost desire will be gratified in regard to us, and He will bring even us stainless and blameless into the blaze of His presence. There we shall all have to stand and let that all-penetrating light search us through and through. How do we expect to be then "found of Him in peace, without spot and blameless?" There is but one way—to live in constant exercise of faith in Christ and grip Him so close and sure that the world, the flesh, and the devil cannot make us loosen our fingers. Then He will hold us up, and His great purpose, which brought Him to earth and nailed Him to the cross, will be fulfilled in us; and at last, we shall lift up voices of wondering praise "to Him who is able to keep us from falling, and to present us faultless before the presence of His glory with exceeding joy."[11]

"Holding, I am held."

---

[11]Alexander Maclaren, *The Epistles of St. Paul to the Colossians and Philemon* (*The Expositor's Bible,* ed. W. Robertson Nicoll), p. 115.

"That You May Know that You Have
Eternal Life"

And this is the record, that God hath given to us eternal life, and this life is in his Son. He that hath the Son hath the life; and he that hath not the Son of God hath not the life. These things have I written unto you that believe on the name of the Son of God, that ye may know that ye have eternal life.

I John 5:11-13

Chapter XVIII

THAT YOU MAY KNOW THAT YOU HAVE ETERNAL LIFE

SOMETIME AGO, a successful businessman of Kansas City, an earnest Christian, was greeted by his banker with the question, "What do you know for sure, Pete?" He immediately replied, "I know the blood of Jesus Christ cleanses me from all sin, I'm a child of God by faith, and I'm on my way to heaven."

Surprised and impressed by the unexpected answer, the banker exclaimed, "Wait a minute! Come into my office; I want to talk with you." My friend had the privilege of talking at length concerning the surpassing grace of God and the glorious things He has provided for all who will believe and trust Him.

The world is hungry to know some things "for sure"—things in which men may place their confidence in a day of confusion and uncertainty. And God is even more concerned that men shall know the things which He has provided, in His all-sufficient grace, for the children of men. Among other things, He wants men to know that they can be sure of eternal life.

Many assert that it is impossible for men to know, here and now, that they have eternal life. According to the Holy Scriptures they are are wrong. But equally wrong are those who assert that all who are certain that they have been converted ought never to question the fact of their personal salvation. They do not agree with Paul that men whom he addressed as "saints" who have been "sanctified in Christ Jesus" should be admonished to examine themselves (II Cor. 13:5) to discover

whether they are yet in the faith, or instead are reprobates in
whom Christ no longer dwells ("*adokimoi*, the very adjective
that Paul held up before himself as a dreadful outcome to be
avoided, I Cor. 9:27."[1]). They do not agree with John that there
is a real and deadly possibility that men who have fully experienced the saving grace of God might abandon the Gospel
of Christ which they once received and thus disown the Son
and forfeit that eternal life which is ours only in Him (I John
2:23-25). They do not agree with Peter that men who "have
obtained like precious faith with us through the righteousness
of God and our Saviour Jesus Christ" and who are now "partakers of the divine nature, having escaped the corruption that
is in the world through lust," yet have need to guard against
the peril of "being led away with the error of the wicked" and
actually sharing the fate of unstable men who "wrest the scriptures unto their own destruction" (II Pet. 3:16-18). But

> He who never doubted of his state,
> Perhaps he may—perhaps too late.

No other knowledge is nearly so important as the assurance
that we have eternal life. Thank God, we may know. But how?
Certainly not by how we feel about the matter. People sometimes say, "I was a backslider for years. But all the while I
was out in sin, I knew in my heart that I was still a child of
God and still saved." We would not question the sincerity of
people who make such statements. But there is reason to question their spiritual intelligence and understanding. Human
feeling is neither a reliable guide to divine truth nor a safe
index of one's personal spiritual status. "Samson knew not
that the Lord had departed from him . . . The heart is deceitful above all . . . There is a way that seemeth right . . . Thou
sayest, I am rich and have need of nothing, and knowest not
that thou art wretched, miserable, poor, blind, and naked . . .
knoweth not whither he goeth . . . deceiveth his own heart. . . ."

---

[1]A. T. Robertson, *Word Pictures in the New Testament*, Vol. IV, p. 270.

How men feel about things does not determine matters. Many unsaved people say with complete sincerity, "I feel that I am all right just as I am." Or, "I am not afraid to die." Or, "I feel that I am just as sure of heaven as anyone in the church." But how men feel about spiritual matters determines nothing. When we begin to determine our spiritual status and to define our doctrines by human experience, feelings, and opinions, we have embarked on a path of error the end of which is everlasting disaster. (Is not this erroneous procedure a prime factor underlying the shameful multiplicity of sects?) None can feel more assured of salvation than men of long ago who justified themselves in their rejection of Jesus in the confidence that 'we are Abraham's seed . . . we have one Father, even God." Reliance on feeling is unwise.

Although Calvin taught that, for the elect, an important means of assurance is the inner witness of the Spirit, he also taught that the reprobate may receive a similar inner witness, actually experiencing the grace of God to such an extent that they imagine themselves to be of the elect. But since they are not, God (as he believed) has no intention that their experience of His grace shall endure. From the outset, His intention is that they shall wither away and die. "There is nothing strange," he writes, "in [God's] shedding some rays of grace on the reprobate, and afterwards allowing these to be extinguished" (3:2:12). This is accomplished, according to Calvin, through 'an inferior operation of the Spirit," the whole purpose of which is "the better to convict them and leave them without excuse" (3:2:11). (To Calvin, this was in perfect accord with ". . . the doctrine which I maintain, that the reprobate are hateful to God, and that with perfect justice, since those destitute of His Spirit cannot produce anything that does not deserve cursing" [3:24:17].)

Contending that the reprobate may respond to the Gospel, exercise faith in Christ and the mercies of God, and actually experience grace to such an extent that they sincerely believe themselves to be of the elect, Calvin wrote (3:2:11, 12):

. . . experience shows that the reprobate are sometimes affected in a way so similar to the elect that, even in their own judgment, there is no difference between them. Hence it is not strange that by the Apostle a taste of heavenly gifts, and by Christ himself a temporary faith, is ascribed to them. Not that they truly perceive the power of spiritual grace and the sure light of faith; but the Lord, the better to convict them and leave them without excuse, instils into their minds such a sense of his goodness as can be felt without the Spirit of adoption. . . . Therefore, as God regenerates the elect only for ever by incorruptible seed, as the seed of life once sown in their hearts never perishes, so he effectually seals in them the grace of his adoption, that it may be sure and stedfast. But in this there is nothing to prevent an inferior operation of the Spirit from taking its course in the reprobate. Meanwhile, believers are taught to examine themselves carefully and humbly, lest carnal security creep in and take the place of assurance of faith. We may add that the reprobate never have any other than a confused sense of grace, laying hold of the shadow rather than the substance, because the Spirit properly seals the forgiveness of sins in the elect only, applying it by special faith to their use. Still it is correctly said that the reprobate believe God to be propitious to them, inasmuch as they accept the gift of reconcilation, though confusedly and without due discernment; not that they are partakers of the same faith or regeneration with the children of God; but because under a covering of hypocrisy, they seem to have a principle of faith in common with them. Nor do I even deny that God illumines their minds to this extent, that they recognize his grace;[2] but that conviction he distinguishes from the peculiar testimony which he gives to his elect in this respect, that the reprobate never obtain to the full result or to full fruition. When he shows himself propitious to them, it is not as if he had truly rescued them from death and taken them under his protection. He only gives them a manifestation of his present mercy. [Footnote: The French adds, 'Comme par une bouffee'—as by fits and starts.] In the elect alone

---

[2]But Paul declared that "the natural man receiveth not the things of the Spirit of God: for they are foolishness unto him; neither can he know them, because they are spiritually discerned" (I Cor. 2:14). Jesus taught that men can know the truth of His teaching only if they sincerely will to do God's will (John 7:17), which is quite the opposite of Calvin's "covering of hypocrisy." Calvin himself declares (1:6:2) that ". . . it is impossible for any man to obtain even the minutest portion of right and sound doctrine without being a disciple of Scripture. Hence the first step in true knowledge is taken when we reverently embrace the testimony which God has been pleased therein to give of Himself. For not only does faith, full and perfect faith, but all correct knowledge of God originate in obedience." And obedience, let us add, is far removed from any "covering of hypocrisy."

ıe implants the living root of faith so that they persevere even to the
ınd. Thus we dispose of the objection that if God truly displays his grace,
t must endure for ever. There is nothing inconsistent in this with the fact
ɔf his enlightening some with a present sense of grace, which afterwards
ɔroves evanescent.

Although faith is a knowledge of the divine favour towards us and a
ull persuasion of its truth, it is not strange that the sense of the divine
ove, which though akin to faith differs much from it, vanishes in those
vho are temporarily impressed. The will of God is, I confess, immutable,[3]
ınd his truth is always consistent with itself; but I deny that the repro-
ɔate ever advance so far as to penetrate to that secret revelation which
Scripture reserves for the elect only. I therefore deny that they either
ınderstand his will considered as immutable, or steadily embrace his
ruth, inasmuch as they rest satisfied with an evanescent impression;
ust as a tree not planted deep enough may take root, but will in process
ɔf time wither away, though it may for several years not only put forth
eaves and flowers, but produce fruit. In short, as by the revolt of the
ırst man the image of God could be effaced from his mind and soul, so
here is nothing strange in His shedding some rays of grace on the repro-
ɔate, and afterwards allowing these to be extinguished.[4]

Calvin recognized that his argument involved him in a seri-
ɔus difficulty. "Should it be objected," he writes, "that believers
have no stronger testimony to assure them of their adoption,
I answer that though there is a great resemblance and affinity
between the elect of God and those who are impressed for a
time with a fading faith, yet the elect alone have that full
assurance which is extolled by Paul, and by which they are
enabled to cry, Abba, Father" (3:2:11).

But Calvin's answer in no way eliminates his difficulty. For
if (as he declared) it is impossible for the reprobate Christian

---

[3]Calvin considered reprobation a positive decree. For a brief discussion of
Calvin's view of reprobation and of his erroneous fundamental assumption, see
Appendix D.

[4]This was Calvin's explanation of the fact that many fall from grace, a fact
which he acknowledged. His theology required him to assume that those who
fall from grace do so by the express design of God. They believe for a while,
only to fall away because they are not of the elect and therefore must perish.
God wills that they perish, for such is the sole purpose and destiny for which
He created them. Calvin's assumption, essential to the defense of the logic of his
theology, is completely contrary to the total affirmation of the Holy Scriptures.

to perceive that the inner witness of which he is conscious is not really valid, and if in his own best judgment it is impossible for him to observe any difference between himself and the true elect, and if the reprobate Christian is completely sincere in believing God to have been propitious to him and to have given him the gift of reconciliation and in believing himself to be truly elect, how can one's personal feeling be reliable ground for "full assurance" of salvation? Actually, according to Calvin's argument one cannot know whether his feeling of assurance is warranted, or only vain presumption.

Along with inner feeling, Calvin also appealed to the doctrine of election as sure ground for confidence:

Those who preclude access and would not have anyone to obtain a taste of this doctrine [election, as understood by Calvin] are equally unjust to God and men, there being no other means of humbling us as we ought, or making us feel how much we are bound to him. Nor, indeed, have we elsewhere any sure ground of confidence (3:21:1).

Advocates of the doctrine of unconditional security often assert that conditional security is contrary to the doctrine of election—meaning, of course, *unconditional* election. (An exception is the late Dr. Henry C. Thiessen who, in his *Introductory Lectures in Systematic Theology* [Eerdmans], states a good case for conditional election while contending for the unconditional security of "those who have had a vital experience of salvation.") An extended consideration of the doctrine of election, with its many facets, is not within the scope of the present volume.[5] But even if one accepts Calvin's definition of the doctrine of election, it affords no ground for the assurance of salvation. For in declaring that apart from the doctrine of election we have no "sure ground of confidence" of salvation, Calvin did not mean that the doctrine affords such ground of confidence merely as an objective doctrine. He believed that it becomes such "sure ground of confidence" only on the basis of specific evidence of one's personal election.

---

[5]The doctrine of election is the subject of a manuscript now in preparation.

But what constitutes such evidence? Here Calvin appeals again to human feelings and definitions of individual personal experience: "In regard to the elect, we regard calling as the evidence of election, and justification as another symbol of its manifestation, until it is fully accomplished by the attainment of glory" (3:21:7).

But Calvin's contention that one's experience of calling and justification is reliable evidence of personal election is completely nullified by his contention that reprobate Christians, as well as the true elect, sincerely believe themselves to have been called and justified. How can it be known whether one's calling and justification are actual, or only imagined? How can it be known whether one's experience of God's grace is divinely intended to be permanent, or only temporary? How can it be known whether God has implanted within him "the living root of faith" which is ordained to endure, or whether his faith eventually must prove to have been only "evanescent"? Obviously, it can be known only as one finally perseveres (or fails to persevere) in faith. There is no valid assurance of election and final salvation for any man, apart from deliberate perseverance in faith. Calvin himself ultimately arrived at this conclusion. In his commentary on Hebrews 6:12, he writes:

12. *But followers,* or imitators, &c. To sloth he opposes imitation; it is then the same thing as though he said that there was need of constant alacrity of mind; but it had far more weight when he reminded them that the fathers were not made partakers of the promises except through the unconquerable firmness of faith.

. . . .

Faith and patience, &c. What is meant is a firm faith which has patience as its companion. For faith is what is chiefly required; but as many who make at first a marvelous display of faith soon fail, he shows that the true evidence of that faith which is not fleeting and evanescent is endurance.

. . . .

13. *For when God made a promise to Abraham,* &c. His object was to prove that the grace of God is offered to us in vain, except we receive the promise by faith and constantly cherish it in the bosom of our heart.[6]

---

[6] Calvin, *Commentary on the Epistle to the Hebrews,* p. 146 f.

Again, commenting on Hebrews 3:6-14, Calvin writes:

. . . the author of this epistle exhorts the Jews who had already made a profession of Christ to persevere in the faith, that they might be deemed as being in God's household. He had said before that God's house was subject to the authority of Christ. Suitably to this declaration is added the admonition that they would then have a place in God's family when they obeyed Christ. But as they had already embraced the Gospel, he mentions their condition if they persevered in the faith.

• • • • • • • • • • • • • • • • • • • •

This passage reminds us that we are always to make progress even unto death; for our whole life is as it were a race.

• • • • • • • • • • • • • • • • • • • •

12. *Take heed, (or, See) brethren, lest there be at any time in any of you a wicked heart of unbelief,* &c. I have preferred to retain literally what the Apostle states, rather than to give a paraphrase as to the wicked or depraved *heart of unbelief,* by which he intimates that unbelief would be connected with depravity or wickedness, if after having received the knowledge of Christ they departed from his faith. For he addressed them who had been imbued with the elements of Christianity; hence he immediately added, *By departing;* for the sin of defection is accompanied with perfidy.

13. He also pointed out the remedy, so that they might not fall into this wickedness, and that was, to *exhort one another.* For as by nature we are inclined to evil, we have need of various helps to retain us in the fear of God. Unless our faith be now and then raised up, it will lie prostrate; unless it be warmed, it will be frozen; unless it be roused, it will grow torpid. He would have us then to stimulate one another by mutual exhortations, so that Satan may not creep into our hearts and by his fallacies draw us away from God. And this is a way of speaking that ought to be especially observed; for we fall not immediately by the first assault into this madness of striving against God; but Satan by degrees accosts us artfully by indirect means, until he holds us ensnared in his delusions. Then indeed being blinded, we break forth into open rebellion.

We must then meet this danger in due time, and it is one that is nigh us all, for nothing is more possible than to be deceived; and from this deception comes at length hardness of heart. We hence see how necessary it is for us to be roused by the incessant goads of exhortations. Nor does the Apostle give only a general precept, that all should take heed to themselves; but he would have them also to be solicitous for the salvation of every member, so that they should not suffer any of those who had been once called to perish through their neglect. And he who feels it his duty so to watch over the salvation of the whole flock as to neglect no one sheep performs in this case the office of a good shepherd.

. . . .

14. *For we are made partakers*, &c. He commends them for having begun well; but lest, under the pretext of the grace which they had obtained, they should indulge themselves in carnal security, he says that there was need of perseverance; for many having only tasted the Gospel do not think of any progress, as though they had reached the summit. Thus it is that they not only stop in the middle of their race, yea, nigh the starting-posts, but turn another way. Plausible indeed is this objection, "What can we wish more after having found Christ?" But if he is possessed by faith, we must persevere in it, so that he may be our perpetual possession. Christ, then, has given himself to be enjoyed by us on this condition, that by the same faith by which we have been admitted into a participation of him, we are to preserve so great a blessing even to death.

---

⁷*Ibid.*, pp. 81-90. The entire portion is excellent, but most of it has been omitted to conserve space. At this point, John Owen, the translator and editor, adds a footnote: "What is implied here is that we may professedly be partakers of Christ, that is of his blessing as a Saviour, and yet be not really so. The proof of the reality is in the perseverance." Such an assumption is necessary, of course, for the defense of the doctrine of unconditional election. But it is contrary both to the assertion of the Scripture passage, and to the tenor of Calvin's comments.

The disparity between Calvin's *Institutes* and some of the material in his *Commentaries* is quite apparent to the observing reader. Strong writes, "The progress in Calvin's thought may be seen by comparing some of his earlier with his later utterances. . . . we must give Calvin credit for modifying his doctrine with maturer reflection and advancing years" (*Systematic Theology*, p. 778). Strong's contention that portions of the *Commentaries* reflect a maturer Calvin than the *Institutes* is justified. But "advancing years" do not wholly account for the disparity, since the *Institutes*, while first written when he was twenty-six, were revised several times, the last revision being in 1559, just five years before his death.

The disparity must be attributed to the fact that, in his *Commentaries*, Calvin's approach to the Scriptures was often much more candid than in his *Institutes*. In his lifelong development of the *Institutes*, Calvin never was able to free himself from the basic concepts which he entertained at twenty-six years of age and tended always to view the Scriptures from the standpoint of his theology which, unfortunately, is grounded more upon logic than upon the Bible itself—a logic which proceeds from the erroneous *a priori* assumption that the will of God has but a single aspect. In his *Commentaries*, however, Calvin

In his commentary on Acts, Calvin is excellent in his comments on Paul's exhortation to the believers at Lystra, Iconium, and Antioch (14:20-22), the gist of which is:

> . . . let not the faithful neglect the Word of God, as if the reading and preaching thereof were unnecessary; because there is no man who hath not need of continual confirmation.
>
> 22. *And exhorting them.* This was the principal way to confirm, in that they provoke the disciples who had before embraced the Gospel and did profess it, to go forward by exhorting them; for we are far from being so ready and stout as we ought. Therefore our laziness needeth pricks, and our coldness must be warmed. But because God will have his exercised with divers combats, Paul and Barnabas admonish the disciples to be ready to suffer tribulation. A very necessary admonition, that we must go on warfare in this world, that we may live well and godly. If the flesh should not molest us, if Satan should attempt nothing, if the wicked should not trouble us with some stumblingblocks, it were no such troublesome thing to persevere; because that were a sweet walk through a soft and pleasant way; but because there arise on every side, and every minute of an hour, infinite assaults which provoke us to fall away, there ariseth the hardness; and therefore it is that the virtue of constancy is so rare. Therefore, to the end we may persist even unto the end, we must be prepared for war.

. . . .

> But this is the best comfort, and which is sufficient enough to confirm their minds, that this way (though it be hard and sharp) leadeth unto the kingdom of heaven.[8]

---

tended to get closer to the Scripture itself. Consequently, there is a startling disparity to be found between the *Institutes* and some portions of his *Commentaries,* a disparity which many have noted. The above comments of Calvin (containing such statements as "But if [Christ] is possessed by faith, we must persevere in it, so that he may be our perpetual possession" and "Christ, then, has given himself to be enjoyed by us on this condition, that by the same faith by which we have been admitted into a participation of him, we are to preserve so great a blessing even to death") can so little be reconciled with the gist of his *Institutes* that Owen finds it necessary to insist that we assume Calvin to have implied an insincere profession of faith. Despite Owen's plea, there is no evidence of such an implication in Calvin's comments.

[8]Calvin, *Commentary on the Acts of the Apostles,* Vol. II, p. 24 f.

It is evident from his writings that Calvin ultimately concluded that, in the last analysis, the only real ground for the assurance of one's election is his deliberate perseverance in faith. Hodge arrived at the same conclusion. In his comments on Romans 8:29, 30, he asserts that "Election, calling, justification, and salvation are indissolubly united; and, therefore, he who has clear evidence of his being called has the same evidence of his election and final salvation."[9] But what is the "clear evidence" of one's call? In his concluding remarks at the close of the chapter, Hodge concedes that "The only evidence of election is effectual calling, that is, the production of holiness. And the only evidence of the genuineness of this call and the certainty of our perseverance is a patient continuance in well doing".[10] In other words, the only real evidence of election is perseverance, and our only assurance of the certainty of persevering is—to persevere!

John Eadie states the same conclusion. In his commentary on Colossians, his excellent comments on 1:23 include:

While . . . the perseverance of the saints is a prominent doctrine of Scripture and a perennial source of consolation, it is not inconsistent with exhortations to permanence of faith and warnings of the sad results of deviation and apostasy. He who stops short in the race, and does not reach the goal, cannot obtain the prize. He who abandons the refuge into which he fled for a season is swept away when the hurricane breaks upon him. The loss of faith is the knell of hope.

.   .   .   .

For man is not acted on mechanically by the grace of God, but his whole spiritual nature is excited to earnest prayer and anxious effort. His continuance in the faith is not the unconscious impress of an irresistible law, but the result of a diligent use of every means by which belief may be fostered and deepened. . . . Thus, as rational beings are wrought upon by motives, so warnings and appeals are addressed to them, and these appliances form a special feature of God's plan of preserving them.

---

[9]Charles Hodge, *Commentary on the Epistle to the Romans,* p. 207.
[10]*Ibid.,* p. 212.

The apostle thus shows them how much is suspended on their presever-ance.[11]

All Calvinist theologians ultimately agree with Hodge, Eadie, and Calvin that the only unfailing evidence and ground for assurance that one is elect is deliberate perseverance in faith in Jesus Christ. Professor John Murray of Westminster Theological Seminary aptly states the matter:

. . . let us appreciate the doctrine of the perseverance of the saints and recognize that we may entertain the faith of our security in Christ only as we persevere in faith and holiness to the end. It was nothing less than the goal of the resurrection to life and glory that Paul had in mind when he wrote, "Brethren, I count not myself to have apprehended: but this one thing I do, forgetting those things which are behind, and reaching forth unto those things which are before, I press toward the mark for the prize of the high calling of God in Christ Jesus" (Phil. 3:13, 14).

The perseverance of the saints reminds us very forcefully that only those who persevere to the end are truly saints. We do not attain to the prize of the high calling of God in Christ Jesus automatically. Perseverance means the engagement of our persons in the most intense and concentrated devotion to those means which God has ordained for the achievement of his saving purpose. The scriptural doctrine of perseverance has no affinity with the quietism and antinomianism which are so prevalent in evangelical circles.[12]

These things being true, it is obviously an error of the gravest sort to assume that a past experience of conversion makes one unconditionally secure and constitutes a guarantee of final salvation. And why should men who concede that perseverance in faith is the only real evidence of personal salvation, and in-

---

[11]John Eadie, *Commentary on the Epistle to the Colossians*, p. 85 f. It is odd that a Calvinist should speak of "how much is suspended on perseverance." For according to "tulip" theology's doctrine of unconditional election, *nothing at all* is suspended on perseverance. Quite to the contrary, perseverance is supposedly suspended on election. But when men get close to the Scriptures, they often get far from their theology. Eadie has it right: *much* is suspended on perseverance, according to the Scriptures—all theology to the contrary notwithstanding.

[12]John Murray, *Redemption—Accomplished and Applied*, p. 193.

deed the very "means which God has ordained for the achievement of his saving purpose," insinuate (as do some) that all
who faithfully exhort Christians to continue in the faith and
be not moved away from the hope of the Gospel are somehow "enemies of grace" and of the Gospel of Christ? And what
warrant have men for turning away the concern of Christians
from the imperative necessity of deliberately persevering in
faith and implying that the only real concern is whether a
past conversion experience was valid by constantly trumpeting
the popular doctrine of "once in grace, always in grace"?
(which, even in the light of Calvin's assertion that reprobate
Christians enjoy a temporary experience of the grace of God
which causes them to believe that they are elect, is a misleading
half-truth, shamefully short of a full and accurate definition of
doctrine). There is a deadly inconsistency in the ministry of
men who believe that God saves and secures men—not apart
from, but *through* means—but whose preaching serves to destroy the concern of their hearers for the essential importance
of continuing in the means. How different was the ministry of
Paul (Acts 14:22, Col. 1:23, I Cor. 15:1, 2, I Tim. 4:16, II Tim.
2:12, etc.).

The New Testament writers sometimes bade their readers
recall their past experience of grace for their encouragement
in present trials. But they never encouraged them to begin
placing confidence in the mere fact of past grace, as if that
settled matters for eternity. Rather, they exhorted them to
press on in the way of faith, as they had in the past. But many
churches today would bar from their pulpits any man who
would dare to preach the urgent warnings of Paul, the other
Apostles, and our Saviour Himself, without carefully "explaining" them into total irrelevance. They have been taught to
believe that a past act of faith and experience of grace constitute infallible assurance of unconditional security. They are
fully confident that they are elect and therefore must continue
in grace, despite any and all eventualities.

Certainly the elect will persevere in faith and grace to final salvation. The fact is indisputable. But while God knows who they are, and has known from the beginning, *men* can know only as they persevere. While it is true that the elect will persevere to the end, that is only *half* the truth; for it is equally true that they who persevere to the end *are* the elect. It is the latter solemn truth which the Holy Scriptures present as a matter for the utmost concern of believers. To ignore the import of the many urgent warnings against the peril of apostasy by appealing to a particular definition of the doctrine of election is to tread a path of folly and presumption. Even if Calvin's doctrine of unconditional election were correct (which it is not[13]), it could never be of more than academic import, since (as Calvin acknowledged) actual perseverance in faith constitutes the only real evidence of personal election. We should be foolish indeed, were we to allow interpretations and definitions and hypotheses of the doctrine of election to dissuade us from giving earnest heed to the Saviour's explicit warning, "Remain in me, and I in you. . . . If a man remain not in me, he is cast forth . . . and withered . . . and burned." Jesus said, "My sheep hear my voice . . . and they follow me." No man who is not listening to His voice and following Him has warrant for assuming that he is one of Christ's sheep. No man who is not deliberately persevering in the way of faith has warrant for assuming that he has eternal life in Christ. No man who is not living in obedient faith has warrant for entertaining the hope of everlasting salvation.

Let us summarize: Calvin taught that, while the elect will certainly persevere in faith and grace, reprobate Christians have a temporary experience of grace during which time they are completely unaware of any distinction between themselves and the elect, sincerely believing God to be fully propitious to them and believing themselves to be truly elect. Calvin also

---

[13]The certainty of election and perseverance is with respect, not to particular men unconditionally, but to the *ekklēsia* corporately. See Appendix E, Sec. 10.

taught that the only real evidence of the election of any individual is his perseverance in faith. Thus, even from the teachings of Calvin, we must conclude that while a past conversion experience and a present sense of grace are precious encouragements, they do not constitute absolute evidence of election to everlasting salvation.

Let us hear the conclusion of the whole matter: Objectively, the elect will persevere, and they who persevere are elect. Subjectively, the individual is elect *only as he perseveres.* This conclusion is inescapable, regardless of one's definition of election.

The important question arises, Is it possible to know whether we are actually persevering? Can we know whether salvation is a present reality, rather than a vain assumption? Thank God, Yes! John writes, "These things have I written unto you that believe on the name of the Son of God, that ye may know that ye have eternal life" (I John 5:13). Much of the First Epistle of John is concerned with the question of how to know we have eternal life. John presents seven important ways to know that salvation is a present reality:

1. First, as there is no salvation apart from Jesus Christ, there is no valid assurance of salvation possible except as one deliberately trusts in Him. Sincere faith in Jesus Christ is, itself, an evidence of salvation. It is "you who believe on the name of the Son of God" who may "know that you have eternal life" (5:13). John also writes, "Whosoever shall confess that Jesus is the Son of God, God dwelleth in him, and he in God. . . . Whosoever believeth that Jesus is the Christ stands begotten of God. . . . Who is he that overcometh the world, but he that believeth that Jesus is the Son of God?" (4:15; 5:1, 5). It is important to recognize that such confessions as John mentions in the preceding verses are not mere casual mental assents. John's statements must be viewed against the background of his day. Whoever made such confessions in that day must be prepared to suffer persecution—perhaps the loss of family,

friends, livelihood, position in the community, and perhaps even life itself. Men did not lightly persist in such confessions. But according to John, it is only as one earnestly believes on the name of the Son of God that he may have both eternal life, and valid assurance of that life. "Assurance" of eternal life on any other basis is vain presumption.

2. One has assurance that he has eternal life in Christ if he is honoring Christ as the Lord of his life and keeping His word and commandments. "And hereby we do know that we know him, if we keep his commandments. He that saith, I know him, and keepeth not his commandments, is a liar, and the truth is not in him. But whoso keepeth his word, in him verily is the love of God perfected: hereby know we that we are in him" (2:3-5. Cf. 3:24; 5:2, John 8:31, 51; 14:21-24; 15:9-14, Heb. 5:8, 9).

3. One has assurance that he has eternal life in Christ if he is walking after the example of his Saviour. "He who saith that he abideth in him ought himself also so to walk even as he walked" (2:6; cf. John 8:12; 14:12). No man not endeavoring to follow the example of Jesus and to walk in His steps has warrant for assuming that he is saved. Jesus is the example for all His followers. An example is not necessarily a saviour; and we need more than an example: we need a saviour. But Jesus cannot be the Saviour of men who do not accept Him as their example.

4. One has assurance that he has eternal life in Christ if he loves the Father and His will, rather than the world. "Love not the world, neither the things that are in the world. If any man love the world, the love of the Father is not in him. For all that is in the world, the lust of the flesh, and the lust of the eyes, and the pride of life, is not of the Father, but is of the world. And the world passeth away, and the lust thereof: but he who perseveres in doing the will of God abides forever" (2:15-17).

5. One has assurance that he has eternal life in Christ if he habitually practices righteousness, rather than sin. "If ye know that He is righteous, ye know that everyone who practices righteousness stands begotten [perfect indicative passive] of him. . . . He who practices sin is of the devil. . . Whoever stands begotten of God does not practice sin; for his seed remaineth in him: and he cannot practice sin, because he stands begotten of God. In this the children of God are manifest, and the children of the devil: whoever does not practice righteousness is not of God, neither he that loveth not his brother" (2:29; 3:8-10).

6. One has assurance that he has eternal life in Christ if he loves the brethren. "We know that we stand passed [perfect indicative] out of death into life, because we love the brethren. He that loveth not his brother abideth in death. Whoever hateth his brother is a murderer: and ye know that no murderer hath eternal life abiding in him. . . . My little children, let us not love in word, neither in tongue; but in deed and in truth. And hereby we know that we are of the truth, and shall assure our hearts before Him" (3:14, 15, 18, 19. Cf. 2:9-11; 3:23; 4:8, 11, 12, 16, 20-5:1; John 13:34, 35).

7. The seventh means of assurance that one has eternal life in Christ is a consciousness of the indwelling presence of the Holy Spirit. "He that keepeth his commandments dwelleth in him, and he in him. And hereby we know that he dwelleth in us, by the Spirit which he hath given us. . . . Hereby know we that we dwell in him, and he in us, because he hath given us of his Spirit. . . . He that believeth on the Son of God hath the witness in himself" (3:24; 4:13; 5:10).

A consciousness of the indwelling presence of the Comforter is the most blessed evidence of the possession of eternal life in Christ that one may have. But one will know the comforting witness of the Spirit only as he manifests the other evidences of salvation which John cites. It is sheer presumption for anyone to "know" he has eternal life who is not trusting in Christ with a sincere heart, keeping His word and commandments, walking as He walked, loving the Father and His will rather than the world, loving his fellow Christians, and practicing righteousness rather than sin. Anyone who presumes to have the inner witness of the Spirit under other circumstances is mistaken.

Not every inner witness is authentic. The Bible warns against both self-deception and deceiving spirits. There is a very real danger of being misled by seducing spirits, especially for people who become greatly concerned about inner feelings. What easy preys seducing spirits find in people who take great account of personal feelings. Satan, who masquerades as an angel of light, cannot perfectly mimic the witness of the Holy Spirit; nor can the demons and seducing spirits. But they can do so sufficiently well to deceive unwary people for whom personal feelings are the most important guide in matters of doctrine and faith. The Spirit has expressly declared "that in the latter times some shall depart from the faith, giving heed to seducing spirits and doctrines of demons" (I Tim. 4:1). John warns us to be on our guard against both false prophets and deceiving spirits (I John 4:1). The peril is real. To become preoccupied with inner feelings is dangerous and wrong in this age in which we are called to "walk by faith, not by sight."

It is a blessed fact that "the Spirit himself bears witness with our spirit that we are children of God" (Rom. 8:16). But this is true only for those who walk, not after the flesh, but after the Spirit. There is no fellowship with God possible for men who are walking in darkness. "God is light, and in him is no darkness at all. If we say that we have fellowship with him and walk in darkness, we lie and do not the truth. But if we walk in the light, as he is in the light, we have fellowship one with another [God and the believer], and the blood of Jesus Christ his Son cleanseth us from all sin" (I John 1:5-7).

There is no valid witness or assurance of salvation apart from obedient faith in Jesus Christ as Saviour from sin. John, who cites numerous ways we may know we have eternal life as a present blessing, here and now, warns us of the necessity of continuing in faith, if we would continue to share the eternal life of God through Christ:

Whoever disowns the Son, the same has not the Father: but he who confesses the Son has the Father also. Let that therefore remain in you which you have heard from the beginning [the true Gospel, in contrast with the false doctrines of the "antichrists" who had "gone out" from the company of the faithful, embracing Gnosticism, which denied essential aspects of the nature and Person of Jesus, with which they now were endeavoring to "seduce" those who still continued true to the authentic Gospel]. If that which you have heard from the beginning shall remain in you, ye also shall remain in the Son and in the Father. And this is the promise that he has promised us, the eternal life. . . . And this is the record, that God has given to us eternal life, and this life is in his Son. He who has the Son has the life; and he who has not the Son of God has not the life. These things have I written to you who believe on the name of the Son of God, that you may know that you have eternal life. . . . He who believes on the Son of God has the witness in himself (I John 2:23-25; 5:11-13, 10).

> Verily, verily, I say unto you, If a man keep my
> word, he shall never see death.
>
> JOHN 8:51

Is Apostasy Without Remedy?

For if we sin wilfully after that we have received the knowledge of the truth, there remaineth no more sacrifice for sins, but a certain fearful looking for of judgment and fiery indignation which shall devour the adversaries. He that despised Moses' law died without mercy under two or three witnesses: of how much sorer punishment, suppose ye, shall he be thought worthy who hath trodden under foot the Son of God and hath counted the blood of the covenant, wherewith he was sanctified, an unholy thing, and hath done despite unto the Spirit of grace?

HEBREWS 10:26-29

Chapter XIX

IS APOSTASY WITHOUT REMEDY?

"I HAVE SINNED—I have betrayed innocent blood!" Such was the cry of wretched Judas in his bitter remorse. Did his anguished cry awaken concern and pity in the hearts of the priests, the official shepherds in Israel? "What is that to us?" was the scornful retort of his fellow-conspirators. "See thou to that."

Hurling into the holy place the coins which mocked his anguish, thirty silver coins for which he had sold Jesus—and his soul, Judas hurried from the temple to . . . where? He was a man without friend, without priest, without God, without hope. Where could he go? To a tree, a noose, and a bloody field—his last way station on a swift journey to hell. "What is that to us?"

The priests were painfully scrupulous about the "lawful" use of the money, now that it was in their pious possession again. What zeal they had for the proprieties of religion! But for the innocence of Jesus, and for the soul of Judas—"What is that to us?"

To the priests, the problem of apostasy was merely academic and quite irrelevant. Not so for Judas. It was a problem with which he could not live, and for which he found no solution. And I daresay it is a problem which weighs heavily on many anxious souls today.

Is apostasy without remedy? Several passages of Scripture seem to affirm that it is. John writes, "If any man see his brother sinning a sin not unto death, he shall ask, and he shall give him life for them that sin not unto death. There is sin unto death; I do not say that he shall pray for that" (I John 5:16).

The writer to the Hebrews warns, "For as touching those who were once enlightened and tasted of the heavenly gift and were made partakers of the Holy Spirit and tasted the good word of God and the powers of the age to come, and fell away, it is impossible to renew them again unto repentance; seeing they crucify to themselves the Son of God afresh and put him to an open shame" (6:4-6 ASV).

Again he warns: "If we sin wilfully after receiving the full knowledge [*epignōsis*] of the truth, there remains no more a sacrifice for sins, but a certain fearful expectation of judgment and a fierceness of fire which shall devour the adversaries. A man who has set at nought Moses' law dies without mercy on the word of two or three witnesses: of how much greater punishment think ye shall he be judged worthy who has trodden under foot the Son of God and has counted the blood of the covenant wherewith he was sanctified an unholy [commonplace] thing, and has done despite unto the Spirit of grace? . . . It is a fearful thing to fall into the hands of the living God" (Heb. 10:26-29, 31).

The writer's consideration of the problem of falling away after having been "partakers of the Holy Spirit" (6:4) and his assertion that deliberate defection constitutes an outrage against "the Spirit of grace" (10:29) strongly associate such apostasy with the blasphemy against the Holy Spirit, concerning which Jesus solemnly warned: "Therefore I say unto you, every sin and blasphemy shall be forgiven unto men; but the blasphemy against the Spirit shall not be forgiven. And whosoever shall speak a word against the Son of man, it shall be forgiven him; but whosoever shall speak against the Holy Spirit, it shall not be forgiven him, neither in this world, nor in that which is to come" (Matt. 12:31, 32 ASV).

Jesus presents no prospect of forgiveness for the sin against the Holy Spirit. Is there a "point of no return" which men may reach, a condition of abandonment from which they cannot be recovered? So the Scriptures affirm. It is recorded of Eli's sons that they refused their father's reproof and "hearkened not unto the voice of their father, because Jehovah was minded to slay them" (I Sam. 2:25 ASV). Lange comments:

They were in a state of inner hardening which excluded the subjective condition of salvation from destruction, and so they had already incurred God's unchangeable condemnation. As hardened offenders, they were already appointed by God to death; therefore the word of instruction had no moral effect on them.[1]

God had determined that "the iniquity of Eli's house shall not be purged with sacrifice nor offering for ever" (I Sam. 3:14).

Contemplating the rise of the ultimate antichrist, "the man of sin" and "the lawless one" whose appearance on the world scene will be accomplished by "the working of Satan with all power and signs and lying wonders," Paul declares of men who "received not the love of the truth, that they might be saved," that "God shall send them strong delusion, that they should believe a lie, that they all might be condemned who believed not the truth, but had pleasure in unrighteousness" (II Thess. 2:9-11). Robertson comments, "Here is the definite judicial act of God (Milligan) who gives the wicked over to the evil which they have deliberately chosen (Rom. 1:24, 26, 28) . . . [the] terrible result of wilful rejection of the truth of God."[2]

It is evident that the sons of Eli and the unbelievers cited by Paul had passed a "point of no return." Many believe this to be the situation of the apostates depicted in Hebrews 6 and 10 and in I John 5:16. Joseph Addison Alexander's poem, "The Doomed Man," gives pause for solemn reflection:

> There is a time, we know not when,
> A point we know not where,
> That marks the destiny of men
> For glory or despair.

---

[1] J. P. Lange, *Commentary on the Holy Scriptures: Samuel*, p. 76.
[2] A. T. Robertson, *Word Pictures in the New Testament*, Vol. IV, p. 53.

> There is a line, by us unseen,
> That crosses every path;
> The hidden boundary between
> God's patience and His wrath.

But other passages indicate that apostasy is not without remedy. Consider Paul's important assertion in Romans 11. He declares that "some of the branches" (individual Jews who rejected Jesus at His appearing) have been broken off because of their unbelief, but can yet be restored if they do not continue in unbelief. "Because of unbelief they were broken off, and thou standest by faith. Be not haughty, but fear: for if God spared not the natural branches, take heed lest he also spare not thee. Behold therefore the goodness and severity of God: on them which fell, severity; but toward thee, goodness, if thou continue in his goodness: otherwise thou also shalt be cut off. And they also, if they abide not still in unbelief, shall be grafted in: for God is able to graft them in again" (Rom. 11:20-23).[3]

Paul himself is an example of one who, when Christ was offered for sin, became a "branch broken off." For he continued with Judaism while, at Calvary, God's redemptive processes shifted from the ordinances of the old economy to Christ's "one sacrifice for sins for ever." The Levitical priesthood and ordinances of animal sacrifice suddenly became invalid in God's sight, and all who continued in such observances only imagined a vain thing. In their rejection of Jesus and the New Covenant in His blood, they were broken off through unbelief. This must necessarily have been the case with Paul who, under the old economy, "touching the righteousness which is in the law [was] blameless" (Phil. 3:6; cf. Luke 1:6). (Paul did not mean, of course, that he had been without sin under the law. In fact, the law had made him painfully aware of

---

[3]Contrary to the assumptions of some, Rom. 11:20-23 does not concern Israel and the Gentiles corporately, but Jews and Gentiles as individuals. For a discussion of the significance of Rom. 9-11, see Appendix C.

sin. But he honored the law, though he could not keep it perfectly, and availed himself of the grace vouchsafed in the ordinances and was thus "blameless" with respect to "the righteousness which is in the law.")

To assert that Paul was not under saving grace in his earlier life and had never known salvation before his encounter with Christ on the Damascus road is to assert that men could not be saved under the old economy. But despite the fact that he had continued "blameless" under the law, when Christ was offered in fulfillment of the law and the prophets and to establish the New Covenant in His blood, Paul became a "branch broken off" through his unbelief in the appointed Saviour and the New Covenant announced in His Gospel. Not until he "continued not still in unbelief" was he "grafted in again" into "the root" of covenant relationship with God enjoyed by the patriarchs and all the faithful of all previous generations. How truly was Jesus "set for the fall and rising again of many in Israel" (Luke 2:34).

God's grace! How rich, how full, how free! Those who first celebrated Calvary in rank apostasy and blasphemed the holy name of Jesus could be restored to grace, if they continued not in unbelief. The desire of God's heart is to "have mercy upon all" (Rom. 11:32) and to answer the prayer of Jesus, "Father, forgive them. . . ."

Again, consider Paul's words to the Galatians. Some of the Galatians had erred from the faith through the influence of the Judaizers and thus became "severed from Christ" who, because of their attempt to ensure justification through fleshly observances, now "profited them nothing" (5:4, 2 ASV). But while not minimizing the tragedy and woe of their present spiritual state through their unwitting defection from Christ, Paul does not despair of their recovery. He assumes that the erring Galatians may be restored and is therefore willing to "travail in birth again until Christ be formed in you" (4:19), as once he did in leading them to their original conversion to Christ (cf. I Cor. 4:15). He has confidence in the Lord that they will come to share his mind (5:10a) that faith in Christ alone, to the exclusion of all confidence in fleshly observances, is the way of justification and salvation. Thus we see that, while the error of the Galatians constituted actual defection from Christ and His saving Gospel and was a mortal error, it was not without remedy. Paul was willing to "travail again" in their behalf, that they might be restored to grace through a return to simple faith in Christ (cf. II Cor. 11:3 and context).

Consider another evidence that apostasy is not without remedy. Paul directed the Corinthians to excommunicate a man guilty of incest (I Cor. 5:1 ff.). Such action was necessary for the purity and testimony of the church. But another purpose was also in view. The offender was to be excommunicated and officially delivered over to Satan for the destruction of the flesh for a salutary purpose: "that the spirit may be saved in the day of the Lord Jesus" (v. 5). The offender's sin, unjudged and unforgiven, had wrought spiritual death within—a state which now was to be publicly acknowledged through excommunication. But the offender was not to be considered beyond recovery. In fact, excommunication itself would tend toward his possible restoration. It would awaken him to the tragedy of his circumstance and his need for forgiveness and restoration. Robertson comments: "Paul's motive is not merely vindictive, but the reformation of the offender. . . . The final salvation of the man in the day of Christ is the goal and this is to be attained not by condoning his sin."[4] We may surmise from II Corinthians 2:5-11 (if the same man is in view) that the salutary purpose in excommunication was realized, and he was restored to grace and welcomed back into the fellowship of the church.

Let us consider another evidence that apostasy is not without remedy. Paul expressed fear that, should he return to Corinth, he should be obliged to "bewail" (*pentheō,* a term of mourning as for the dead) many who had sinned flagrantly

---

[4]Robertson, *op. cit.*, p. 113.

and had not repented (II Cor. 12:21). He warns the Corinthians that, should he come, he will not spare the rod of
reproof (13:2) against those who have lapsed into lascivious
living and have not repented. Knowing that they may be unaware of their tragic spiritual circumstance, he admonishes
them (13:5) to examine themselves to see whether they are
still in the faith, as they presume to be, or have instead become reprobate ("*adokimoi*, the very adjective that Paul held
up before himself as a dreadful outcome to be avoided, I Cor.
9:27"[5]), in which case Jesus Christ no longer dwells in them.
But it is fully evident (12:21) that Paul assumes that the offenders who have not as yet repented may do so, if they will,
and so be restored to a saving relationship with Christ.

James concludes his letter with a word of both warning
and encouragement: "Brethren, if any of you do err [*planaō*,
wander away, go astray] from the truth, and one convert him
[*epistrephō*, cause to return, bring back], let him know that he
who converts the sinner from the error of his way shall save a
soul from death, and shall hide a multitude of sins" (5:19, 20).
Robertson writes:

It was easy then, and is now, to be led astray from Christ, who is the
Truth. . . . A *soul from death* . . . the soul of the sinner (*hamartōlon*) won
back to Christ, not the soul of the man winning him. . . . It is ultimate
and final salvation here meant by the future (*sōsei*).[6]

(The duty of believers to recover those who err from the truth
and depart from the faith is emphasized in other passages,
e.g., II Tim. 2:25, 26 [note context, v. 18], Jude 22, 23, and
Gal. 6:1, cf. Thayer on *paraptōma* and *katartizō*.)

Finally, let us consider the gracious appeal of the risen
Christ to the church in Laodicea (Rev. 3:14-22), a church in
which He found not one thing to commend. The Laodicean
church had lost all distinction from the world around it, being
"neither hot nor cold." (How many churches there are in our

[5]*Ibid.*, p. 270.
[6]Robertson, *op. cit.*, Vol. VI, p. 67.

day in the disastrous circumstance of the church at Laodicea!)
Jesus expresses His wish that they were either hot or cold—
anything but "lukewarm," a condition exactly like that of the
environment around them. They have lost their spiritual distinction from the pagan world and differ nothing, being actually a part of the world rather than of the kingdom of Christ.
Professing themselves to be wealthy and in need of nothing,
they are in reality wretched, pitiable, poor, blind, and naked—
lacking the garment of the righteousness of Christ to cover
their spiritual nakedness. They are spiritually dead. But they
have not yet passed a "point of no return;" Jesus has not yet
spewed them out of His mouth. In their present state, they
are as distasteful to Christ as a beverage which is intended
to be hot, but is only lukewarm; or a beverage which should
be cold, but has become lukewarm. He is on the point of
spewing them from His mouth, and there is nothing about
them in their present state which will allow Him to do otherwise. But He still loves them and therefore entreats them,
while there is yet opportunity, to "be zealous therefore and
repent." There seems little prospect that the church, as a whole,
will heed His warning and repent and be restored to grace.
Nevertheless, individuals within the church may heed His
call, if they will. Therefore, standing outside the door of the
Laodicean church, Christ tenderly entreats: "Behold, I stand
at the door and knock: if any man hear my voice and open
the door, I will come in to him and will sup with him, and he
with me. To him that overcometh will I grant to sit with me
in my throne, even as I also overcame and am set down with
my Father in His throne" (vv. 20, 21). They are mistaken who
assume that apostasy is necessarily without remedy.

One of the passages often cited by those who contend that
apostasy is necessarily without remedy is I John 5:16. John
does not define the "sin unto death" in his statement. But the
context of his entire epistle suggests that the sin of which he
writes is the ostentatious renunciation of the Saviour through
open denial that Jesus is actually the Christ come in the flesh,

the holy Son of God. (Cf. 4:15; 5:1, 5, 9, 10, 13, 20; 1:2.) Such denial is fatal and marks one as an antichrist (4:2,3). The attempts of the antichrists to "seduce" the faithful by persuading them to join them in discarding the cardinal doctrines of Christ constitute a real threat to their spiritual safety, against which John urgently warns them (4:1-3, II John 7-11, I John 2:18-28). But though John warns believers to have nothing to do with the antichrists and does not enjoin prayer in their behalf, neither does he forbid such prayer nor expressly affirm that their restoration is impossible. Westcott writes:

St. John does not command intercession when the sin is seen, recognized by the brother, in its fatal intensity; but on the other hand he does not expressly exclude it. Even if the tenour of his words may seem to dissuade such prayer, it is because the offender lies without the Christian Body, excluded from its life, but yet not beyond the creative, vivifying power of God.[7]

Nothing is impossible for God that is consonant with His character and His eternal purposes.

Another passage cited by those who assume that apostasy is necessarily without remedy is Hebrews 6:4-6. But we need not conclude that the passage teaches that the renewal of apostates to repentance is necessarily impossible. Westcott comments on verse 6:

The use of the active voice limits the strict application of the words ["it is impossible to renew them again unto repentance"] to human agency. This is all that comes within the range of the writer's argument.[8]

Certainly the Bible teaches that repentance is essentially the work of God and, in any instance, is the response of the individual to divine influences from God through the Spirit. But God uses human beings as His agents in accomplishing His purposes. While it pleases God to save all who believe, it pleases Him also to employ men as His agents in preaching

---

[7]B. F. Westcott, *The Epistles of St. John*, p. 210.
[8]B. F. Westcott, *The Epistle to the Hebrews*, p. 150.

and teaching the Gospel of Christ which is His power unto salvation to all who believe. There is a definite place for human agency in effecting the repentance and salvation of the lost. Westcott doubtless is correct in his assertion that the impossibility of renewing to repentance the apostates depicted in Hebrews 6 is limited to human agencies. (Contra. Jas. 5:19, 20, Jude 22, 23, Gal. 6:1, II Tim. 2:25, 26, where human agency is encouraged and the prospect of success is implied.) What is said by the writer to the Hebrews to be impossible for men is not impossible for God, with whom all things right and good are possible.

Again, Westcott writes:

The present participles (contrast *parapesontas* of the definite past act of apostasy) bring out the moral cause of the impossibility which has been affirmed. There is an active, continuous hostility to Christ in the souls of such men as have been imagined.[*]

The apostasy in view in Hebrews 6 takes its character, not merely from a past act of defection, but also from a present deliberate hostility toward Christ. The impossibility of renewal to repentance and salvation rests, not on the mere fact of a past act, but on the fact of a present condition of opposition. The marginal reading of the American Standard Version is suggestive: "It is impossible to renew them again unto repentance, the while they crucify to themselves the Son of God afresh and put him to an open shame." The present condition of deliberate, open hostility may conceivably be remedied and the persons renewed to repentance and salvation.

There is hope implied also in the verses which immediately follow: "For a piece of ground that drinks in the rains so frequently falling on it, and continues yielding vegetation useful to those for whose sakes it is cultivated, receives from God His blessings. But if it continues to yield thorns and thistles, it is considered worthless and in danger of being

---

[*]*Ibid.*, p. 151.

cursed, and its final fate is burning" (vv. 7, 8 Williams). The ground which has yielded only thorns and thistles has already been adjudged worthless, and is now rejected; but it is said to be only "near to a curse." It awaits eventual burning; but that fate as yet is only in prospect. Perhaps it may be averted. The branch pruned away from the vine (John 15:6) immediately withers, because it is severed from the source of life; but it is not immediately gathered and cast into the fire and burned. The branches broken off through unbelief may yet be grafted in again, if they abide not still in unbelief (Rom. 11:20-23). "God is able to graft them in again!" The Laodicean church is dead; there is not one sign of spiritual life in it. The risen Christ is on the point of spewing them from His mouth and ending all prospect of restoration. But He has not done so as yet, and He bids them hasten to repent and know again His saving grace. Restoration is not impossible for apostates, including those depicted in Hebrews 6.

Shepardson takes a similarly hopeful view of Hebrews 10, declaring that the apostasy in view is

. . . purposeful and continuous apostasy from Christianity. The word "sin" is in the present participle, which denotes not a single act of unbelief, but a state or condition of unbelief. [Cf. Lange on Heb. 10:26, ". . . the pres. *hamartanontōn* marks *habitual* in contrast with transient denial."] Those described are those who . . . turn away from Christ and continue . . . to turn away.

. . . .

. . . just as long as we continue in this state of willful apostasy we put ourselves beyond the possibility of forgiveness.

. . . .

The revealed character of God makes it certain that such apostasy, if continued, must sooner or later bring terrible punishment. Holy love will compel some adequate recognition in penalty of such a crime. Whatever judgment comes to men will be commensurate with their character and opportunities. Because of what He is, He must not only punish the wicked, but also care for His own; judgment for all will be unquestionably just. For those who are in Christ, judgment will have no terrors; but for those who have separated themselves from Him and are now living "without God and without hope in the world," it will be seen to be "a fearful thing to fall into the hands of the living God." Such is our author's renewed warning against the awfulness of continuous apostasy from [Christ], this apostasy being regarded from the point of view of the judgment and looked back upon as a completed thing.[10]

Shepardson's contention that the fearful judgment of Hebrews 10:29 f. is regarded from the point of view of the coming Day of Judgment and is seen in retrospect as a thing completed is fully warranted by language. The verb *axiōthēsetai* is future passive indicative. It is declared by the writer to the Hebrews that one who proves himself to be a willful, persistent apostate "shall be judged worthy" of infinite punishment. Final condemnation may yet be averted, while life and opportunity continue.

Westcott likewise contends that the apostasy in view in Hebrews 10 is not necessarily without remedy: "It must be observed that the argument assumes that the sacrifice of Christ is finally rejected and sin persisted in *(hamartanontōn)*. The writer does not set limits to the efficacy of Christ's work for the penitent."[11]

We have earlier associated the apostasy depicted in Hebrews 6 and 10 with the sin of blasphemy against the Holy Spirit. The charge of the Pharisees that Jesus cast out demons by Beelzebub was blasphemy against the Holy Spirit in that it constituted a denial of His testimony to Jesus, who performed His ministry "in the power of the Spirit." The testimony of the Spirit to Jesus today is the proclamation of His saving Gospel and the personal witness of believers in whom He dwells. Men who reject that witness, including all who apostatize, are as guilty of blaspheming the Holy Spirit as were the Pharisees who ridiculed Christ's ministry of deliverance. But let us observe that it is a mistake to view such blasphemy as the isolated act of a single moment. Although in both Mat-

---

[10]Daniel Shepardson, *Studies in the Epistle to the Hebrews,* pp. 457-461.
[11]Westcott, *The Epistle to the Hebrews,* p. 327.

thew 12:32 and Mark 3:29 the act of blaspheming the Holy
Spirit is expressed by aorist subjunctives, it does not follow that
the act must be considered as momentary and punctiliar.
Burton declares that the aorist of the dependent moods ". . .
when indefinite may refer to a momentary or extended action
or to a series of events."[12] Likewise an aorist participle (Luke
12:10) "when indefinite . . . may be used of momentary or
extended actions or of a series of events."[13] Language therefore
does not specify that the unforgivable blasphemy against the
Holy Spirit is the act of a single moment. Other considerations
indicate that such blasphemy is unforgivable only as one
finally persists in it.

It is encouraging to read that, despite the intensity of the
hatred and resentment toward Jesus which so generally prevailed among the priests and the Pharisees during His earthly
ministry, in the early days of the church "a great company of
the priests were obedient to the faith" (Acts 6:7) and many
of the Pharisees became believers (Acts 15:5). Must we assume that the blasphemous verdict that Jesus cast out demons
by the power of Beelzebub was never general among the
Pharisees, and that not one man who once held that opinion
ever became a believer? What, then, must have been the original opinion of Saul the Pharisee concerning the exorcisms of
Jesus, whom he considered a rank fraud and an enemy of
Moses, the law, and the God of Abraham, Isaac, and Jacob?
Did he not originally concur in the judgment of those who
charged that Jesus cast out demons by Beelzebub? Did he
not share in their guilt and condemnation? But where sin
abounds, there grace does much more abound, free to all who
will receive it with contrite hearts.

The mercy of God is great. "That mercy is wider than all
humanity, deeper than all sin, was before all rebellion, and
will last for ever. And it is open for every soul of man to receive

---

[12]E. D. Burton, *Syntax of the Moods and Tenses in New Testament Greek*,
Sec. 98.
[13]*Ibid.*, Sec. 133.

it if he will."[14] Even after declaring that apostates are "reserved unto the day of judgment to be punished" (II Pet. 2:9) and that "to them the mist of darkness is reserved for ever" (v. 17) and that "the day of judgment and perdition of ungodly men" (3:7) already has been determined upon, Peter declares that the Lord "is longsuffering to us-ward, not willing that any should perish, but that all should come to repentance" (v. 9) and asserts that the long delay in judgment ("the longsuffering of our Lord," v. 15) is for salvation. God takes no pleasure in the death of the wicked. His heart of mercy finds no delight in the punishment of sinners which His righteousness and the moral integrity of His universe demand. He prefers mercy to judgment. To men who "have forsaken the Lord, [who] have provoked the Holy One of Israel to anger, [who] are gone away backward," a merciful God implores, "Seek ye the Lord while he may be found, call ye upon him while he is near. Let the wicked forsake his way, and the unrighteous man his thoughts: and let him return unto the Lord, and he will have mercy upon him; and to our God, for he will abundantly pardon" (Isa. 1:4; 55:6, 7).

It is evident that blasphemy against the Spirit of grace is unforgivable, not as it stands as the isolated act of a single moment, but only as it remains the final attitude of the individual in his rejection of the appeals and proffered mercies of God. Surely there is warrant for believing that only in rare instances (e.g., Eli's sons) may apostasy be irremediable before the occasion of death; and certainly not in any instance in which the individual becomes concerned about his spiritual circumstance and sincerely penitent toward God.

Many dear souls mistakenly fear that they have so blasphemed the Holy Spirit that they have passed a "point of no return." It is easy so to imagine. For who of us has not sorely grieved the Blessed Comforter? Who has not quenched His holy influence? Who has not ignored His still, small voice and

---

[14]Alexander Maclaren, *Expositions of Holy Scripture: Ephesians*, p. 88.

His faithful guidance? But men who fear that they have so blasphemed the Holy Spirit that they are forever beyond recovery are mistaken. Their fear is evidence that such is not the case.

Many, however, regard their very fear as cause for despair. The assertion that, for those who apostatize, there remains only "a certain fearful expectation of judgment and fiery indignation which shall devour the adversaries" (Heb. 10:27) has struck terror to the hearts of many who have imagined that the writer meant that there was no possibility of recovery and that, for all who once withdraw from Christ, there remains no prospect other than to live out their days in constant dread and fearful anticipation of inevitable final condemnation. Their fear, itself, has been regarded as infallible evidence that their situation is hopeless and their doom is sealed for eternity. But they have misunderstood the writer's statement. The rendering of *ekdochē* as "looking for" or "expectation" has been most unfortunate. Alford writes:

. . . reception (i.e., *meed, doom:* not, as I believe universally interpreted without remark, *expectation.* The word used *(ecdochē)* appears never to have this sense, and this is the only place where it occurs in the New Test. All which *remains* is the reception of the doom of judgment, and the *fiery indignation,* &c.) of judgment. . . .[15]

The writer's meaning is that the certain prospect before apostates (except they repent) is fiery judgment (cf. RSV, Williams, Goodspeed). The picture of men abandoned to perdition living out their days in dreadful anticipation of fiery judgment is completely contrary to the Scriptures. To the contrary, the few passages which refer to men in such circumstance portray them as brazen and self-confident, anticipating no such fiery judgment. There is no fear apparent in Eli's sons following their warning. There is no suggestion of fear present in the men cited by Paul in II Thess. 2:10-12. Men abandoned to final reprobation during "the tribulation, the great" (Rev. 7:14,

---

[15]Henry Alford, *The New Testament for English Readers,* p. 1548.

the Greek text is emphatic) are depicted as utterly devoid of penitence and the fear of God. Their only response to the righteous judgments of God will be increasing impenitence and blasphemy (Rev. 9:20, 21; 16:9, 11, 21). All who feel a revulsion and horror at the thought of such impudence may be sure that they are not beyond the holy influences of the Spirit of grace and the possibility of redemption. Let them recognize that "the goodness of God leadeth thee to repentance," and the feeling of repentance within their hearts is the gracious call of a loving God. "The sacrifices of God are a broken spirit: a broken and a contrite heart, O God, thou wilt not despise" (Ps. 51:17).

Some have been distressed by the fact that Judas is said to have repented, but his repentance availed nothing. Matthew records that "Judas, which had betrayed him, when he saw that he [Jesus] was condemned, repented himself, and brought again the thirty pieces of silver to the chief priests and elders" (27:3). But the Greek text does not state that Judas actually repented *(metanoeō)*, but merely that he regretted *(metamelomai)*. The words are synonyms; but there is an important distinction between them. *Metamelomai* signifies regret or remorse; but such remorse does not necessarily involve actual modification of the moral purpose and intention of the individual. *Metanoeō* is the more comprehensive term, involving not only remorse for the past, but also a deliberate change of mind, heart, purpose, and intention for the future. Although Thayer contends that the distinction between the two is not so great as some have supposed, he concedes that ". . . *metanoeō* is the fuller and nobler term, expressive of moral action and issues, [and this fact] is indicated not only by its derivation, but by the greater frequency of its use, by the fact that it is often employed in the imperative *(metamelomai* never), and by its construction with *apo, ek* (cf. *hē eis theon metanoia*, Acts xx. 21)."[16] Most translators have recognized that *met-*

---

[16] J. H. Thayer, *A Greek-English Lexicon of the New Testament*, p. 405.

amelētheis indicates that the remorse of Judas fell short of actual repentance toward God, and have translated accordingly. Robertson comments:

. . . mere sorrow avails nothing unless it leads to change of mind and life *(metanoia)*, the sorrow according to God (II Cor. 7:9). This sorrow Peter had when he wept bitterly. It led Peter back to Christ. But Judas had only remorse that led to suicide.[17]

Another passage which has troubled many is found in Heb. 12. It is recorded that Esau, a profane (earthly minded) person, "for one morsel of meat sold his birthright. For ye know how that afterward, when he would have inherited the blessing, he was rejected: for he found no place for repentance, though he sought it carefully with tears" (Heb. 12:16, 17). The picture of Esau tearfully seeking repentance, but all in vain—forever rejected, has terrified many troubled souls who have imagined themselves to be in such fearful predicament.

First, let us recognize that in the case of Esau, the "rejection" had nothing to do with his salvation. Westcott comments:

The son who had sacrificed his right could not undo the past, and it is this only which is in question. No energy of sorrow or self-condemnation, however sincere, could restore to him the prerogative of the firstborn. The consideration of the forgiveness of his sin against God, as distinct from the reversal of the temporal consequences of his sin, lies wholly without the argument. . . . It would be equally true to say that in respect of the privileges of the first-born which Esau had sold, he found no place for repentance, and that in respect of his spiritual relation to God, if his sorrow was sincere, he did find a place for repentance.[18]

(Irrespective of the chicanery of Rebekah and Jacob, God had rejected Esau as the heir to the Abrahamic Covenant and the progenitor of the Messianic line—a matter which has nothing to do with the question of his salvation.)

Lünemann makes a strong case for applying the clause, "for he found no place for repentance," to Isaac rather than to

---

[17]Robertson, *op. cit.*, Vol. I, p. 222 f.
[18]Westcott, *The Epistle to the Hebrews*, p. 408 f.

Esau.[19] This view is in complete accord with the account in Genesis (27:33 ff.) and was adopted by the translators of the American Standard Version: "when he afterward desired to inherit the blessing, he was rejected; for he found no place for a change of mind *in his father,* though he sought it diligently with tears." What Esau vainly sought was not his own repentance, but a change of mind in Isaac and the bequest of the blessing pertaining to the firstborn, which was now impossible, much to the sorrow of both Isaac and Esau. There is no warrant for the popular picture of Esau tearfully endeavoring to arrive at a condition of repentance, but forever unable to do so, forever beyond redemption.

But while the issue with respect to Esau himself pertained only to the matter of his temporal blessing as the firstborn, rather than to his salvation, it is nevertheless true that the writer to the Hebrews presents the episode as an object lesson to warn his readers not to trifle with their heavenly birthright as sons of God by becoming earthly minded, after the example of profane Esau. As Esau lost the temporal heritage which might have been his, so the writer warns Christians that they may lose the heavenly heritage which is theirs. But it was some years after carelessly consenting to sell his birthright that Esau finally lost, through the deception of Rebekah and Jacob, the heritage which he earlier had considered as of trifling consequence in comparison with the immediate satisfaction of his physical appetite.

Eventually there came a time when the heritage which Esau had treated with disdain became irretrievably lost. After the blessing of Isaac had been pronounced, Esau's loss could not be remedied. Isaac's first blessing and the rights of primogeniture had been bestowed upon Jacob; the issue was closed, and Esau's tears and loud protests were forever in vain. Just so, for every Christian whose love of this present world leads him

---

[19]Gottlieb Lünemann, *Meyer's Critical and Exegetical Hand-Book to the New Testament: The Epistle to the Hebrews,* p. 710 f.

to trifle away his heavenly birthright as an heir of God and joint-heir with Christ, there must come a time (except he repent) when judgment becomes final, and the heritage lost can never be recovered.

But that time is not yet, so long as life and the day of grace continue. For were this not so, the many appeals of God to those who have gone astray would be vain mockery, and many encouraging passages in the Scriptures would be outright deception of the cruelest sort. The door of hope is not closed against those who, having become "not my people" because of their wickedness and unfaithfulness, may yet cry, "Come, and let us return unto the Lord: for he hath torn, and he will heal us; he hath smitten, and he will bind us up" (Hos. 6:1). But let none presume upon time, for life and opportunity are uncertain, and the day of grace must come to an end. "Seek ye the Lord while he may be found, call ye upon him while he is near: Let the wicked forsake his way, and the unrighteous man his thoughts: and let him return unto the Lord, and he will have mercy upon him; and to our God, for he will abundantly pardon" (Isa. 55:6, 7).

But despite the many Scriptures to the contrary, some persist in denying that restoration is possible for those who actually have fallen from grace, on the ground that a second birth is an impossibility. "Jesus did not say, 'Ye must be born again and again,'" say they. "There can be but one spiritual birth for an individual, just as there can be but one physical birth." The objection seems valid to men whose concept of the new birth is inadequate and unscriptural and who assume that an equation exists between physical and spiritual birth. But such is not the case, as we have considered in Chapter 7. Furthermore, although there was but one physical birth for Lazarus of Bethany, he experienced a resurrection to a resumption of the physical life which began with his birth. Shall we assume that the God who can recall dead men to a resumption of physical life cannot restore fallen men to a resumption of spiritual life in Christ?

Distinguishing between conversion and restoration, Westcott comments on Hebrews 6:4-6:

Some divine work then may be equivalent to this renewing, though not identical with it (Matt. xix. 26). The change in such a case would not be a new birth, but a raising from the dead.

. . . .

The end of this renewal is *metanoia*, a complete change of mind consequent upon the apprehension of the true moral nature of things. It follows necessarily that in this large sense there can be no second *metanoia* (comp. v. 1). There may be, through the gift of God, a corresponding change, a regaining of the lost view with the consequent restoration of the fulness of life, but this is different from the freshness of the vision through which the life is first realised. The popular idea of repentance, by which it is limited to sorrow for the past, has tended to obscure the thought here.[20]

Delitzsch, however, contends that there is no prospect of restoration for the apostates depicted in Hebrews 6: "No more salvation (says the writer of the epistle) for those who, having learned by the Holy Ghost to know Jesus as the very Son of God, assume the same position toward their Saviour as those unbelievers who brought Him to the cross."[21] But what, then, of Peter? He fully knew Jesus to be "the Christ, the Son of the living God" (Matt. 16:16); and not by mere human insight, but by divine revelation: "Flesh and blood hath not revealed this unto thee, but my Father which is in heaven." And what holy privilege was his! On the mount, with James and John, he beheld His glory—the glory as of the only begotten of the Father—and heard the Voice out of the cloud, "This is my beloved Son" (Matt. 17:5). And yet, in the hour of trial, he denied even the remotest acquaintance with Jesus: "I do not know the man!"—as though He were quite an ordinary person, thus conceding that the judgment of His enemies was, in his opinion, entirely correct. How persistent he was in his denial—

---

[20]Westcott, *The Epistle to the Hebrews*, p. 150.
[21]Franz Delitzsch, *The Epistle to the Hebrews*, Vol. I, p. 293.

three times! And how deliberate and emphatic was his denial! He cursed and swore under oath, "I know not the man!"

And yet, Peter found forgiveness. Is that not encouraging for us all, as we think of the many times and ways we have so shamefully denied our Holy Saviour? Have we not sworn by deed and life, if not in word, "I know not the man"? Have we no need to go out and weep bitterly with Peter? But still He comes—the Man of Sorrows, forever scarred—and gently asks, "Lovest thou me?"

To every weary prodigal—disillusioned, hungry, heartsick of the far country—the Saviour offers precious encouragement and assurance that the Father longs for his return. There is room for him in the old accustomed place at the Father's table where there is bread enough and to spare—Living Bread broken for us, of which we may eat and live for ever. Even now, the Father watches for his return. He has but to rise and return in humble confession, "Father, I have sinned—against heaven, and in thy sight, and am no more worthy to be called thy son." With what compassion the Father will welcome him! How fervent will be His embrace and kiss! With what joy will He cry, "Bring forth the best robe—the righteousness of Christ; put it on him, and put a ring on his hand and shoes on his feet. Let us eat and be merry! For this my son was dead, and is alive again; he was lost, and is found!"

Appendices

Appendix A

New Testament Passages Establishing the Doctrine of Conditional Security, and a List of Passages Cited by Chafer as "Misunderstood" by Arminians.

In his *Systematic Theology,* Vol. III, pp. 290-312, Dr. Lewis Sperry Chafer cites fifty-one passages of Scripture to which, in his opinion, Arminians might understandably appeal in their arguments against the doctrine of unconditional security, because of their incomplete apprehension (as he believed) of the total revelation of the Holy Scriptures. Following is a comparison of Chafer's list with a list of eighty-five New Testament passages which establish the doctrine of conditional security. Duplications of parallel passages in the Synoptic Gospels are avoided, and no passages are included, the meaning of which is not clearly established in the immediate context. Numerous decisive passages, the meaning of which must be established by comparison with other Scriptures, are therefore omitted. No claim is made that the list is complete, even within the above limits.

Of the fifty-one passages cited by Chafer, only one is from the Old Testament. A list of pertinent passages from the Old Testament would be lengthy. For our purpose, no such list is required. Chafer's objection that certain passages are "dispensationally misapplied" constitutes an admission that the doctrine of unconditional security cannot be established in the Old Testament, or in other than the Christian era. It also constitutes a contention that, in an essential aspect, saving faith in the present era differs intrinsically from saving faith in other eras.

333

Dr. Chafer's many omissions include some of the most decisive passages. It may be assumed that his omissions, far from deliberate, were the consequence of his earnest conviction that the Bible affirms unconditional security for believers in the present dispensation—a conviction which apparently so completely conditioned his study of the Scriptures that the significance of many warning passages escaped his notice. In that respect, Dr. Chafer may be regarded as representative of many godly men and earnest Bible scholars.

The fifty-one New Testament passages cited by Chafer are given as he lists them. It will be observed that many of his references differ somewhat from mine. I sincerely believe that, had he considered them in their larger context, his conclusions might well have been different.

N. T. Passages Establishing the Doctrine of Conditional Security:	Passages Cited by Chafer as Misunderstood by Arminians:
	1. Matt. 5:13 (cited with I Jn. 3:10)
	2. Matt. 6:23 (cited with I Jn. 3:10)
	3. Matt. 7:16-19 (with I Jn. 3:10)
1. Matt. 18:21-35	4. Matt. 18:23-35
2. Matt. 24:4, 5, 11-13, 23-26	5. Matt. 24:13
3. Matt. 25:1-13	6. Matt. 25:1-13
4. Luke 8:11-15	7. Chafer cites the parallel passage, Matt. 13:1-8, the language of which is not so definitive.
5. Luke 11:24-28	8. Luke 11:24-26. The key to the meaning of the parable is in vv. 27, 28, which Chafer omits (cf. John 8:51).
6. Luke 12:42-46	
7. John 6:66-71	
8. John 8:31, 32	9. John 8:31
9. John 8:51	
10. John 13:8	10. John 13:8
11. John 15:1-6	11. John 15:2
	12. John 15:6
	13. Acts 5:32

12. Acts 11:21-23

13. Acts 14:21, 22

14. Rom. 6:11-23

15. Rom. 8:12-14, 17

16. Rom. 11:20-22

17. Rom. 14:15-23

18. I Cor. 9:23-27

19. I Cor. 10:1-21

20. I Cor. 11:29-32

21. I Cor. 15:1, 2

22. II Cor. 1:24

23. II Cor. 11:2-4

24. II Cor. 12:21-13:5

25. Gal. 5:1-4

26. Gal. 6:7-9

27. Eph. 3:17

28. Phil. 2:12-16

29. Phil. 3:4-4:1

30. Col. 1:21-23

31. Col. 2:4-8

32. Col. 2:18, 19

33. I Thess. 3:1-8

34. I Tim. 1:3-7, 18-20

35. I Tim. 2:11-15

36. I Tim. 4:1-16

37. I Tim. 5:8

38. I Tim. 5:11-15, 5, 6

39. I Tim. 6:9-12

40. I Tim. 6:17-19

41. I Tim. 6:20, 21

42. II Tim. 2:11-18

43. II Tim. 2:22-26

44. II Tim. 3:13-15

45. Heb. 2:1-3

46. Heb. 3:6-19

47. Heb. 4:1-16

14. Acts 13:43 (cited with I Jn. 3:10)

15. Acts 14:22 (with I Jn. 3:10)

16. Rom. 8:6, 13 (with I Cor. 11:29-32)

17. Rom. 8:17 (with I Cor. 9:27)

18. Rom. 11:21

19. I Cor. 9:27

20. I Cor. 11:29-32

21. I Cor. 15:1, 2

22. Gal. 5:4

23. Phil. 2:12

24. Col. 1:21-23

25. I Thess. 3:5 (with I Jn. 3:10)

26. I Tim. 1:19 (with I Jn. 3:10)

27. I Tim. 2:14, 15 (with I Jn. 3:10)

28. I Tim. 4:1, 2 (with I Jn. 3:10)

29. I Tim. 5:8

30. I Tim. 5:12

31. I Tim. 6:10

32. II Tim. 2:12 (with I Jn. 3:10)

33. II Tim. 2:18

34. Heb. 3:6, 14

48. Heb. 5:8, 9
49. Heb. 6:4-9
50. Heb. 6:10-20
51. Heb. 10:19-31
52. Heb. 10:32-39
53. Heb. 11:13-16
54. Heb. 12:1-17
55. Heb. 12:25-29
56. Heb.13:9-14
57. Heb. 13:17, 7
58. Jas. 1:12-16
59. Jas. 1:21, 22
60. Jas. 2:14-26
61. Jas. 4:4-10
62. Jas. 5:19, 20
63. I Pet. 1:5-9, 13
64. II Pet. 1:5-11
65. II Pet. 2:1-22
66. II Pet. 3:16, 17

67. I John 1:5-2:11
68. I John 2:15-28

69. I John 2:29-3:10
70. I John 5:4, 5
71. I John 5:16
72. II John 6-9
73. Jude 5-12
74. Jude 20, 21
75. Rev. 2:7
76. Rev. 2:10, 11

35. Heb. 5:8, 9
36. Heb. 6:4-9

37. Heb. 10:26-29

38. Jas. 2:17, 18, 24, 26

39. II Pet. 1:10, 11
40. II Pet. 2:1-22
41. Chafer cites v. 17 in connection with I Jn. 3:10, but misses the significance because he ignores v. 16.

42. Chafer cites v. 19 in connection with Heb. 3:6, 14, which he dismisses as being concerned only with outward profession.
43. I John 3:10
44. I John 5:4, 5
45. I John 5:16

46. Jude 3-19

47. Chafer cites v. 10 in connection with I Cor. 9:27, but misses its significance because he ignores v. 11.

77. Rev. 2:17
78. Rev. 2:18-26
79. Rev. 3:4, 5
80. Rev. 3:8-12
81. Rev. 3:14-22
82. Rev. 12:11
83. Rev. 17:14

48. Chafer disposes of Rev. 2:7, 11, 17, 26; 3:5, 12, 21 by asserting that the term "overcomer" is the equivalent of *Christian*, and all who become saved are immediately made eternal overcomers through the experience of the new birth, which is, itself, the final and irrevocable act of overcoming (p. 306). Such an assertion ignores the fact that the messages are directed, not to the unsaved, but "unto the churches," and the warnings and appeals to overcome are addressed to men who already have come into the experience of the new birth.

84. Rev. 21:7, 8

49. Rev. 21:8, 27. By associating v. 8 with v. 27 and ignoring v. 7, Chafer misses the significance of v. 8.

85. Rev. 22:18, 19

50. Rev. 22:19. Chafer asserts that the passage is a "warning to all men." But according to his theology's "sovereign grace" and "sovereign election" (unconditional), it is impossible that any man's part should be taken away out of the book of life and out of the holy city. The reprobate, by eternal decree, were forever excluded from God's purposes in grace. They have no part in the book of life or the holy city to be taken away for any cause whatever, for they never were included.

APPENDIX B

Whom Does the Father Give to Jesus?

The Scriptures affirm that certain individuals are given by the Father to the Son, that no man can come to Jesus except the Father draw him (John 6:44), and that all that the Father gives to Jesus will come to Him (v. 37). The question arises, Whom does the Father "draw" and give to the Son? Is there anything in man of which the Father takes account, or is the choice merely arbitrary on the part of God?

Many have charged that for God to take account of anything in men would make Him "a respecter of persons." But the Scriptures declare that for God to *fail* to do so would indeed make Him a respecter of persons and arbitrary and unjust in His dealings with men. (Consider the following verses, with context: Acts 10:34, Rom. 2:11, Eph. 6:9, Col. 3:25, I Pet. 1:17). It is only some men's theology which asserts that to take account of anything in men would make God a respecter of persons. The Scriptures declare exactly the opposite.

Proponents of the doctrine of unconditional election have made much of the fact that in John 6:37, 44, 65; 17:2, Eph. 1:4, II Thess. 2:13, and certain other passages (notably Rom. 9:6-29, for a discussion of which see Appendix C), no assertion is made of the existence of any factor in man of which God takes account in election. But it is folly to assume that, since there are passages in which no conditioning factor is asserted, therefore none exists. For elsewhere in the Scriptures, the existence of such a factor is expressly affirmed.

Jesus said, "It is written in the prophets, And they shall be all taught of God. Every man therefore that hath heard and hath learned of the Father cometh unto me" (John 6:45). But Jesus further declared that, for every person, the effect of the Father's teaching (of which Jesus was the annointed vehicle, John 7:16; 12:49, 50; 17:8) is directly determined by something within, and of, the individual himself: "If any man wills to do His will, he shall know of the doctrine, whether it be of God, or whether I speak of myself" (John 7:17; cf. 5:40-47, Luke 7:30 RSV, John 3:14-21). All who "will to do His will" are persuaded of the truth of His teaching, and therefore "hear" and "learn" of the Father and are drawn to Jesus as the Father's gift to the Son, that He might "see of the travail of His soul and be satisfied."

There is nothing about God's gift of believers to be the heritage of the Son who died for them which somehow transforms the Gospel's "whosoever will" into a "whosoever must" and a "most of you shan't." There is nothing about it which binds men in the strait jacket of an antecedent decree of positive unconditional election and reprobation, while insisting that they are "free." There is nothing about it which conjures up some dark, inscrutable paradox, loudly insisting upon the impossibility of reconciling Holy Scripture's revelation of both the sovereignty of God and the moral freedom and accountability of men. It is only some men's theology which does such things. All theologians to the contrary notwithstanding, the Scriptures declare that, with respect to both the saved and the lost, God takes fully into account the faculty of spiritual initiative and decision with which He endowed man in creation. He has respect for His own creation.

APPENDIX C

The Significance of Romans 9-11.

Proponents of the doctrine of unconditional election presume to find in Romans 9-11 (especially 9:6-29) complete confirmation of their contention that election to eternal salvation is without respect to anything in men. Many seem to have approached Rom. 9-11 with the assumption that Paul's purpose in that portion of his letter to the Romans was to expound the theological doctrine of the sovereignty of God. Not so. His purpose was to answer an urgent question which disturbed Jewish believers everywhere, of whom doubtless there were many at Rome.

In the days of the Apostles, the Gospel of Christ was truly "to the Jew first." Wherever the Apostles went, it was customary for them to enter the synagogues and preach the Gospel first to the Jews of the community. Many Jews became believers, and assemblies which were predominantly Gentile usually had strong nuclei of Jewish converts. This was the situation at Rome. Writing to believers at Rome, Paul addresses them sometimes as Gentiles (1:13-15; 11:13 ff.) and sometimes as Jews (2:17ff.; 4:1 ff.; 7:1 ff.).

Having reached a glorious climax in his consideration of the cardinal questions of sin, and of salvation, justification, and righteousness by grace through faith in Jesus Christ, Paul turns to a consideration of the present circumstance of Israel—a question of utmost concern for Jewish believers. They had accepted Jesus as the promised Messiah and now anticipated the fulfillment of the Messianic promises concerning Israel—perhaps soon (Acts 1:6, 7; 3:19-26). But grounds for their hope seemed to be fading. Why the delay? Had Israel been cast away? Were the glorious promises of God to the fathers to be ignored? More and more, it seemed either that the promises must fail, or that Jesus was not really the promised Messiah.

The question was of more than academic concern. Doubts arising from incomplete understanding and nourished by disappointment threatened to destroy the faith of many. It was a vexing question among Jewish believers everywhere, and one which required a firm and positive answer. Paul doubtless had often met the question elsewhere, and he now writes at length to answer it for Jewish converts at Rome. Let us consider a brief analysis of his answer:

1. [9:6-13] God's word has not been proved ineffective. There is an "Israel" *within* Israel—even as, historically, only the descendants of Isaac and Jacob were reckoned as the children of the covenant-promise, to the exclusion of all other descendants of Abraham.

2. [9:14-31] God is sovereign and therefore has the right to do as He pleases with individuals and nations. He is free to bestow favors on some, and to deny them to others, without becoming answerable to any creature. This absolute sovereignty extends to Isaac and Ishmael (vv. 7-9), to Jacob and Esau (vv. 10-13), to Moses (vv. 15, 16), to Pharaoh (v. 17), to all other individual men (vv. 18-24), and, collectively, to Israel and the Gentiles (vv. 25-31). God, as sovereign, has an absolute right to make of the common lump of humanity some vessels to honor, and others to dishonor; some for wrath and destruction, and others for mercy and glory. He has an absolute right to say of Israel, "not my people." It is not for men to call God into question. (To do so is not only presumptious; it is positively dangerous, since such an attitude is incompatible with faith. Hence the sharpness and vigor of Paul's reply to presumed objectors.)

3. [9:30-10:21] Israel's failure to "arrive," however, is not at all due to some absolute unconditional decree arising arbitrarily from the fact of the sovereignty of God, without respect to anything in men. The cause of Israel's present frustration is their own unbelief and disobedience. They have only themselves to blame. God continues to stretch forth His hands toward them, but in vain.

4. [11:1-6] Actually, despite the allegations of some, God has not cast away His people. Even though Israel, nationally, is "not my people," God still has His remnant in Israel-after-the-flesh. Paul, himself, is one among them (11:1). As in past generations, God has His "Israel" *within* Israel. Jewish believers in Christ constitute His present remnant in Israel and are of the election, not of works, but of grace.

5. [11:7-10] The present hardening of Israel, nationally—far from being the consequence of an arbitrary act of God in casting them off (11:1, 2)—is the consequence of their own failure to obtain the righteousness which they sought. Their failure (as Paul has affirmed, 9:31-10:21) stemmed from the fact that they sought righteousness by their own works, rather than by faith, thus stumbling over Christ, whom they found an offence. Their stumbling and consequent hardening were foretold by Isaiah and David (as well as others).

6. [11:11, 12, 15] God is able to turn Israel's present lapse to good account, both for the immediate proclamation of salvation among the Gentiles, and for the ultimate recovery of Israel herself. Having accomplished good through their lapse, God will multiply blessing for all nations through the recovery and restoration of Israel.

7. [11:13-24] During the present lapse of Israel, nationally, the salvation of individuals, both Jews and Gentiles (10:12, 13), remains a separate and distinct consideration, entirely independent of the question of the circumstance of Israel, nationally. It is evident from vv. 14, 23, 24 that the "hardening" of "the rest" (as distinguished from "the election," v. 7) is not the consequence of an arbitrary decree of unconditional reprobation; it is not absolute, but only relative.

8. [11:25-27] The recovery and restoration of Israel, nationally, is certain in the purpose of God. They will again become "my people" (9:25, 26).

9. [11:28, 29] Even in the present era of national unbelief, while "enemies concerning the gospel," Israel-after-the-flesh is

still beloved for the fathers' sake, and God's promises to the fathers will yet be honored and fulfilled.

10. [11:30-32] God's constant sincere purpose is to have mercy on all, both Jews and Gentiles, and includes any and all individual men, as they believe (10:12, 13; 11:20-24).

Many have failed to recognize that Paul's consideration in Rom. 9:6-29 is the question of the circumstance of Israel, rather than the personal salvation of individual men, and that his argument serves only to affirm that God, as a sovereign Creator, is free to order all things as He pleases and to bestow or deny favors as He chooses without becoming answerable to men—a truth which Paul earnestly desired to establish in the minds of Jewish Christians who were profoundly disturbed over the question of the circumstance of Israel and in danger of denying the wisdom and righteousness of God. Paul asserts only the inherent freedom of God, as a sovereign Creator, to act without becoming accountable to His creatures. But this must not be construed to mean that God is not governed by moral principles inherent in His own holy character and that He is at liberty to be arbitrary or capricious. God is governed in His actions, not by the judgment of His creatures, but by the moral integrity of His own Person. Those who have assumed that Rom. 9:6-29 affirms that God is merely arbitrary in His dealings with men, including the unconditional choice of some to salvation and the arbitrary consignment of others to perdition, have misconstrued the passage. They have also ignored much that follows in Rom. 9-11 and the consistent testimony of the Holy Scriptures, including categorical assertions that God wills to have all men to be saved and does not will that any should perish, but that all should come to repentance.

Liddon comments: "Throughout this section (ix. 6-29) no attempt is made by the Apostle to harmonize the absolute Freedom and Omnipotence of God with man's self-determination and responsibility. For the moment, the former truth is stated with such imperious force that the latter appears to be quite lost sight of: and the necessity for this 'one-sidedness' of statement lay in the presumption entertained by the Jews, that in virtue of their theocratic position God *must* be gracious to them. Without attempting to determine the relation of interdependence which exists between Divine and human freedom, (secured by the truth that the former is ruled by God's essential Sanctity and is consequently conditioned by moral facts on the side of man), S. Paul passes on to consider the other side of the phenomenon before him, viz. the responsibility of the Jews themselves for their failure to attain the [righteousness of God]."[1]

The Bible affirms both the sovereignty of God and the freedom of the human will. Many have insisted that the two truths, as revealed in the Scriptures, cannot be reconciled. But the irreconcilability which they have insisted upon exists, not between the two truths as revealed in the Scriptures, but between the Bible's categorical assertions of the freedom and responsibility of men and the unwarranted conclusions which many have drawn from certain passages in which the human factor simply is not affirmed—conclusions which are but groundless assumptions.

The sovereign God who is free to order all things as He pleases has declared that He is pleased, by the foolishness of preaching, to save them that believe (I Cor. 1:21); that He is pleased with the faith of men who diligently seek Him (Heb. 11.6); and that He takes no pleasure in the death of the wicked (Ezek. 33:11; 18:20-32), but wills to have all men to be saved and to come to the knowledge of the truth (I. Tim. 2:4), not willing that any should perish, but that all should come to repentance (II Pet. 3:9).

---

[1]H. P. Liddon, *Explanatory Analysis of St. Paul's Epistle to the Romans,* p. 174.

APPENDIX D

Calvin's View of Reprobation, and His Erroneous Fundamental Assumption.

Calvin considered reprobation a positive decree. "By predestination we mean the eternal decree of God by which he determined with himself whatever he wished to happen with regard to every man. All are not created on equal terms, but some are preordained to eternal life, others to eternal damnation; and, accordingly, as each has been created for one or other of these ends, we say that he has been predestinated to life or to death" (3:21:5). "We say, then, that Scripture clearly proves this much, that God by his eternal and immutable counsel determined once for all those whom it was his pleasure one day to admit to salvation, and those whom, on the other hand, it was his pleasure to doom to destruction. We maintain that this counsel, as regards the elect, is founded on his free mercy, without respect to human worth, while those whom he dooms to destruction are excluded from access to life by a just and blameless but at the same time, incomprehensible, judgment" (3:21:7). "Now if, in excuse of themselves and the ungodly, either the Pelagians, or Manichees, or Anabaptists, or Epicureans (for it with these four sects we have to discuss this matter), should object the necessity by which they are constrained, in consequence of the divine predestination, they do nothing that is relevant to the cause" (3:23:8). In the same paragraph, however, he writes, "Moreover, though their perdition depends on the predestination of God, the cause and matter of it is in themselves."

Thus, according to Calvin, by eternal decree before creation, God "determined with himself whatever he wished to happen with regard to every man." Some He "preordained to eternal life, others to eternal damnation," without regard to anything in man, either of the elect or of the reprobate—"they do nothing that is relevant to the cause." And yet, somehow, "the cause and matter of [the peridition of the reprobate] is in themselves."

It cannot be questioned that men, as guilty sinners, are deserving of perdition. But according to Calvin's view of reprobation, the guilt of the reprobate is a consequence rather than a cause. For if by eternal decree God unconditionally "preordained" specific men to eternal damnation without respect to anything in them, but simply because "it was his pleasure to doom them to destruction," it cannot be true that "the cause and matter" of their perdition is to be found within the reprobate themselves, as Calvin asserts, because God's decree was antecedent to any act of man. According to Calvin's definition of election and reprobation, the guilt of the reprobate is, itself, the direct consequence of God's positive decree of reprobation. God created the reprobate for no other purpose than guilt and everlasting damnation, and the real "cause and matter" of their perdition is to be found in God's decree, rather than "in themselves," as Calvin asserts.

Calvin becomes involved in the same sort of contradiction in his consideration of the fall of angels. He writes: "Paul gives the name of *elect* to the angels who maintained their integrity. If their steadfastness was owing to the good pleasure of God, the revolt of the others proves that they were abandoned. Of this no other cause can be adduced than reprobation, which is hidden in the secret counsel of God" (3:23:4). Obviously, this makes the revolt of the angels the direct consequence of an act of God. According to Calvin, the whole company of angels were going along in a business-as-usual sort of way when— bang! God suddenly sprang the trap under some of them by withdrawing His sustaining grace and "abandoning" them to perdition. This was simply "owing to the good pleasure of God," and "no other cause can be adduced than reprobation, which is hidden in the secret counsel of God."

But elsewhere in his *Institutes*, Calvin declares that ". . . . at their first creation they were the angels of God, but by revolting they both ruined themselves and became the instruments of perdition to others. . . . Everything damnable in [Lucifer] he brought upon himself by his revolt and fall. Of this Scripture reminds us, lest, by believing that he was so created at first, we should ascribe to God what is most foreign to his nature. For this reason Christ declares (John viii. 44) that Satan, when he lies, 'speaketh of his own,' and states the reason, 'because he abode not in the truth.' By saying that he abode not in the truth, he certainly intimates that he once was in the truth, and by calling him the father of lies, he puts it out of his power to charge God with the depravity of which he was himself the cause" (1:14:16).

Thus, on one page, there is "no other cause" for the fall of angels except "the good pleasure of God" in suddenly withdrawing His sustaining grace from some and "abandoning" them to perdition, while continuing to secure the "steadfastness" of others who "maintained their integrity." On another page, however, there is no other cause than that which we may find in the angels themselves, who, without provocation or necessity or excuse, wickedly revolted against God and His divine will.

It is difficult to read at length from Calvin without concluding that he was a master at eating his cake and having it too. The left hand giveth, and the right hand taketh away. Calvin's difficulty stemmed from the fact that he labored under an erroneous fundamental assumption. His cardinal error was his failure to acknowledge that the will of God has more than a single aspect, which led to his consequent denial that God desires to have all men to be saved. It is apparent from his writings that Calvin reasoned thus: If God truly wished all men to be saved, then all men would be saved. But most men are not saved. Therefore, we must conclude that God does not wish all men to be saved. Calvin's logic is unassailable; but it is based on the erroneous assumption that the will of God has but a single aspect.

Calvin deplored the fact that his opponents ". . . recur to the distinction between will and permission, the object being to prove that the wicked perish only by the permission, but not by the will of God. But why do we say that he permits, but just because he wills?" (3:23:8). Certainly anything within His permission is within God's will. But this does not establish the fact that His will has but a single aspect. All that occurs in the universe is within the permissive will of God. Neither men nor angels nor devils can go beyond the limits of God's permissive will. But it is by no means true that all that occurs is in accord with the perfect will of God.

One may argue that, since the world is filled with greed, lust, violence, debauchery, hatred, and impenitence, God evidently wishes it to be so and is well pleased. But the Scriptures declare otherwise. Although God allows these things to exist in the world, He has revealed His displeasure and wrath with respect to all such things and has commanded all men to repent. Thus it is evident that there are two aspects of the will of God with respect to sin: His permissive will allows it; but His perfect will forbids it and will bring all sin into judgment.

There are two aspects of the will of God for men with respect to salvation. Numerous Scriptures reveal God's perfect will to "have all men to be saved and to come to the knowledge of the truth" (I Tim. 2:4); but the fact that not all men are saved reflects God's permissive will. If a man is saved, it is in accordance with God's perfect will that all men should be saved; if a man is lost, it is in accordance with God's permissive will that men, being free moral agents rather than mere puppets, may refuse to obey Him. The latitude between God's perfect will and His permissive will is the area within which men function with freedom as responsible moral intelligences, accountable before God in solemn judgment. God is at work in humanity "bringing many sons unto glory" (Heb. 2:10) through the redemptive process rooted in His grace and wrought in Christ. But as moral intelligences created in His image, men must of their own free will concur in God's redemptive process if they are to share His everlasting glory as His sons. The fact that men are responsible, as free moral agents, is a corollary of the fact that the will of God has two aspects, rather than one.

The fact that the will of God has two aspects, rather than one, is fully apparent in numerous passages of Scripture. Consider the following: "If any man wills to do His will, he shall know . . ." (John 7:17). "Not every one that saith unto me, Lord, Lord, shall enter into the kingdom of heaven; but he that doeth the will of my Father . . ." (Matt. 7:21). "But the Pharisees and lawyers rejected the counsel [boulē, purpose] of God for them, being not baptized of John" (Luke 7:30). According to the Scriptures, men may choose to do God's will, or *not* to do His will. Since everything that happens is necessarily within the bounds of God's will, yet (according to the Scriptures) much that happens is *contrary* to the will of God, it is evident that the will of God has two aspects, rather than one.

Calvin does assert that God has "a double will" (3:24:17). But he means only that God has one will for the elect and another for the reprobate, both of which are simply corresponding manifestations of the one immutable will of God. (But if His will has but a single aspect, God is necessarily insincere; for He is ostensibly angry toward impenitent sinners with whom He secretly must be pleased, since they are but fulfilling His immutable will for them.) Calvin's assumption that the will of God has but a single aspect involved him in a fundamental error which warped both his theology and his interpretation of the Scriptures.

Much of Calvin's exposition of the Scriptures is excellent, including his interpretations of the warnings against apostatizing and the exhortations to persevere. He insists that believers must persevere in faith if they are to remain in grace. He frankly acknowledges that the Scriptures declare that some do actually fall from grace (reprobate Christians whose faith and experience of grace, by divine decree, are intended to be only temporary). He rightly asserts that the elect will persevere in faith and continue in grace to ultimate final salvation. But he views the perseverance of specific individual men as the *consequence* of election, rather than as a condition. Therefore, he is under the necessity of denying that God desires to have all men to be saved. For if God desires to have all men to be saved, then perseverance must necessarily be a condition, rather than a consequence, of election. Hence, his interpretations of the explicit declarations of Scripture that God wills to have all men to be saved, and that Christ died for all men, are ingenious and artificial. The reason is apparent: had he accepted the obvious meaning and import of such simple categorical declarations of Holy Scripture, his definition of election and the whole logic of his theology would have disintegrated. Calvin therefore rejected the face value of numerous passages of Scripture, in the interest of his theology, which he was able to substantiate by appealing to selected proof passages and by assigning ingenious interpretations to some of the most explicit declarations in the Holy Scriptures.

An example of Calvin's interpretation of passages incompatible with his theology is found in his comments on I Tim. 2:4-6. He writes that "[Paul] demonstrates that God has at heart the salvation of all, because he invites all to the acknowledgment of his truth."[1] Having made such a concession (in full accord with the obvious meaning of Paul's words), Calvin immediately begins his retraction by asserting, "This belongs to that kind of argument in which the cause is proved from the effect." In other words, since many are not saved, it cannot be true that God really wishes all men to be saved. Conceding that "if 'the gospel is the power of God for salvation to everyone that believeth' (Rom. i. 16), it is certain that all those to whom the gospel is addressed are invited to the hope of eternal life," Calvin yet insists that only "they whom God makes partakers of his gospel are admitted by him to possess salvation"—who are, of course, only such as have the good fortune of having been included in God's "secret election." We must not believe, therefore, that

---

[1] John Calvin, *Commentaries on the Epistles to Timothy, Titus, and Philemon,* p. 54.

God really desires that all men should come to the knowledge of the truth and be saved. Paul's simple statement must be "interpreted" to bring it into conformity with Calvin's theology. According to Calvin, God "invites all to the acknowledgment of His truth;" but He makes sure that only the right ones answer His universal invitation. He has taken all necessary steps to ensure that none of the wrong ones shall obey His righteous command to all men everywhere to repent or answer His gracious invitation to "whosoever will."

In defense of his theology, Calvin asserts that "all" does not mean *all*, but rather only *some men of each of all classes*. He declares that in affirming that God wills to have all men to be saved, ". . . the Apostle simply means that there is no people and no rank in the world that is excluded from salvation; because God wishes that the gospel should be proclaimed to all without exception. Now the preaching of the gospel gives life; and hence he justly concludes that God invites all equally to partake salvation. But the present discourse relates to classes of men, and not to individual persons; for his sole object is to include in this number princes and foreign nations."[2] In other words, when Paul declared that God "wills to have all men to be saved and to come to the knowledge of the truth," he really meant only that God wills to have *some* men of each of all nations and classes, including a few kings, to be saved and to come to the knowledge of His truth.

Again, Calvin writes, "The universal term *all* must always be referred to classes of men, and not to persons. . . ."[3] Such an assumption is necessary for the defense of Calvin's theology. And it does seem a modest concession for Calvin to ask, in view of the fact that the whole of his elaborate theology is at stake. But we wonder why Paul depended so much on "interpreters" instead of simply saying that God desires to have some men of each of all different classes to be saved and to come to the

---

[2] *Ibid.*, p. 54 f.
[3] *Ibid.*, p. 57.

knowledge of the truth, and that Jesus gave Himself a ransom for some men of each of all classes.

Elsewhere Calvin writes, "By this [Paul] assuredly means nothing more than that the way of salvation was not shut against any order of men; that, on the contrary, he had manifested his mercy in such a way that he would have none debarred from it" (3:24:16). But of course Calvin does not really mean that God actually "had manifested his mercy in such a way that he would have none debarred from it." Such a statement contradicts his theology. For according to Calvin, most men were created for the specific purpose of being forever barred from the mercy of God. Calvin therefore means only that God has barred the reprobate from His mercy, not on the basis of "class" or "order of men," but rather as specific individuals whom He created for perdition and for whom His mercy was never intended. Against any who might be reluctant to accept his "interpretation" of such a simple categorical statement of Scripture and his necessary definition of the word *all* as only *some men of all classes,* Calvin fumes, "For if they persist in urging the words, 'God hath concluded all in unbelief, that he might have mercy upon all' (Rom. xi. 32), I will, on the contrary, urge what is elsewhere written, 'Our God is in the heavens: he hath done whatsoever he hath pleased' (Ps. cxv. 3)" (3:24:16). To Calvin, of course, belongs the exclusive right to define "whatsoever he hath pleased" to do.

"Hence we see the childish folly," writes Calvin, "of those who represent this passage [I Tim. 2:4-6] to be opposed to predestination [i.e., to Calvin's particular hypothesis of election and reprobation]. 'If God,' say they, 'wishes all men indiscriminately to be saved, it is false that some are predestinated by his eternal purpose to salvation, and others to perdition [i.e., unconditionally]. They might have had some ground for saying this, if Paul were speaking here about individual men; although even then we should not have wanted the means of replying to their argument; for, although the will of God ought not to be judged from his secret decrees, when he reveals them to us by outward signs, yet it does not therefore follow that he has not determined with himself what he intends to do as to every individual man."[4]

Thus, all in the same breath, Calvin declares that "God has at heart the salvation of all . . . yet it does not therefore follow that he has not determined with himself what he intends to do as to every individual man"—some of whom He created for salvation, and others for perdition. Again, as so often with Calvin, the left hand giveth, and the right hand taketh away. "God has at heart the salvation of all [and] invites all to the acknowledgment of his truth." But He also has at heart the everlasting perdition of men whom He created for no other purpose or destiny—men to whom, from before creation, He utterly denied all prospect of arriving at the acknowledgment of His truth and salvation. "God has at heart the salvation of all"—and the damnation of most! Without regard to anything in men, God is pleased to consign to everlasting perdition many whose salvation He "has at heart." Why? Perhaps to confirm the logic of Calvin's theology.

Calvin resorts to similar exegetical artifice in his interpretation of passages which affirm that Christ died for all mankind. For example, according to his interpretation of I John 2:2, John did not mean that Jesus is actually the propitiation "for the sins of the whole world." Instead, he meant only that He is the propitiation for the sins of the elect wherever they may happen to be throughout the whole world, and in whatever generation they may happen to live on earth. ". . . the design of John was no other than to make this benefit common to the whole Church. Then under the word *all* or whole, he does not include the reprobate, but designates those who should believe as well as those who were then scattered through various parts of the world. For then is really made evident, as it is meet, the grace

---

[4]Calvin, *Commentaries on the Epistles to Timothy, Titus, and Philemon*, p. 54.

of Christ, when it is declared to be the only true salvation of the world."[5]

It must have come as an amazing revelation to John's readers to learn that Jesus Christ is the propitiation for the sins of the elect quite as much in one part of the world as in another, and as much in one generation as in another. What nonsense! But of course John's simple statement must be properly "interpreted." The logic of Calvin's theology demands a limited atonement. (In his introduction to Eerdmans' edition of the *Institutes,* John Murray writes, "[Calvin's] exegesis, in a word, is theologically oriented." That is only too true, in a sense which Murray did not mean. The profound pity is that Calvin's theology was not exegetically oriented.)

While many Calvinists concede that such a doctrine is manifestly unscriptural, a limited atonement remains an essential tenet of Calvin's theology. The "Five Pillars of Calvinism" are five in number, not four. But Calvinists who advocate a limited atonement have no moral right to assure any man that Christ died for him, personally. For according to their theology, their statement may, or may not, be true; and in most instances is not.

Calvinists who reject the erroneous doctrine of limited atonement, while more Scriptural, are correspondingly less logical. Quite inconsistent are moderate Calvinists who reject a limited atonement while advocating an unconditional election. Why should Jesus bear the sins of men who have no prospect of forgiveness and whose inevitable destiny, by decree of God, is eternal perdition? Why should God sacrifice His Son for men whom He does not desire to save and whom He does not love? Or, how is it true that God *loves* men whom he deliberately creates for no other end and purpose than everlasting estrangement from Himself? It is a strange "love" which creates men for naught but wrath. Or, if one insist that reprobation is "not a

---

[5]Calvin, *Commentaries on the Catholic Epistles,* p. 173.

positive decree," as do some "Calvinists" (a thing impossible
to establish, if election be unconditional), how is it true that
God loves men whom He simply "passes by" while saving others
no more deserving of His mercy? A God who "passes by" the
mass of helpless sinners in casual unconcern is not unlike the
priest and the Levite in our Saviour's parable. If it be protested
that sinners have offended God and are undeserving of His
mercy, let us ask whether our Saviour taught us to love our
enemies and to forgive those who have offended us. Let us also
ask whether, according to our Saviour's teaching, to love and
forgive and to seek reconciliation would make us *like* God, or
unlike Him (Matt. 5:43-48). The only claim the robbers' vic-
tim had on the good Samaritan was the character of the Samaritan himself—the spirit of love and brotherhood which he had
toward his fellow men. The only claim guilty sinners have on
the mercy of God is the gracious character of God Himself.
That claim was enough to send Jesus to Golgotha and to a
shameful death as the propitiation "for the sins of the whole
world." The guilt of men who persist in disobedience is com-
pounded many-fold by the fact that Jesus "gave himself a ransom for all" and God desires that none perish, but that all come
to repentance and to the knowledge of His truth and saving
grace.

Chafer, who rejects the doctrine of limited atonement, tacitly
admits the inconsistency of contending for both unlimited redemption and unconditional election: "To the unlimited re-
demptionist, the seeming inequity of a judgment falling upon
[the reprobate] after Christ has borne that judgment is but
one more mystery which the finite mind cannot understand."[6]
But the "mystery" and the inconsistency are not present for men
who recognize that the will of God has more than a single
aspect, and that the Scriptures present both an unlimited atonement and a conditional election (with respect to particular in-

---

[6]Lewis Sperry Chafer, *Systematic Theology*, Vol. III, p. 188.

dividuals). We can be consistent (and Scriptural) only as we recognize that the love which provided an infinite atonement "for the sins of the whole world" finds expression in God's sincere desire that none should perish, but that all should come to repentance and salvation. Conditional election is the inevitable corollary of unlimited redemption. "God was in Christ reconciling the world unto himself, not imputing their trespasses unto them . . . [therefore] as though God did beseech you by us, we pray you in Christ's stead, be ye reconciled to God" (II Cor. 5:19, 20).

It is true, as Calvinists delight to contend, that there is a hard core of logic at the center of Calvin's theology. But it is a logic which proceeds on the erroneous assumption that the will of God has but a single aspect, and which is totally invalid. It is therefore inevitable that, despite its core of logic, there should be much in Calvin's theology which is horribly illogical—a fact which Calvinists concede, but which they excuse on the plea that the frightful paradoxes are "mysteries" which our finite minds cannot comprehend. It is odd that men who glory in the "logic" of Calvin's theology are so ready to accept all that is grossly illogical in it. Even more distressing is the fact that they are quite ready to accept the many ingenious and artificial interpretations of simple, explicit statements of Holy Scripture which the defense of Calvin's theology requires.

Calvin's profound intolerance toward all who questioned any of his opinions was not merely the evidence of a vanity easily offended; it was a reflection of his sincere estimate of his *Institutes of the Christian Religion:* "I dare not bear too strong a testimony in its favour and declare how profitable the reading of it will be, lest I should seem to prize my own work too highly. However, I may promise this much, that it will be a kind of key opening up to all the children of God a right and ready access to the understanding of the sacred volume. . . . And since we are bound to acknowledge that all truth and sound doctrine proceed from God, I will venture boldly to declare what I think of this work, acknowledging it to be God's work rather than mine."[7]

We would not question Calvin's sincerity in assuming his *Institutes* to be a comprehensive expression of holy truth quite free from error, and the indispensable key to understanding the Scriptures. But we deny the wisdom of sharing his assumption. It is cause for regret that, in the past four centuries, many have seemed to regard Calvin's *Institutes*, not merely as the expression of a system of theology, but actually as a sort of infallible norm by which to judge all exegesis and doctrine. Such an assumption militates against the possibility of any really objective study of the Holy Scriptures and the formulation of a truly Biblical theology. "To the law and to the testimony: if they speak not according to this word, it is because there is no light in them."

But we do well to honor Calvin for his earnest purpose to be ever "prompt and sincere in the work of the Lord," and for his zeal and labors to lead men into the light of holy truth, as best he saw it. Jealous for the glory of God and indignant against the presumptions of "unholy men in holy office" who trafficked in the souls of men, arrogating to themselves the provinces of God, Calvin labored diligently to expound the Scriptures, and especially to defend the doctrine of the sovereignty of God, according to his conception and definition.

---

[7]Calvin, *The Institutes of the Christian Religion*, p. 22 f.

Appendix E

Other Scriptures to Which Advocates of the Doctrine of Unconditional Security Commonly Appeal.

It has been our purpose in the course of this treatise to consider the major passages of Scripture to which advocates of the doctrine of unconditional security commonly appeal. In addition to those considered in the foregoing chapters, there are others which warrant brief discussion:

1. "The gifts and calling of God are without repentance" (Rom. 11:29). Some assert that Paul's statement indicates that, regardless of subsequent circumstances, God cannot withdraw from any individual the gift of justification and salvation, once it has been bestowed. But Rom. 11:29 is not a general principle applicable to any and every situation in God's dealings with men; for such would contradict many passages of Scripture. The meaning of Paul's statement is governed by context (Rom. 9-11, esp. 11:26-29). Context indicates that Paul's affirmation concerns the corporate election of Israel. Despite the present unfaithfulness of Israel, collectively, God's promise to the fathers will yet be fulfilled in a generation who will seek the King of glory and who will be willing in the day of His power (Ps. 24:6; 110:3; cf. Hos. 3:4, 5; 5:15-6:3; Zech. 12:10; 13:6 ff., etc.). Meanwhile, even those in whom the promise cannot be fulfilled—a rebellious generation—are yet "beloved for the fathers' sakes." God's gifts and calling of Israel to the privileges of their corporate election, though temporarily unrealized through the general unbelief of rebellious generations, will never be finally withdrawn and will ultimately be realized in a "willing" generation. Rom. 11:29 has no application to the question of individual salvation and security (contra. vv. 20-23). Paul's statement in v. 29 was written, not concerning saved men, but concerning men who were "enemies concerning the gospel" (v. 28).

2. "Who art thou that judgest another man's servant? to his own master he standeth or falleth. Yea, he shall be holden up: for God is able to make him stand" (Rom. 14:4). This verse, with its context, only points out that one whose convictions may differ from our own concerning the exact definition of practical Christian living is not necessarily disapproved of God, simply because his convictions differ somewhat from ours. God, whose servant he is, has the sole responsibility of judgment. Although he may differ from us in minor respects, he may still stand approved in God's sight (perhaps more so than we) and, since he is a servant of God, His grace will sustain him. But it is only by faith that one continues to stand in the grace of God (Rom. 11:20-22, II Cor. 1:24).

3. "If any man's work shall be burned, he shall suffer loss: but he himself shall be saved, yet so as by fire" (I Cor. 3:15). Some contend that Paul's words indicate that, while it is possible for Christians to lose the rewards which faithfulness secures, it is impossible for them to lose salvation. But let us observe that, while it is true that all believers must appear before the judgment seat of Christ (Rom. 14:10-12, II Cor. 5:10), I Corinthians 3:12-15 is specifically concerned with the judgment of ministers of the Gospel (cf. v. 5 ff.). (There is doubtless a secondary application, in principle, to all believers.) The sole issue in view in the passage is how men build who "build on this foundation"—Jesus Christ. Those who "suffer loss" will be men who, though they did not build well, yet built (and remained) on the one adequate Foundation and therefore, despite their poor labors, are nevertheless saved. The passage in no way affirms that it is impossible for men to abandon "this foundation" and to be moved away from the hope of the Gospel, thus to forfeit salvation. The peril of apostasy, so prominent in many other passages from the pen of Paul, is not under consideration in this passage.

4. "And the Lord said, Simon, Simon, behold, Satan hath desired to have you, that he may sift you as wheat: but I have

prayed for thee, that thy faith fail not: and when thou art converted, strengthen thy brethren" (Luke 22:31, 32). Jesus foresaw, not only Peter's denial, but also his restoration. But what was true in Peter's case does not govern what may be true in other instances. To assume that Peter's experience implies a universal principle and that restoration is inevitable in every instance and final apostasy is therefore impossible is to deny the plain record and testimony of the Scriptures. Jesus, our Advocate with the Father, prays for all who trust in Him. But we are warned not to abandon faith, thus to depart from our High Priest (Heb. 4:14-16; 10:19-39).

5. "All that the Father giveth me shall come to me; and him that cometh to me I will in no wise cast out" (John 6:37). Many assert that Jesus here promised that no one who comes to Him will subsequently be cast out, and that a saving relationship with Christ, once effected, is therefore indissoluble. But such an assumption contradicts numerous plain warnings of Jesus, for example John 15:1-6. The promise of Jesus in John 6:37 is, as Robertson comments, a "definite promise of Jesus to welcome the one who comes."[1]

6. "And this is the Father's will which hath sent me, that of all which he hath given me I should lose nothing, but should raise it up again at the last day" (John 6:39). It is not the Father's will that any who come to Jesus should subsequently be lost. But neither is it His will that any should perish (II Pet. 3:9) or fail to come to the knowledge of the truth and be saved (I Tim. 2:4). But there is a vast difference between God's perfect will and His permissive will (cf. Appendix D). The freedom of men to act, and their consequent responsibility, cannot be abrogated. In His intercessory prayer on the eve of His betrayal, Jesus prayed, "Those that thou gavest me I have kept, and none of them is lost, but the son of perdition" (John 17:12). The faithfulness of the Good Shepherd to safeguard His sheep

---

[1] A. T. Robertson, *Word Pictures in the New Testament*, Vol. V, p. 108.

does not relieve them of the necessity of listening to His voice and following Him (John 10:27-29).

7. "To whom coming as unto a living stone, rejected indeed of men but chosen of God and precious, ye also, as living stones, are built up a spiritual house, an holy priesthood, to offer up spiritual sacrifices acceptable to God by Jesus Christ" (I Pet. 2:4, 5). Some have contended that, if the saved may become lost, the spiritual house of which Peter writes (cf. Eph. 2:22) may, to some extent, be dismantled. Such a contention assumes that the "spiritual house" is being built only for future use and must remain incomplete until the consummation of the age. But this is not so. The "spiritual house" is always complete and ready for the "offering up of spiritual sacrifices" in the worship and service of God. Irrespective of the number of "living stones," God's spiritual house on earth is constantly complete, being composed of all who are in Christ through obedient faith. Likewise, the "body of Christ" (I Cor. 12:27), while continually increasing (Eph. 4:16, Col. 2:19), is nevertheless constantly whole and complete.

8. "They went out from us, but they were not of us: for if they had been of us, they would have continued with us: but they went out, that they might be made manifest that they were not all of us" (I John 2:19). Some have asserted that John's statement indicates that all who are false professors will eventually withdraw from the company of true believers (which is contrary to many passages of Scripture) and that all who withdraw never were true believers (which is contrary to both the warning passages and the record of actual instances of apostasy). With respect to the antichrists cited by John, there are two possibilities. Their professions of faith may have been false from the beginning; or, they may have been actual apostates who abandoned faith and withdrew from Christ. Either circumstance could be true. John asserts only that, at the time they withdrew from the spiritual fellowship of true believers,

"they were not of us;" otherwise they would have continued in fellowship with the faithful.

Let it be observed that, whatever may have been the circumstance of the antichrists in view, John was writing of specific instances, rather than stating a universal principle. Let us beware the fallacy of assuming that all truth can and must be compressed into a single sentence of Scripture, and that the precise circumstance in one instance of defection necessarily governs the circumstance in all other instances. There are some whose professions of faith are false from the beginning, and there are others who abandon faith and withdraw from a saving relationship with Christ. The Scriptures recognize both circumstances, and the precise circumstance of the antichrists cited by John determines nothing with respect to the circumstance in other instances. Let us observe that, after citing the tragic record of the antichrists who denied that Jesus is the Christ (vv. 18-23), John urgently warns his children in the faith to beware the peril of succumbing to the seductions of the antichrists by embracing their fatal heresy, thus failing to retain the true saving Gospel and to remain in the Son and in the Father, sharing the eternal life in Him (vv. 24-28).

9. "And as many as were ordained to eternal life believed" (Acts 13:48b). Proponents of the doctrine of unconditional election and security presume to find strong support in Acts 13:48, contending that Luke's statement implies that believing the Gospel is a consequence of election and an evidence of individual predestination to eternal life, and that one who has sincerely believed therefore has infallible evidence that he is of the elect and unconditionally secure for all eternity.

Commentators are divided over the question of the precise significance of *tetagmenoi*, which the Authorized Version (following the Vulgate) renders "ordained." Lange contends that "the words bear no other sense than that all those, and those alone, were really converted, who were ordered, appointed, by

God to eternal life."[2] But he also insists that "the free self-determination of the human will is as little denied as it is asserted in this passage; a *decretum absolutum* is by no means involved in *tetagmenoi*."[3] Meyer concurs. While insisting that the literal meaning is "the divine destination to eternal salvation," he declares: "It was dogmatic arbitrariness which converted our passage into a proof of the *decretum absolutum*. For Luke leaves entirely out of account the relation of 'being ordained' to free self-determination. . . . Indeed, the evident relation in which this notice stands to the apostle's own words, *epeidē* . . . *zōēs*, ver. 46, rather testifies *against* the conception of the *absolute* decree, and *for* the idea, according to which the destination of God does not exclude, comp. ii. 41, individual freedom. . . ."[4]

Alford comments: "The meaning of [*tetagmenoi*] must be determined by the context. The Jews had *judged themselves unworthy of eternal life:* the Gentiles, as many as were disposed to eternal life, believed. *By whom* so disposed, is not *here* declared: nor need the word be in this place further particularized. We know that it is God who worketh in us the will to believe, and that the preparation of the heart is of Him:[5] but to find *in this text* pre-ordination to life asserted is to force both the word and the context to a meaning which they do not contain. The key to the word here is the comparison of [I Cor. 16:15 and Rom. 13:1]: in both of which places the *agents* are expressed, whereas here the word is absolute. See also ch. xx. 13. . . . Wordsworth well observes that it would be interesting to enquire what influence such renderings as this of *praeordinati* in the Vulgate version had on the minds of men like St. Augustine and his followers in the Western Church in treating the great questions of free will, election, reprobation,

---

[2]Lange, *Commentary on the Holy Scriptures: Acts,* p. 258.
[3]*Ibid.*
[4]Meyer, *Critical and Exegetical Hand-Book to the Acts of the Apostles,* p. 264.
[5]But in so doing, God does not act arbitrarily. Cf. Appendix B, C.

and final perseverance: and on some writers in the reformed churches who, though rejecting the authority of that version, were yet swayed by it away from the sense of the original here and in ch. ii. 47. The tendency of the Eastern Fathers, who read the original Greek, was, he remarks, in a different direction from that of the Western School."[6] Wordsworth's observations merit serious reflection.

All who assume that *tetagmenoi* in Acts 13:48 implies that those who believed the Gospel at that particular time and place did so as the consequence of an absolute decree of unconditional election unwittingly embrace a second assumption, completely absurd: All present in the congregation who ever were to believe the Gospel did so immediately. There could be no further opportunity to consider the Gospel, and no man who failed to believe that day could ever believe and be saved; for all who were predestined to believe did so immediately. A preposterous assumption! Such a pattern fits neither the case of Paul nor the universal experience of the Church through all generations.

It should be obvious that *tetagmenoi* in the passage before us can have no meaning or significance which is incompatible with its context[7] or with explicit categorical assertions that God wills to have all men to be saved (I Tim. 2:4) and does not will that any should perish, but that all should come to repentance (II Pet. 3:9). In any event, let us observe that, regardless of the precise significance of *tetagmenoi* in Luke's statement, the doctrine of unconditional security finds no support in Acts 13:48. It is certain that the elect will believe the

---

[6]Alford, *The Greek Testament*, p. 153 f.

[7]Verse 46. Certainly Paul did not mean that the Jews who rejected the Gospel did so because, in their humble opinion of themselves, they deemed (a common meaning of *krinō*) themselves unworthy of eternal life. His meaning then is that, with respect to God and His eternal purposes in grace, through their rejection of His word they pronounced judgment and condemnation (a more frequent meaning of *krinō* in the N.T.) on themselves as unworthy of eternal life which God freely offered them through the sincere call of the Gospel.

Gospel. But Luke's statement does not in any wise establish either that election is unconditional, or that everyone who once believes the Gospel is eternally elect and will necessarily continue in faith. The Scriptures cite numerous instances of actual apostasy (which would not be possible if Acts 13:48 implied what some have assumed) and believers are urgently warned against failing to continue in faith. "The just shall live by faith: but if he draws back, my soul shall have no pleasure in him." The fact of past faith affords no guarantee against either the possibility or the disastrous consequence of abandoning faith and departing from the Saviour. To find support for the doctrine of unconditional security in Acts 13:48 is to read into Luke's statement something that is not there.

10. "For whom he did foreknow, he also did predestinate to be conformed to the image of his Son, that he might be the firstborn among many brethren. Morever, whom he did predestinate, them he also called: and whom he called, them he also justified: and whom he justified, them he also glorified" (Rom. 8:29, 30). This passage has often been called "an unbreakable chain"—foreknowledge, predestination, calling, justification, glorification. For the elect, it is indeed an unbreakable chain; and only the elect are comprehended in Paul's affirmation (v. 33). The calling, justification, and glorification constitute the implementation of the predestination (conformity to the image of the Son) which God purposed for the elect. For them, calling and justification will issue in ultimate glorification, in accordance with the eternal purpose of God to "bring many sons unto glory" (Heb. 2:10), the glory of full conformity to the image of His Son. But there is nothing about Paul's affirmation which establishes that election is unconditional or that all who experience calling and justification are necessarily eternally elect and will inevitably persevere. Certainly it is true that the elect (who are foreknown to God) will persevere. But that is only *half* the truth; for it is equally true that they who persevere are elect. The latter solemn truth is presented in the Holy

Scriptures, not as the inevitable outcome of some inexorable divine decree with respect to specific individuals unconditionally, but as a matter for the constant concern and holy endeavor of believers.

The certainty of election and perseverance is with respect, not to particular individual men unconditionally, but rather with respect to the *ekklēsia,* the corporate body of all who, through living faith, are in union with Christ, the true Elect and the Living Covenant between God and all who trust in His righteous Servant (Isa. 42:1-7; 49:1-12; 52:13—53:12; 61:1, 2). Consider the following:

God's eternal purpose in grace:
> Eph. 1:4, He chose us in Christ that we should be *hagious kai amōmous* before Him.
> Col. 1:22, He reconciled us to Himself in Christ, through His death, to present us *hagious kai amōmous* before Him.

Fulfillment corporately (certain):
> Eph. 5:27, Christ will present the *ekklēsia* to Himself *hagia kai amōmos.*

Fulfillment individually (contingent):
> Col. 1:23, He will present us *hagious kai amōmous* before Him—if we continue in the faith grounded and settled and be not moved away from the hope of the Gospel.

To assume that eternal glory is the inevitable terminus of "an unbreakable chain" for everyone who once experiences saving grace is to ignore the explicit warnings, not only elsewhere in the Scriptures, but in the very passage before us. Paul warns: "Therefore, brethren, we are debtors, not to the flesh, to live after the flesh. For if ye live after the flesh, ye shall die: but if ye through the Spirit do mortify the deeds of the body, ye shall live. For as many as are led by the Spirit of God, they are sons of God" (Rom. 8:12-14). "And if children, then heirs; heirs of God, and joint-heirs with Christ; if so be that we suffer with him, that we may be also glorified together" (v. 17).

Let not vain assumptions concerning the meaning of such passages as Rom. 8:29, 30 destroy our concern for heeding the many warnings and exhortations to persevere in the faith. God will present us holy and unblameable and unreprovable before Him only if we continue in the faith and be not moved away from the hope of the Gospel. "If we endure," writes Paul, "we shall also reign with him: if we deny him, he also will deny us." "He that overcometh," promises the risen Saviour, "the same shall be clothed in white raiment; and I will not blot his name out of the book of life, but I will confess his name before my Father, and before his angels. . . . Be thou faithful unto death, and I will give thee the crown of life. He that hath an ear, let him hear what the Spirit saith unto the churches. He that overcometh shall not be hurt of the second death."

BIBLIOGRAPHY

Alford, Henry, *The Greek Testament*. London: Rivingtons, 1868.

Barnhouse, Donald Grey, *Life by the Son*. Philadelphia: American Bible Conference Association, 1939. Used by permission of the publishers of *Eternity* magazine, Philadelphia.

Berkouwer, G. C., *Faith and Perseverance*. Translated by Robert D. Knudsen. Grand Rapids: Eerdmans, 1958. Used by permission.

Bloomfield, S. T., *The Greek Testament with English Notes, Critical, Philological, and Exegetical*. Boston: Perkins and Marvin, 1837.

Burton, Ernest De Witt, *Syntax of the Moods and Tenses in New Testament Greek*. Third Edition. Edinburgh: T. & T. Clark, 1898.

Calvin, John, *Commentary on the New Testament*. 15 vols. Translated by Henry Beveridge, John Owen, John Pringle, and William Pringle. Grand Rapids: Eerdmans.

————, *Institutes of the Christian Religion*. 2 vols. Translated by Henry Beveridge. Grand Rapids: Eerdmans.

Chafer, Lewis Sperry, *Major Bible Themes*. Wheaton: Van Kampen Press, 1953. Used by permission of Dallas Theological Seminary, Dallas, Texas.

————, *Systematic Theology*. 8 vols. Dallas: Dallas Seminary Press, 1947. Used by permission of Dallas Theological Seminary.

Clarke, William Newton, *An Outline of Christian Theology*. New York: Charles Scribner's Sons, 1898.

Dargan, Edwin Charles, *The Doctrines of Our Faith*. Nashville: The Sunday School Board of the Southern Baptist Convention, 1920. Used by permission.

Delitzsch, Franz, *Biblical Commentary on the Psalms*. 3 vols. Translated by Francis Bolton. Edinburgh: T. & T. Clark, 1873.

————, *Commentary on the Epistle to the Hebrews*. 2 vols. Translated by Thomas L. Kingsbury. Grand Rapids: Eerdmans.

Denney, James, *Studies in Theology*. London: Hodder and Stoughton, 1895.

————, *The Christian Doctrine of Reconciliation*. New York: George H. Doran Company, 1918.

————, *The Death of Christ*. New York: The American Tract Society, 1903.

Eadie, John, *Commentary on the Epistle of Paul to the Colossians*. Grand Rapids: Zondervan.

368

Godet, Frederick L., *Commentary on the Epistle to the Romans.* Translated by A. Cusin and revised and edited by Talbot W. Chambers. Grand Rapids: Zondervan.

————, *Commentary on the Gospel of John.* 2 vols. Translated by Timothy Dwight. Grand Rapids: Zondervan.

Goodspeed, Edgar J., *The New Testament: An American Translation.* Chicago: The University of Chicago Press, 1935. Used by permission.

Hengstenberg, E. W., *Commentary on the Gospel of St. John.* Edinburgh: T. & T. Clark, 1868.

Hodge, Charles, *A Commentary on the Epistle to the Romans.* Philadelphia: William S. Martien, 1851.

Knox, R. A., *The New Testament of Our Lord and Saviour Jesus Christ.* New York: Sheed and Ward, 1945. Used by permission.

Kuyper, Abraham, *The Work of the Holy Spirit.* Translated by Henri De Vries. New York: Funk & Wagnalls, 1900.

Liddon, H. P., *Explanatory Analysis of St. Paul's Epistle to the Romans.* London: Longmans, Green, and Company, 1893.

Lightfoot, J. B., *Saint Paul's Epistles to the Colossians and to Philemon.* Grand Rapids: Zondervan.

————, *The Epistle of St. Paul to the Galatians.* Grand Rapids: Zondervan.

Lockyer, Herbert, *Blessed Assurance.* Grand Rapids: Zondervan, 1955. Used by permission.

Maclaren, Alexander, *Expositions of Holy Scripture.* 32 vols. New York: Hodder and Stoughton, and George H. Doran Company.

————, *The Epistles of St. Paul to the Colossians and to Philemon* (*The Expositor's Bible,* ed. W. Robertson Nicoll). New York: Hodder and Stoughton, and George H. Doran Company.

Mayor, Joseph B., *The Epistle of St. James.* Grand Rapids: Zondervan.

Meyer, H. A. W., *et al., Critical and Exegetical Hand-Book to the New Testament.* Translated and edited by Frederick Crombie and William Stewart. New York: Funk & Wagnalls, 1884.

Moffatt, James, *The New Testament: A New Translation.* New York: Harper & Brothers, copyright 1922, 1935, and 1950. Used by permission.

Montgomery, Helen Barrett, *The New Testament in Modern English.* Philadelphia: The American Baptist Publication Society, 1924. Used by permission.

Moule, H. C. G., *Colossian Studies.* London: Hodder and Stoughton, 1909. Used by permission of Pickering & Inglis, Ltd., Glasgow.

————, *Thoughts on Christian Sanctity.* Chicago: Moody Press.

Moulton, James Hope, and George Milligan, *The Vocabulary of the Greek Testament*. Grand Rapids: Eerdmans.

Murray, John, *Redemption—Accomplished and Applied*. Grand Rapids: Eerdmans, 1955. Used by permission.

Pierson, A. T., *Keys to the Word*. Grand Rapids: Zondervan.

————, *The Heart of the Gospel*. London: Passmore and Alabaster, 1892.

Robertson, A. T., *A Grammar of the Greek New Testament in the Light of Historical Research*. Nashville: Broadman Press, 1934. Used by permission of the Sunday School Board of the Southern Baptist Convention, Nashville.

————, *Word Pictures in the New Testament*. 6 vols. New York: Harper & Brothers, 1930. Used by permission of the Sunday School Board of the Southern Baptist Convention, Nashville.

Ryle, J. C., *Expository Thoughts on the Gospels*. 4 vols. Grand Rapids: Zondervan.

Shepardson, Daniel, *Studies in the Epistle to the Hebrews*. New York: Revell, 1901.

Strong, Augustus H., *Systematic Theology*. Philadelphia: The Judson Press, 1907. Used by permission.

Thiessen, Henry C., *Introductory Lectures in Systematic Theology*. Grand Rapids: Eerdmans, 1949. Used by permission.

Tholuck, Augustus, *Commentary on the Gospel of St. John*. Edinburgh: T. & T. Clark, 1860.

Verkuyl, Gerrit, *Berkeley Version of the New Testament*. Grand Rapids: Zondervan, 1945. Used by permission.

Vincent, Marvin R., *Word Studies in the New Testament*. Grand Rapids: Eerdmans, 1946. Used by permission.

Westcott, B. F., *The Epistles of St. John*. Grand Rapids: Eerdmans.

————, *The Epistle to the Ephesians*. Grand Rapids: Eerdmans.

————, *The Epistle to the Hebrews*. Grand Rapids: Eerdmans.

————, *The Gospel According to St. John*. London: John Murray, 1903.

Weymouth, Richard Francis, *The New Testament in Modern Speech*. New York: Harper & Brothers. Used by permission.

Williams, Charles B., *The New Testament: A Translation in the Language of the People*. Chicago: Moody Press, 1950. Used by permission.

Wuest, Kenneth S., *The Gospels: An Expanded Translation*. Grand Rapids: Eerdmans, 1956. Used by permission.

————, *Treasures from the Greek New Testament for the English Reader*. Grand Rapids: Eerdmans, 1943. Used by permission.

INDEX

Abel, his acceptable sacrifice offered "by faith," 23, 236

Abiding in Christ, more than "fellowship" and "consecration," 97

Abraham, an example of enduring faith, 110, 178, 234f.

Adam, necessity of persevering faith in his original state, 22f., 236

Adeney, W. F., 33

Alexander, Cecil F., 264

Alexander, Joseph Addison, 311f.

Alford, Henry, 61, 109, 323, 363

Animal sacrifice, offered as an act of confession and faith, 24

Aorists, do not specify point-action, require definition by context, logic, and analogy, 77f.

Apostasy, not the act of unbelievers, 156; meaning of term, 157; actual instances cited in N. T., 173ff; usually not without remedy, 312ff.

Assurance of salvation, seven means of, 301-304

Atonement, objective and unlimited, individual in application, 26, 132

Auber, Harriett, 118

Augustine, 103, 150, 363

Barnhouse, Donald Grey, 132, 260-262

Berkouwer, G. C., 165-170, 177

Beza, Theodore, 36

Blasphemy against the Holy Spirit, not immediately unforgivable, 320f.

Bloomfield, S. T., 36

Branches in the Vine, true believers only, 44-47

Browne, E. Harold, 23

Burton, E. D., 56, 62, 77, 79, 321

Calvin, John, 45, 146-148, 289-297, 300, 345-357

Chafer, Lewis Sperry, 39, 54f., 67-70, 95f., 133, 333-337, 355

Chastening, two possible responses rather than one, 142

Christ, the supreme example of faith, 242ff.; died as Son of *man*, 245; voluntary in His death, 246ff.

Clarke, William Newton, 87

Clephane, Elizabeth C., 25

Cromwell, Oliver, 266

Dargan, Edwin Charles, 64

Davidic Covenant, Calvin's erroneous application, 146-148

Death, both spiritual and physical, the penalty of sin—suffered by Jesus on the cross, 25f.

Delitzsch, Franz, 144, 148, 149, 163, 199, 328

Denney, James, 26, 64, 127

Eadie, John, 297

Election to final salvation, comprehends *ekklēsia* corporately, individual men only secondarily, 364-367

Eli's sons, apostasy final, 311, 322

Eternal life, a quality of life emanating from God, rather than mere endless existence, 21; not the believer's inalienable personal possession *ipso facto*, 52

Faith, esential to Adam's felicity in Eden, 22; saving faith a working faith rather than merely speculative, 7, 8, 218f.

Faithfulness of God, cannot avail for unfaithful men, 109f.

Forgiving spirit, an essential aspect of saving faith, 38-40

Godet, F. L., 59, 117, 146, 198, 208, 220

Havergal, Frances Ridley, 220f.

Hengstenberg, E. W., 45, 58, 208

Hodge, Charles, 7, 297

Holy Spirit, seal of God's ownership, earnest of believer's inheritance, 105; is no surety of the believer's faithfulness, 111; blasphemy against not immediately unforgivable, 320

Huther, J. E., 271

Judas, an example of apostasy, 179ff.; without true repentance, 324f.

Justification, by faith rather than ordinances or works, 3-6, 255-260, 263-265

Kendrick, A. C., 165

Kenosis, 244ff.

371

INDEX OF GREEK WORDS

INDEX OF SCRIPTURE REFERENCES